DATE DUE

DEMCO 38-296

Politics, Persuasion, and Educational Testing

Politics, Persuasion, and Educational Testing

Lorraine M. McDonnell

Harvard University Press

Cambridge, Massachusetts, and London, England

Several chapters from this book have been adapted and used with permission
from the National Center for Research on Evaluation, Standards, and Student
Testing (CRESST). Copyright © 1997 by The Regents of the University of
California and supported under the Institute for Education Science (IES), U.S.
Department of Education.

Library of Congress Cataloging-in-Publication Data

McDonnell, Lorraine, 1947–
     Politics, persuasion, and educational testing / Lorraine M. McDonnell.
        p.   cm.
     Includes bibliographical references and index.
     ISBN 0-674-01322-0 (alk. paper)
     1. Educational tests and measurements—United States.   2. Educational
evaluation—United States.   3. Education—Standards—United States.
I. Title.
LB3060.83.M33   2004
371.26—dc22   2004040586

In memory of my father, Lawrence McDonnell,
who taught me so much

Contents

Acknowledgments

Because I was a political scientist venturing into the realm of psychometricians when I began this research, I had much to learn and benefited from many excellent teachers. I am especially grateful to Eva Baker, Joan Herman, and Bob Linn, the co-directors of the National Center for Research on Evaluation, Standards, and Student Testing (CRESST) at UCLA. Fifteen years ago, they invited me to "come play with them" at CRESST. Not only did they tutor me in all the technical details associated with student testing, but they supported me and defended my research to funders who questioned whether anything useful could ever be learned from a political analysis of testing. Chapters 3 and 5 are based on technical reports that I prepared for CRESST and are used with the center's permission. However, the findings and opinions expressed in this book do not reflect either the position or policies of CRESST or its funder, the Institute for Education Science (IES), U.S. Department of Education.

I have also benefited from all I have learned while serving on the National Research Council's Board on Testing and Assessment for six years. My fellow board members' wide-ranging expertise, coupled with our spirited discussions, have taught me as much about thoughtful deliberation as about assessment. Equally important to my education about testing was what I learned listening to the policymakers, administrators, teachers, and concerned citizens in California, Kentucky, and North Carolina who were willing to share their perceptions and experience with me. I only hope that my analysis has given full voice to their concerns and insights.

Obtaining the data analyzed in this book depended on the work of a skilled group of research assistants: Craig Choisser, Kirstin Falk, Diane Johnson, Marguerite Kamp, Sara Wakai, and Leah Watts. I especially appreciate the dedicated competence of Lawrence Messerman, my "fellow schlepper" through the three states. Gloria Applegate, Audrey Carter, Barbara Espinoza, and Sara Wakai ably coded the instructional artifact data analyzed in Chapter 5.

I have been fortunate over the past decade to have a congenial intellectual home in the political science department at the University of California, Santa Barbara. My colleagues have consistently shown me the importance of a focused disciplinary lens, even if studying children instead of war, peace, or presidents. One of my departmental colleagues, Stephen Weatherford, is also my spouse, and for thirty years, he has served as my scholarly exemplar as we have engaged in "the big chat" about all manner of politics and policy.

This book never would have appeared without the support and efforts of two people. The first is Elizabeth Knoll, the senior editor for the behavioral sciences at Harvard University Press, who has been the model of a supportive, gracious, and patient editor. The other is Florence Sanchez, my department's faculty assistant, whose high standards and meticulous attention to detail made final preparation of this manuscript possible.

Finally, this book is dedicated to my father, who died just as I was completing it. Like many good parents, much of what he taught me about duty, empathy, and intellectual discipline he did through example and steady encouragement. Even during his last days, he would gently prod me by asking, "How is the book progressing?" For his wisdom and for all the help I received from friends and colleagues, I am deeply appreciative.

Tables and Figures

Abbreviations

APC	Assessment Policy Committee
API	Academic performance index
AYP	Adequate yearly progress
CAP	California Assessment Program
CARE	Campaign for Academic Renewal in Education
CATS	Commonwealth Accountability Testing System
CLAS	California Learning Assessment System
CRESST	National Center for Research on Evaluation, Standards, and Student Testing
CRI	Capitol Resource Institute
CSBA	California School Board Association
CTA	California Teachers' Association
CTBS	Comprehensive Test of Basic Skills
CWA	Concerned Women of America
DPI	Department of Public Instruction
EPCRA	Emergency Planning Committee Right-to-Know Act
ESEA	Elementary and Secondary Education Act
IEP	Individualized education program
IES	Institute for Education Science, U.S. Department of Education
II/USP	Intermediate Intervention/Underperforming School Program
KDE	Kentucky Department of Education
KERA	Kentucky Education Reform Act
KIRIS	Kentucky Instructional Results Information System
NAEP	National Assessment of Educational Progress
NCAE	North Carolina Association of Educators
NCLB	No Child Left Behind Act
NCTM	National Council of Teachers of Mathematics
NELS	National Educational Longitudinal Survey
OBE	Outcomes-based education
OTL	Opportunity to learn
PIE	Parents Involved in Education

PPIE	Parents and Professionals Involved in Education
QSP	Quality School Portfolio
SBE	State Board of Education
SDE	State Department of Education
SPI	Superintendent of Public Instruction
STAR	Standardized Testing and Reporting program
TAAS	Texas Academic Assessment System
TRI	Toxics Release Inventory
TVC	Traditional Values Coalition
USJF	United States Justice Foundation

Politics, Persuasion, and Educational Testing

1

Testing from a Political Perspective

Americans may dread taking tests, but most accept them as necessary and legitimate tools of modern life. We take tests to demonstrate our competence to drive cars and to work as barbers, teachers, undertakers, lawyers, and at a host of other occupations. Tests are used in allocating some of the most valued societal benefits, including high school diplomas, college educations, and well-paying jobs. Yet few of us would consider testing to be a lens through which we might view contemporary politics or understand the value conflicts that shape so many political debates. If people outside the field of education even think about testing, they likely see it as something developed by experts and administered by educators—a somewhat mysterious enterprise, shrouded in secrecy and dominated by technical issues.

At one level, testing lies in the domain of experts who must ensure that the scores test-takers receive truly reflect their relevant knowledge and skills, and that these scores are reasonably consistent from one test administration to the next. But at another level, tests fall squarely in the political realm. Beginning with the early use of written examinations in U.S. schools during the nineteenth century, standardized tests have raised questions that are fundamentally political.[1]

In political debates surrounding the uses of standardized tests, perennial questions have arisen about whether particular tests are sufficiently reliable and valid to be used in allocating benefits such as college admissions, and when tests are used in such allocation decisions and produce unequal distributions, whether they merely reflect preexisting inequalities in society or compound them and create additional barriers. These questions persist today in debates about whether test scores should be used to decide if students should be promoted to the next grade, and whether students whose primary language is other than English should be tested in English. Debates about testing and its uses have not only defined the politics of education at key points during the past century, but they are also emblematic of broader political conflicts about race, ethnicity, class, and the criteria by which public goods are distributed.

1

Although the use of standardized tests has highlighted societal divisions around questions of equity and social justice, recent controversies about their content have also made testing a major venue for debates about which cultural values should prevail in American public life. This book focuses on that debate by examining the design and implementation of new student assessments in three states—California, Kentucky, and North Carolina—during the early 1990s. It takes an explicitly political perspective, and portrays these state tests as attempts to change teachers', students', and the public's opinions about what knowledge and skills should be taught in the nation's schools through an appeal to values. In focusing on the role of values as a policy tool, the book examines how public officials and education professionals attempted to persuade their constituents to accept a particular vision of schooling. The analysis looks from the bottom up as well as from the top down. It examines how assessment policy has served as a focal point for grassroots mobilization to contest the values embodied in a particular test.

New state assessments continue to raise enduring questions about equality and fair treatment, especially when the assessments are used to impose consequences on individual students.[2] However, because these tests are designed to measure performance on academic content standards that reflect value choices about what students should learn and how they should be taught, they pose yet another set of political questions. In this case, the politics of testing emerges from a reliance on values as the motivating force for holding schools accountable and for improving the quality of their instruction. Although many education reformers assumed that these values would be uncontested, broad-based consensus has been elusive. Abiding philosophical issues such as which educational decisions should be the prerogative of the state and which should remain within the purview of the family have been linked with practical questions about when students should use calculators and what role phonics, spelling, and grammar should play in an inquiry-oriented curriculum. The political arena has thus become a primary venue for deciding what should be taught and tested.

The Central Argument

In focusing on state assessment policies, this book makes three arguments. First, although standardized tests are primarily measurement tools to obtain information about student and school performance, they are also strategies for pursuing a variety of political goals. Over the past decade, elected officials have increasingly relied on student testing as a tool for holding schools accountable to externally imposed standards. In doing so, these officials have sought not just to hold schools accountable for their performance as public institutions, but also to influence classroom instruction through their choice of what knowledge and which skills are tested on state assessments. Both the decision to impose external standards through a testing regime and the choice of those standards have often sparked intense political debate. Consequently, the effect of state assessments on education and the broader society cannot be understood independently of the assessments' political functions.

Second, the curricular values underlying student assessments are often critical elements in advancing a state's education policy goals. Even when state governments decide to attach tangible consequences to test results, they also have the option of using persuasion and values-based appeals in motivating policy targets to change their behavior. The testing policies that have gained the greatest public attention recently are those that award cash bonuses to schools with high or improving test scores, "take over" low-performing schools, or inform decisions about whether students are promoted or graduate from high school. Yet even when the results of state assessments have tangible consequences, much of their force as policy strategies depends on whether the social and curricular values they embody are broadly accepted by parents, educators, students, and the public. Consequently, in designing testing policies as tools to increase student learning, officials have a choice in the extent to which they rely on more coercive strategies rather than values-based appeals. Each approach has its advantages and disadvantages, and while this study focuses primarily on the values dimension of student testing policy, it also compares each strategy's potential as a policy instrument.

Third, assessment policy is a useful lens for developing broader theoretical and empirical understandings of politics and policy. By examining state assessments as instances of policy strategies based on persuasion, we can begin to formulate a general theory of how policies operate that rely on information and values to accomplish their intended goals. Focusing on the political dynamics of assessment policy can also contribute to a better understanding of the so-called culture wars—what divides opponents and how their differences might be bridged. Because it has been the focal point for conflicts over societal values, student testing also serves as a vehicle for examining some of the conditions under which the public becomes engaged in technically complex policies. Assessment policy largely reflects the values of the education professionals and testing experts responsible for its design. However, because it is based on a well-defined set of values, assessment policy also provides the motivation and even to some extent the institutional mechanism to mobilize citizen action that may be either supportive of or opposed to those values. In fact, as I will argue, assessment policy, with its accompanying link to curriculum standards, has provided a major opportunity for shifting the balance away from professional values to grassroots, lay notions of what constitutes a good education.

The remainder of this chapter establishes the groundwork for these arguments by briefly discussing the policy uses of standardized assessments and the reasons for their appeal to policymakers and the public. Three state cases are also outlined, and the study methods described.

The Policy Purposes of Assessment

From their earliest administration more than a hundred years ago, standardized tests have been used for a variety of policy purposes, and often the same test serves multiple functions. For example, tests are used as one source of information in making instructional decisions about individual students, such as whether they need special education or other kinds of supplemental services. Since many educational interventions have improved student achievement as their intended effect, standardized tests also play an important role in program evaluations: whether or not participants' test scores improve after intervention is a key indicator of program effectiveness.

For our purposes, the most important policy uses of standardized tests are as accountability mechanisms and as levers to change classroom instruction. Because they are public institutions, schools are accountable to citizens and their elected representatives for how well they educate children, with standardized tests an integral part of the process. Providing information to the public about school performance is one aspect of the accountability relationship. When the only purpose of an assessment is to provide information, it is considered a "low stakes" test because it has no significant, tangible, or direct consequences attached to the results, and information alone is assumed to be a sufficient incentive for people to act. In this case, the theory is that a standardized test can reliably and validly measure student achievement; that politicians, educators, parents, and the public will then act on the information generated by the test; and that actions based on test results will improve educational quality and student achievement.

However, 27 states now attach consequences at the school level to assessment results. These consequences may include funding gains and losses; warnings; assistance from outside experts; loss of accreditation status; and in a few places, the eventual state takeover of schools (Quality Counts, 2003, pp. 87–88). In addition, 22 states use their assessments to impose consequences on individual students: they may be rewards or benefits in the form of special diplomas, graduation from high school, or promotion to the next grade; or they may be sanctions that typically consist of the withholding of those permissions (Council of Chief State School Officers, 2001). Once consequences are attached to test scores, the assessment becomes a "high stakes" test. Policies based on high stakes assessments assume that information alone is insufficient to motivate educators to teach well and students to perform to expected standards. Hence the promise of rewards or the threat of sanctions is needed to accomplish expected changes. Rewards in the form of financial bonuses may be allocated to schools or teachers, and sanctions imposed through external oversight or takeover by higher-level authorities.

When testing is used as a lever to change classroom instruction, it may be implemented with either a high or a low stakes assessment. Although standardized tests have long been used as an education reform strategy for changing classroom instruction, this use has become more common with the advent of the standards reforms now promoted by states and the federal government. This movement seeks to improve educational quality by setting high content standards that define the knowledge and skills that teachers should teach and students should learn, and by holding them accountable for meeting performance standards that specify what constitutes mastery of that content. It assumes that educators and the public can agree on a set of curricular values; that those values can be translated into a set of standards; and that assessments can measure how well students perform on the standards.

About half the states have revamped their assessment systems during the past decade to align them more closely with specific content and performance standards, and most of the remainder are in the process of alignment or planning alignment. Many have also diversified their testing format beyond reliance solely on multiple-choice items, with 44 states now including items that require students to provide extended written responses (Council of Chief State School Officers, 2001).

The growth of the standards movement during the past decade, with its link to state assessments, represents a marked change in testing policy. Traditionally, standardized tests were designed to measure students' knowledge and skills at a very general level. Because they were used to test students attending different schools and exposed to different curricula, standardized tests typically measured basic skills and did so in a few broadly defined areas. The standards movement has meant that expectations for what students should know have become both more rigorous and more precise, and while states differ in how directive they are with local school districts, the assumption is that state standards will lead to more uniform learning goals among communities.[3]

The values embodied in these standards are of several types. First, there is an emphasis on equity, exemplified in the rallying cry "High standards for all students." Standards advocates assume that a major reason some children have not received the full benefits of public education is that adult expectations for their achievement have been low, and because they have not been given an opportunity to learn high-level, demanding content. The assumption is that by clearly communicating the notion "All students can learn to high standards," teachers and students alike will understand what is expected of them and schools will move to equalize students' opportunities to learn (O'Day and Smith, 1993; Ravitch, 1995). This overarching value raises basic philosophical and practical questions that remain unanswered. For example: Can and should standards be applied to all students? What exactly does "all" mean? (McDonnell, McLaughlin, and Morison, 1997). Nevertheless, at least at a rhetorical level, one message of the standards movement is that those who are concerned about equalizing educational opportunities should embrace this approach.

The equity focus is evident most recently in the federal No Child Left Behind Act (NCLB). The act (PL 107–110), signed by President G. W. Bush in early 2002, amends the Elementary and Secondary Education Act (ESEA) and requires for the first time that all students in grades 3 though 8 be tested annually in mathematics and reading in order for states to continue receiving ESEA Title I funds. NCLB also requires that states develop measurable objectives for improved achievement by all students, with consequences for schools that fail to meet these progress targets including required improvement plans, student transfer options, and even major restructuring. To ensure that schools work to improve the achievement of all students, they are required to disaggregate and report test scores by demographic and educational subgroups such as specific ethnic groups, economically disadvantaged students, and those with limited English proficiency. At the time of its enactment, NCLB, endorsed by huge majorities in both houses of Congress, represented a remarkable consensus between the two national political parties, and reflected President Bush's campaign pledge to "leave no child behind."

A second set of values, and the main focus of this book, revolves around what should be taught and how it should be taught. The standards movement is unique in that the concept has been promoted by political elites on the left and the right, and it enjoys widespread public support. Presidents G. H. W. Bush and Bill Clinton both advocated establishing national standards; state-level standards have been developed with the active involvement of both Democratic and Republican governors; and in national opinion polls, a large majority of the American public expresses strong support for establishing clear standards for what students should be taught and then testing them on those standards (Hochschild and Scott, 1998; Rose, Gallup, and Elam, 1997; Johnson and Immerwahr, 1994). The use of standards and assessments as vehicles for defining what should be taught and learned was further solidified with the passage of NCLB, because the act requires that states align their assessments with their academic content and performance standards.

However, as the experience of the states analyzed in this book indicates, consensus around the desirability of establishing standards has broken down over the specifics of what those standards should be. Education reformers and others within the education establishment—especially teachers and their subject-matter associations such as the National Council of Teachers of Mathematics (NCTM)—dominated the first round of state standards-setting. The educational vision guiding the initial content standards has been a progressive one. Learning goals emphasize conceptual understanding, application, problem-solving, and linkages between academic content and students' lives. Students are expected to play an active part in their learning, constructing knowledge through discussion, experimentation, and other modes of discovery. Teachers are viewed as facilitators of learning, rather than as imparters of information.

This vision of schooling is still reflected in state standards, most notably in science and mathematics, for which a number of states have adapted standards developed by the National Academy of Science and NCTM. However, the underlying philosophy has come under increasing criticism from those who espouse a more traditional view of schooling and its purposes. These attacks have taken a variety of forms, including disagreements about what literature should define the "canon" in language arts courses, whose history should be included in social studies, how much time should be devoted to memorization and the acquisition of basic skills, and whether children should be exposed to ideas and values that may challenge religious teachings and social values taught by their families.

As the analysis in Chapters 3 and 4 indicates, the reasons for opposing state assessments have been varied, but most opponents pointed to the tests' underlying curricular values as a primary reason. A sampling of comments from California parents who opposed their state's test provides a sense of those arguments:

I think they're pushing concepts rather than facts. They're pushing critical thinking skills which is good on the surface, but when you're teaching somebody how to think you're also teaching them what to think.

In an English section, they would ask questions about how you feel about this story, attempting to generate a response from the children as if they were rats you had to give an electric shock to, rather than asking questions such as "how did the author create a mood of intense anticipation through plot structure?" Kids come into the system perfectly capable of feeling, but they aren't capable of realizing the subtleties of plot development, proper grammar, how to analyze a sentence, how to spell.

We would like to see more emphasis on basic skills in teaching and less emphasis on creating new cultures. And we would like to have the teachers not usurp the rights of parents by deliberately trying to educate their students to another point of view.

Such disputes are not new, and they reflect contested views about the purposes of education that have historically manifested themselves in debates about what curriculum should be taught. The recent controversies are different, however, in that the scope of the standards movement has made them more visible, and expanded the arenas for conflict beyond local school districts and the courts (where such disputes have traditionally been aired) to state legislatures, Congress, and the national media.[4] Conflicts about the social and curricular values underlying state standards are also more visible now because antagonists have linked them to broader political debates about multiculturalism, the place of religious values in public life, the quality of public education, and the use of public funds to pay for sectarian schooling.

A third set of values embodied in the standards movement reinforces the first two by appealing to a diverse array of professional, economic, and political motives. For example, an often-heard argument in favor of adopting a standards-based strategy is that it will help make the United States more economically competitive in global markets. Politicians, business leaders, and education reformers have all made the claim, basing it on the argument that other countries that compete with us economically and whose students score higher on international mathematics and science tests have well-defined standards and assessments tied to those standards. Although researchers have suggested that "inferences about the positive effects of U.S. standard setting are unwarranted based on education in other countries" (Porter, 1994, p. 425), the assumed connection persists in the minds of policymakers. They see the United States as lacking an emphasis on the outcomes of schooling, and standards and assessment as a way to focus the attention of educators on those outcomes. In this case, the values appealed to are national pride and economic competitiveness.

Appeals to teachers have been based on professional values, including their desire to do well by their students and to be competent professionals whose teaching reflects the most up-to-date standards set by the national associations. Political concerns have been tapped in arguments that uniform standards will mitigate the worst effects of the highly decentralized and fragmented U.S. educational system, and will make those responsible for public education more accountable (Smith and O'Day, 1991). These arguments have been framed differently in different places, but they are all designed to persuade a variety of policy targets, especially educators, to change their behavior and to accept a particular set of educational values.

An obvious question that arises from this discussion is: why have policymakers, education reformers, and the public placed so much faith in tests? One reason stems from testing's low cost and its effectiveness as a policy instrument, but part of the perceived power of testing may be more myth than reality.

Testing's strong appeal is largely attributable to the lack of alternative policy strategies that fit the unique circumstances of public schooling. In distinguishing among types of governmental bureaucracies, Wilson (2000) categorizes schools as "coping organizations" because school administrators, policymakers, and their constituents can observe neither the outputs (day-to-day activities) nor the outcomes of classroom teaching. School administrators can observe teachers only infrequently, and their presence in classrooms may alter teachers' behavior. As for the outcomes of teaching, standardized tests are one of the very few, albeit incomplete, ways to measure them. Consequently, assessment has become a critical accountability tool, one of the few mechanisms that top-level managers and policymakers have for determining whether school staff are accomplishing what is expected of them.

But those who rely on assessments view them as more than just devices to monitor unobservable outcomes. As discussed earlier, policymakers and their constituents want to do more than just collect *ex post* information on educational outcomes; they also want to shape those outcomes. However, because so few of a school's core activities are observable, and because the operational distance between state legislatures and individual classrooms is huge, elected officials and other policymakers have few tools at their disposal to accomplish that goal. Standardized tests are one of the most effective levers they have for influencing what happens in local schools and classrooms. A growing body of research suggests that school and classroom practices do change in response to these assessments (Firestone, Mayrowetz, and Fairman, 1998; Herman and Golan, 1993; Corbett and Wilson, 1991; Smith and Rottenberg, 1991; Madaus, 1988).[5]

Furthermore, compared with other educational interventions, assessments are inexpensive. Even the most expensive assessments that require students to conduct experiments and answer open-ended questions cost only about $30–$50 per tested student (Stecher and Klein, 1997; Picus, 1996), while commercially developed, multiple-choice tests cost even less at $2 to $20 per student.

Equally important in explaining the appeal of testing is the widespread belief that it can produce truly objective data. Test scores are only snapshots of someone's performance at a single point in time, and even the best tests can measure only a sample of the skills and knowledge represented in a set of academic standards. Yet policymakers, the public, and even educators often view test scores as considerably more than incomplete proxies for student achievement, and they vest them with greater meaning than technical experts argue is warranted.

Like most public policy myths, the belief that assessments can produce impartial and comprehensive data about student achievement is an influential one (DeNeufville and Barton, 1987). It is in the interest of policymakers and their constituents to believe that judgments about local schools and individual students are based on information that is technically sound and free of bias. Assumptions about objectivity and impartiality become even more important when some schools and students are being rewarded and others are being sanctioned. When "winners and losers" are created through policy actions, decisions need to be based on what appear to be objective grounds. For that reason, the myth of objective test data persists in the mind of both policy elites and the public, despite numerous expert critiques seeking to dispel it (for an overview, see Heubert and Hauser, 1999).

Despite an obvious technical dimension and the scientific mystique surrounding them, state assessments are essentially political strategies. The politics of assessment stems from its function as a mechanism for holding schools and students accountable, and for promoting a particular vision of schooling. The widely shared belief that test scores are objective and comprehensive measures of student achievement has legitimized state assessment policies and reinforced public support for the concept, if not always for specific tests.

The Three State Assessments: A Brief Overview

California, Kentucky, and North Carolina were selected for study because their policies represent a range of assessment formats and uses, and because they were among the earliest states to change their assessment systems. They also differ in the size and diversity of their student populations. As the most populous state in the United States, California had more than 5.5 million elementary and secondary students enrolled in the fall of 1995, 60 percent of whom were students of color, with Latinos representing the largest single group (39 percent). North Carolina had approximately 1.2 million students, two-thirds white and 31 percent black. Kentucky enrolled 659,000 students, the overwhelming majority of them (89 percent) white (National Center for Education Statistics, 1997).

State assessments in California and Kentucky represented a major departure from the traditional reliance on multiple-choice testing. Both states included constructed (open-ended) response items and performance tasks in their tests, and Kentucky's assessment also included portfolios of students' work. Kentucky attached school-level rewards and sanctions to its assessment system, while California did not. North Carolina's assessment, on the other hand, represented less of a divergence from its previous testing program. Most of the test still consisted of multiple-choice items, but it also included some constructed responses and a writing sample in several grades. It did not include any performance tasks or the use of portfolios. In all three states, the new assessment was directly linked to state curriculum standards or frameworks.

This analysis focuses on the initial enactment and implementation of the new assessments. It should be noted that, in all three states, the assessments now in place differ significantly from those implemented in the early 1990s, when the data for this study were collected. Kentucky's assessment, which represented the most radical deviation from past policy, has changed the least since its initial administration in 1992. Yet its format has been altered substantially, and its name changed to distance the current version from what had been viewed by teachers and the public as a problematic centerpiece of the state's massive education reform. California's policy has undergone the greatest change, shifting from one of the most innovative assessments in the country to an "off-the-shelf" multiple-choice test; it also has moved from a low stakes assessment system that imposed no consequences on schools or students to one with potentially significant consequences for both. North Carolina has moved within the past several years from a relatively uncontroversial, low stakes test to one that is high stakes and whose uses and consequences mobilized opposition by civil rights groups and teacher organizations. As we will see, these transformations were not entirely unexpected given the political dynamics that shaped the initial policies. Nevertheless, they illustrate both the volatility of contemporary education politics and the willingness of politicians and their constituents to use policy to reach far down into the classroom to change what is taught.

California

Educators and testing experts looked to the California Learning Assessment System (CLAS) as an exemplar for new forms of student assessment. When fully operational, CLAS was intended to test all the state's students in grades 4, 8, and 10 in reading, writing, mathematics, science, and social studies. Although the tests contained multiple-choice items, students were also required to answer open-ended questions that asked them about their reactions to literary passages or how they arrived at solutions to mathematics problems. The tests were tied to state curriculum frameworks that stressed the ability to understand underlying principles and to apply them in solving real-world problems, as well as to master subject-matter knowledge.

The impetus behind CLAS was Republican governor George Deukmejian's 1990 veto of appropriations for the state's prior test, the California Assessment Program (CAP).[6] Fifteen months after the CAP veto, CLAS, or the "new CAP" as it was originally called, was enacted through a rare consensus among the three centers of education power in California—Deukmejian's successor, Governor Pete Wilson; the legislature (in the person of former state senator Gary Hart, then chair of the Senate Education Committee), and the former State Superintendent of Public Instruction, Bill Honig. Yet just before the second administration of the test in 1994, culturally conservative groups attacked the language arts portion of CLAS, arguing that many of the literary selections on which students were being tested promoted inappropriate values such as violence and the questioning of authority. They filed lawsuits to stop administration of CLAS, mobilized grassroots groups to protest it at the state and local levels, and urged parents not to allow their children to take the test. Although these groups represented only a small minority, a bill authorizing the continuation of CLAS was vetoed by Wilson in September 1994. For several years, California had no statewide assessment. When one was once again administered in 1998, the State Board of Education (SBE) chose an existing multiple-choice test prepared by a commercial test publisher.

By late 1998, California had a new set of academic content standards in language arts, mathematics, science, and social studies. They were a product of a process that sought to be more inclusive and less divisive than the one surrounding the implementation and eventual demise of CLAS. The standards-setting process was only partly successful in avoiding controversy and in reaching a consensus on what California teachers should be expected to teach at each grade level. The resulting standards, particularly in mathematics and science, were considerably more traditional than the previous curriculum frameworks.

With the 1998 election of Gray Davis, the first Democratic governor in 16 years, California's assessment system became high stakes. Within three months of his inauguration, the state legislature passed several education reform bills proposed by Davis. One ranks all schools in the state on the basis of their students' test scores; those in the bottom ranks are potential targets for a state intervention program, and those that fail to improve over several years can be taken over by the state. Schools that meet their performance goals can qualify for reward funding. A second bill established a high school exit exam, first offered in 2001 and required for graduation beginning with the class of 2004.

Because of its innovative approach to assessment, CLAS encountered many technical problems during its short existence, and its development and administration were further constrained by cost considerations. However, as the analysis in Chapter 3 indicates, political factors reflecting the different values of key policymakers and their constituents were more significant in explaining both the initial enactment of CLAS and its quick demise.

Kentucky

The student assessment system in Kentucky, the Kentucky Instructional Results Information System (KIRIS), was one component of what is probably the most comprehensive state education reform in this century. In 1989, in response to a lawsuit challenging the constitutionality of the state's school finance system, the Kentucky Supreme Court ruled not just that the finance system was unconstitutional, but that the entire state school system was unconstitutional. The court ordered the legislature to redesign Kentucky's education system in its entirety. The Kentucky Education Reform Act (KERA), signed into law in April 1990, pumped more than $700 million in new funds into the system in its first two years of implementation. KERA made many sweeping changes that ranged from how the duties of local school boards are defined to how teachers are licensed and what is taught in classrooms. It required that elementary schools teach younger children in "ungraded primaries" that combine students from kindergarten through third grade in the same classrooms; it mandated that each school establish a site council to govern its curricular, personnel, and budgetary decisions; and it created a network of family-service and youth-service centers located at or near schools with large concentrations of poor students.

KIRIS stood at the heart of the KERA reforms. As part of the comprehensive overhaul of its educational system, Kentucky developed six learning goals. From those goals, 75 "valued outcomes" were defined, setting the standards for what Kentucky teachers would be expected to teach and students expected to master. All students in grades 4, 8, and 12 were tested in five subjects using an assessment system that consisted of short-answer questions, performance tasks, and portfolios.[7] Student performance on these assessments was scored as "novice," "apprentice," "proficient," or "distinguished," based on a set of standards for what students were expected to know. Once baseline scores (derived from a combination of student assessment scores and other data such as attendance and graduation rates) were calculated for each school, schools were required to improve by a specified percentage or threshold score every two years. Those that exceeded their threshold score were eligible for monetary awards; those that failed to improve or declined by fewer than five percentage points were provided various forms of assistance; those that declined by more than five percentage points risked being put on probation. Under the last condition, parents would have the option of transferring their children out of the school, and school staff faced the possibility of dismissal.

KIRIS confronted many of the same technical and political problems as CLAS, but Kentucky policymakers responded differently from those in California, and the original assessment continued to be administered until 1998. State officials were able to sustain KIRIS in the face of serious problems because they modified the test in response to criticisms by testing experts, educators, and political opponents while still maintaining its basic framework. They eliminated two of the state's six learning goals—dealing with individual self-sufficiency and responsible group membership—that were targets of the most intense criticism; they delayed the imposition of sanctions on underperforming schools until 1996; and they shifted the high school assessment from the twelfth to the eleventh grade. In February 1995, the state first awarded $26 million to the 480 of the state's approximately 1,400 schools that had reached their improvement goals. Depending on the degree of improvement, awards to individual schools ranged from $1,300 to $2,600 per teacher.

However, by 1996 it had become clear that problems with KIRIS were so severe—and educators' and the public's confidence in it so diminished—that unless more substantial changes were made, the entire assessment might be abandoned. In April 1998, the governor signed legislation creating a new state assessment, the Commonwealth Accountability Testing System (CATS). Features of CATS include a national, norm-referenced portion so that Kentucky students can be compared with those across the country; reporting of individual student scores to parents; and financial rewards (for schools that successfully meet their thresholds) to be used by the schools, rather than distributed as bonuses to teachers. Once it is completely implemented, CATS may become something other than KIRIS in a new suit, but the overall strategy that Kentucky pioneered in the early 1990s appears to have survived in the guise of new policy.

North Carolina

The state's new assessment, first administered in 1993, represented a less significant departure from its previous testing program than those in California and Kentucky. Students in grades 3–8 were tested at the end of each year in reading, mathematics, and social studies, using a combination of multiple-choice items and open-ended questions. In addition, students in grades 4 and 6–8 were required to produce writing samples.[8] The North Carolina assessment does not include any group exercises or performance tasks (for example, working with scientific apparatus), nor does it require student portfolios. However, the assessment is linked to the state's *Standard Course of Study*, which is a fairly detailed set of curricular standards. Exams are scored at three levels of proficiency—basic, proficient, and exemplary or exceptional.

At the time of this study, North Carolina had a low stakes test, having attached few tangible consequences to its assessment results. The state appropriated about $250 per teacher which local districts, and eventually individual schools, could either allocate as part of a differentiated pay plan or use for staff professional development. Similarly, North Carolina had a takeover plan that allowed the state to intervene directly in school districts performing at substandard levels. However, state takeover was not a realistic threat for most districts: no more than 4 percent of the state's districts were likely to be affected, and those most likely to be were chronically poor, low-performing districts whose status was already well-known.

However, with the passage of new legislation in 1995, the ABCs of Public Education, the North Carolina assessment became a high stakes test. In the elementary and middle school grades, students are tested in reading, mathematics, and writing, using the same type of assessment implemented in 1993. Schools are assigned scores based on the percentage of students at or above grade level and on the schools' progress toward increasing the percentage of students at that level. Teachers at schools that reach their "expected growth" (a calculation that takes into account the school's past performance and statewide average growth) receive bonuses of $750 each; those at schools that achieve "exemplary growth" (10 percent above the statewide average growth) receive $1,500 apiece. In 1998, the state awarded $116 million in bonus funding to teachers.

The state also identifies low performing schools that fail to meet minimum growth standards and have a majority of students performing below grade level. In 1997, 123 of the state's 1,600 schools were identified as low performing, and the state sent assistance teams to 15 of those schools. In 1997, the legislature passed the Excellent Schools Act, which required that all certified staff in low performing schools with assistance teams must take a general knowledge test, and that the principals in those schools be suspended. The North Carolina Association of Educators threatened to sue the state, and the approximately 250 affected teachers, principals, and counselors planned to boycott the exam. However, just a few days before the scheduled testing date in 1998, the legislature reversed itself. No one had to take the test and in the future, staff would be evaluated by the assistance teams and only teachers with poor evaluations that suggest a lack of general knowledge (as opposed to ineffective instructional techniques) would be required to take the test. Since 1993, North Carolina had maintained essentially the same assessment format, with its link to the well-established *Standard Course of Study*, but the state had significantly altered the consequences of that test.

Study Approach and Data Sources

Because testing policy involves many people and many levels of government, understanding its politics requires a variety of data. These data need to capture complex institutional processes through which ideas about education reform are shaped into assessment policies, those policies transformed from legislative goals into specific tests and curricular guidelines, and then interpreted by classroom teachers. But much of this study is also about the values that underlie assessment policies, how they are framed, and how they motivate behavior. Consequently, the data for this study needed to measure key actors' motivations and perceptions, as well as their behavior.

Three kinds of data were collected. The first consisted of interviews with participants in the three states, ranging from state legislators to classroom teachers and parents. In all, 262 face-to-face interviews were conducted between 1992 and 1995, and an additional 44 school administrators and school counselors in Kentucky and North Carolina were interviewed by telephone in 1994.[9]

At the state level, legislators and their staffs, governors' education aides, officials in state departments of education, and interest group representatives were interviewed. Local, in-person interviews in Kentucky and North Carolina focused on two schools in each of three districts for a total of 12 schools in the two states. In each school, the research team interviewed four teachers, the principal, and the counselor; we also interviewed the superintendent, a school board member, the director of testing, and a district-wide curriculum director in each of the six districts.

Since one purpose of the research was to determine the extent to which teachers had accepted the values underlying the state assessment and had incorporated them into their teaching, we had planned to examine local implementation in California in the same way as in the other two states. However, when CLAS was discontinued after only two administrations, it did not make sense to study its effect on classroom teaching. At the same time, the circumstances under which grassroots organizations were mobilized and the test was ultimately abandoned by the state provided another lens through which to view the role of values in policy implementation. Consequently, we chose to focus on seven California schools where opposition to CLAS was particularly intense. In 1995, about four months after CLAS was discontinued, we conducted face-to-face interviews with the principal at each of the seven schools, teachers in the tested grades, one or more school district officials responsible for curriculum and testing, several school board members, leaders of local opposition groups, and a newspaper reporter. In addition, we interviewed three to five parents at each school who had opposed CLAS and had opted their children out of taking the test, as well as an equal number of parents who were knowledgeable about the school but who did not actively support or oppose CLAS. (The analysis of these "outlier" schools is included in Chapter 4.)

For all the interviews at the state and local levels, we used a structured, open-ended protocol, with the interviews ranging in length from about 30 to 90 minutes. The interview data were aggregated and analyzed in several different ways. The state-level interviews were analyzed by making structured comparisons of respondents in the three states on several key variables, including the basis on which respondents supported or opposed the state assessments, their more general beliefs about the role of the state in public education, and their views of the resources and constraints the state faced in implementing a new assessment. The teacher and administrator interviews from Kentucky and North Carolina were analyzed by systematically comparing respondents on a small set of implementation-related variables, including respondents' understanding of the policy's intent, their assessments of the adequacy of the resources available to them, and their perceptions of the extent to which school and classroom practice had changed in response to the state assessment. To ensure more systematic comparisons of the 48 teachers in the sample, those data were entered into a computer database so that responses could be coded and counts made for the major variables. For the local California data, a site summary was prepared for each of the seven schools; it aggregated the interview data according to several key variables — namely, respondents' attitudes toward CLAS, reasons for opposition, mobilization strategies, district and school response to the controversy, and effects of the controversy. As with the teacher interview data, the 51 California parent interviews were entered into a computerized database for more systematic analysis. The appendix and Chapters 3 through 5 provide additional detail about the interview data, and the appendix includes copies of sample protocols.

Because a major purpose of the study was to track the process by which values are incorporated into policy and policy then changes behavior, the study design emphasizes depth of understanding rather than representativeness. At the state level, the approximately 17 policy actors who were interviewed in each state include virtually all the major players in that state's assessment policy development and politics. But the teacher samples in Kentucky and North Carolina are too small to be representative of all teachers in the two states, and the California schools were purposely chosen because they are outliers and thus by definition unrepresentative of all schools in the state. (The appendix contains a discussion of how local schools and communities were selected and it compares the respondent sample with the relevant universe.) However, for several aspects of the research, we were able to supplement our data with that from other studies. For example, in analyzing the responses of the Kentucky teachers in our sample, we drew on data from two state-representative surveys of teachers and principals.

Newspaper articles were a second data source. All news articles, opinion columns, editorials, and letters to the editor about the state assessment and related education reforms that appeared in the *Los Angeles Times,* the *Lexington Herald-Leader,* and the *Charlotte Observer* between January 1990 and December 1997 were obtained through a computerized search. Articles appearing in other newspapers in the three states were obtained on a less systematic basis, most notably when respondents mentioned particular articles as relevant to debates about the state assessment.[10]

These data served two functions. First, newspaper accounts were used to validate interview responses. Because the newspaper reports were closer in time to events that, in some cases, had occurred several years before, they served as a reliability check on respondents' recall. Second, newspaper coverage of state assessments provided one indicator of the issue's visibility and how it had been framed in public debates. Consequently, we undertook a systematic content analysis of the three newspapers' coverage of the state assessments between 1994 and 1997, the years of greatest political and policy activity. Each article was coded by its type (news, editorial, op-ed, letter to the editor); its overall tone with regard to the assessment (positive, negative, or neutral); and for those that were either positive or negative in tone, the arguments or issues they raised (for example, on the positive side, that the test was measuring higher-order skills; on the negative side, that it was promoting a biased cultural agenda). For California, all 216 articles that appeared in the *Los Angeles Times* were coded, as were the 61 that appeared in the *Charlotte Observer.* However, because the number of articles published in the *Lexington Herald-Leader* was so large (n = 725), only a random sample of 195 was coded. (The results of the content analysis are reported in Chapter 3.)[11]

As a third data source, assignments were collected from 23 of the Kentucky teachers and 23 of the North Carolina teachers who had been interviewed in 1993 and 1994.[12] Participating teachers were asked to provide us with all their in-class and homework assignments, quizzes, exams, projects, and any other written work assigned to students over a two-week period during the fall semester of 1994. Teachers were also asked to complete a one-page log form each day during the two-week period.[13] In addition, they were asked to provide copies of all those assignments made over the entire fall semester that they thought were most like the state assessment.[14]

The use of instructional artifacts (teachers' assignments) as an indicator of the extent of policy implementation is a relatively new strategy for measuring classroom effects (see Burstein et al., 1995 for an extended discussion of the methodology). Detailed classroom observations are likely to provide the most in-depth information from which to make inferences about the effect of new assessments on the curriculum. However, the time and expense involved in classroom observations mean that they are usually conducted on very small samples, with data collected over a limited time period.

Consequently, we analyzed instructional artifacts as an alternative. This strategy allowed us to compare teacher reports about changes in instruction with their actual assignments, and to collect data during an entire semester. Instructional artifacts provided a more valid measure of whether teaching was consistent with the state assessment than did either teacher surveys or open-ended interviews. The disadvantage is that the artifacts provided no information about how students received and responded to the curriculum, in the way that classroom observation data do. This data collection strategy also limits generalizability because the sample size is small and not representative of all the state's teachers. Still, the use of instructional artifact data is a significant improvement over past implementation studies that rely almost entirely on participants' self-reports with no independent validation.

The artifact data consist of an average of 15 ten-day assignments per teacher (n = 670),[15] 11 daily logs (n = 503), and nine assignments (n = 399) that teachers judged to be similar to the state assessment.[16]

Information was extracted from the instructional artifacts by six experienced teachers (two for each of three subject areas) who were familiar with the tenets of recent curriculum reforms and the move to standards-based education. They used a coding instrument that asked them to determine what proportion of each teacher's assignments contained a set of general characteristics that were common to the subjects and the two states (for example, requiring open-ended responses of several sentences, requiring students to explain their reasoning), and a set of characteristics specific to a particular subject (for example, requiring students to apply mathematical concepts to real-world solutions or problems). The coders then assessed each teacher's assignments to determine how consistent they were with the instructional goals specific to his or her particular state.[17]

Together these data advance the book's major arguments. They depict in rich detail the ideas and values that shaped each state's assessment, the process by which those values were both contested and sustained in the political arena, and the extent to which a policy mechanism based on persuasion was able to translate ideas about teaching and learning into everyday classroom practice. The in-depth interviews highlight the varied perspectives of those initiating, opposing, and implementing the new assessments, while the newspaper content analysis and the instructional artifacts allowed us to assess the validity of those perspectives and to link testing policy both to the broader politics of the state and to the unique circumstances of local schools and classrooms.

Organization of the Book

Chapter 2 presents a conceptual framework for analyzing hortatory policies that rely on either information or values to motivate action consistent with a policy's goals. When public officials and analysts consider the range of strategies available to advance policy goals, they typically think of ones that rely on tangible rewards and sanctions to motivate action or change behavior. However, policymakers have another tool at their disposal that relies on deeply held values and the ability to persuade. The policy research literature recognizes such persuasive tools, but little empirical or theoretical work has been done on their properties — the types of policy problems these tools are intended to address, their underlying assumptions, and how they can be combined with other instruments. Although student assessment is the policy being studied, the conceptual framework detailed in Chapter 2 applies to other policy domains, and the chapter discussion draws upon examples from other areas, such as consumer safety and environmental protection.

Chapters 3 through 5 compare assessment policies in the three states. Chapter 3 focuses on the state politics of testing, examining the ideas that framed each state's assessment, policymakers' expectations for what the new assessment would accomplish, and the political opportunities and constraints that shaped it. In its focus on state-level opposition to California's and Kentucky's tests, the chapter illustrates the difficulty that political elites have in controlling the direction of values-based policy strategies. While using one set of values to motivate targets, hortatory policies may also serve as a catalyst for mobilization around competing values that are counterproductive to the policy's intent, as was the case with the cultural conservatives who opposed the new assessments.

Chapter 4 reverses the top-down look at policy, and focuses on grassroots opposition to CLAS. It examines how local opponents mobilized and how the state and local communities facing the most intense opposition responded. The chapter also illustrates a dimension of education policy sometimes forgotten by those initiating new policies: local officials often have to mediate conflicts stemming from top-down policies not of their making, and those conflicts can disrupt well-established patterns of school–community relations. In this case, those who were least responsible for the design of CLAS, knew the least about it, and had the least capacity to respond effectively bore the brunt of the controversy. That burden included school board members unable to act in ways they perceived to be in the best interests of their constituents because of state restrictions; administrators and teachers who could not talk knowledgeably to parents about the test because they had not been allowed to see it; and schools where the controversy generated such intense emotions that friends and colleagues became estranged from one another and even students were called upon to take sides.

Chapter 5 addresses the question of whether new state assessments make a difference in what is taught and how, or, posed differently, whether hortatory policies can actually change policy targets' behavior. Although only limited inferences can be drawn from the small sample studied, the analysis suggests that policies grounded in appeals to values do prompt targets to alter their behavior, but that other dimensions of the implementation process — such as the time frame and prior institutional capacity — often limit the extent of that change. Nevertheless, if they are linked with adequate capacity-building tools and tap widely shared curricular values, hortatory testing policies can be quite effective in changing the content and manner of classroom instruction, and may serve as viable alternatives to the current emphasis on high stakes testing.

Chapter 6 outlines the implications of the study for the design and implementation of future assessment policies and suggests what this research implies for policies that require a strong values consensus among diverse groups. At one level, the lessons are similar to those learned from other studies that have examined the implementation of top-down policy: seemingly inexpensive reforms, from the perspective of policymakers, simply shift the cost and time burden to lower levels of the system; reforms cannot succeed unless those charged with implementing them have both the will and the capacity to change; consequently, investment in the enhanced capacity of local implementors becomes a critical ingredient in successful implementation.

But the story of student assessment policy during the past decade is more than just another data point in the history of education policy implementation. Because of their political prominence and the variety of ways they can be used, state assessments have become a focal point for debates about how society should allocate its educational benefits, as well as about what schools should teach. In focusing on the controversy about underlying curricular values, this book may seem out-dated since the policy agenda has shifted to new issues of test use for student promotion and graduation decisions. However, the story of assessment policy in the 1990s has enduring implications for both the wider politics of education and for other policies that rely on values to effect social change.

In fact, assessment policy suggests lessons often ignored in education and policymaking more generally. Hortatory policy requires an open, inclusive, and deliberative process, in contrast to the closed, expert-dominated process that has characterized assessment policy. Although expanding the process and involving more people may seem desirable and straightforward, such a remedy poses its own set of problems. Not only does it make the policymaking process longer and more cumbersome, but it forces participants to confront their differences and then to work to develop common understandings. In the case of education policy, a more inclusive politics will also require a fundamental re-ordering of the balance between the professional authority of educators and the political authority of elected officials and their constituents.

2

Persuasion as a Policy Instrument

Analysts have focused on policy instruments or tools as a way to compare policies and to understand how policy design influences implementation and ultimate effects. Policy instruments are generic mechanisms that translate substantive policy goals (improved student achievement, reduced air pollution) into concrete actions (McDonnell and Elmore, 1987; Linder and Peters, 1988; Schneider and Ingram, 1990, 1997). Policy instruments are, in effect, "the basic building blocks of public policy" (Linder and Peters, 1988, p. 11). Although researchers differ in how they conceptualize categories of policy instruments and in the number of distinct instruments they identify, they agree that different types of instruments embody different assumptions about how a policy problem is defined, the causal process through which government action can change the behavior of policy targets, and what the expected effects of an action will be.

Two classes of policy instruments are included in all categorizations and are familiar to policymakers and the public alike: *mandates* impose rules on targets and are intended to produce compliance (for example, speed limits), and *inducements* provide money and other tangible pay-offs on the condition that targets perform specified actions (for example, various grant-in-aid programs). However, there is another type of policy instrument that relies not on material rewards or sanctions, but on persuasion.

Schneider and Ingram (1990, 1997) call this a hortatory or symbolic tool. Although this policy instrument is expected to change people's behavior, it imposes no tangible consequences on them. Yet hortatory policies are meant to be more than rhetorical tools and are intended to produce measurable effects. In her typology of policy instruments, Stone (1997) includes one that relies on persuasion. This instrument, analogous to the notion of a hortatory tool, is defined as a policy that changes "people's behavior by operating on their minds and their perceptions of the world, rather than through rewards and punishments or through clearly delineated permissions or prohibitions" (p. 260). Weiss (1990) analyzes a similar type of policy

23

instrument, and conceptualizes it as based on ideas. Ideas "work as policy instruments by inviting people to *think* differently about their situation, by providing them with information about new alternatives or about the advantages or disadvantages of existing alternatives, making some perspectives more salient than others, directing attention toward some phenomena and away from others, or leading people to accept different values or preferences" (p. 179).

Information and values are the two elements that distinguish hortatory policies from ones that rely on other mechanisms to motivate action. Sometimes the two elements are used separately, but often they are combined. Examples of information-based policies include food labeling and community right-to-know statutes dealing with hazardous materials. Appeals to values are represented in energy conservation policies and recycling programs.[1]

As mechanisms through which governments seek to achieve their substantive goals, all public policies reflect particular sets of values or preferences. Furthermore, much of politics is about persuading political elites and voters to accept some preferences and not others, and the policy process itself is characterized by appeals to values, persuasion, and the triumph of one set of ideas over another. The difference between hortatory policy and other types is that information and values are not just part of the policymaking process, they are the policy. This policy tool assumes that objective costs and benefits do not have to be altered to elicit desired behavior (Weiss, 1990). Rather, people can learn to value different goals or to change their priorities through new information and value frames. Ideas and information substitute for tangible rewards and sanctions as the motivating policy tools.

Although most literature on policy instruments identifies this persuasive tool as one of the strategies available to policymakers, little theoretical or comparative empirical research has been conducted on its properties. Public policy textbooks typically devote only a few pages to this policy instrument, if they consider it at all. There is empirical research on policies that rely on hortatory tools, but studies of these individual policies have not examined them within a broader theoretical framework. Consequently, we know something about how such policies operate within single policy domains, but little about the generic properties of hortatory policy.[2]

This chapter represents an initial attempt to analyze the major characteristics of hortatory policy by taking an inductive approach and looking across several different policy areas to identify a few basic properties common to most policies of this type. The resulting theoretical framework focuses on the assumptions that hortatory policy makes about how policy-induced change occurs, its links to other policy instruments, and the types of policy problems most amenable to hortatory solutions. Its generic properties are illustrated with examples from assessment policy, and from other policy domains such as environmental protection and consumer safety.

The Theory of Hortatory Policy

As a basis for understanding the differences between hortatory policy and other approaches to solving policy problems, Table 2.1 compares several types of generic policy instruments. In their ideal forms, they are designed to mitigate different types of problems, doing so through different mechanisms and making quite different assumptions about how policy targets will behave and with what expected effects. As we will see later in this chapter, public policies are rarely based on a single instrument, with most combining several. However, whether used singly or integrated with other strategies, the hortatory elements of a policy are distinguishable from other approaches because they seek to change behavior through the use of the less-tangible mechanisms of information and values rather than rules, money, or grants of public authority.

All policies embody an implicit theory of change; they assume that if governments initiate certain actions, the targets of those actions will alter their behavior to be consistent with the policy's goals. For example, a mandate such as a speed limit assumes that by promulgating the rule, imposing sanctions for non-compliance, and enforcing the law, government will cause motorists to drive only at permissible speeds. However, for the theory to be valid, certain causal assumptions must be operational. In this case, the sanctions have to be severe enough and the likelihood of enforcement high enough for motorists to decide that the costs of speeding outweigh the benefits of arriving at their destinations sooner.[3]

Hortatory policies also embody a theory about how to effect change in human behavior. In its simplest form, the theory posits that if information is provided or beliefs and values appealed to, policy targets will act in a manner consistent with the policy's goals and their actions will lead to desired changes. This theory is perhaps clearest for a variety of right-to-know policies that provide information to the public about the health risks and benefits associated with various drugs, food products, and toxics. The assumption is that disclosure will correct the information asymmetries between producers and consumers, and will allow the public to make informed purchases in the private sector and to participate on a more equitable basis in public sector decisions.[4] With regard to the public sector, the theory is that if citizens have reliable information about governmental performance, they will be better able to hold elected officials and bureaucrats accountable for

Table 2.1. Policy instruments compared

Instrument	Primary Elements	Policy Problem	Policy Targets and Expected Effects	Examples
Mandates	Rules	Undesirable behavior or goods being produced. Lack of uniform standards.	Have capacity to comply; most will do so, though some shirking is likely.	Speed limits Environmental regulation Nondiscrimination laws
Inducements	Money (procurement)	Valued goods or services not being produced with desired frequency or at sufficient levels of quality and innovation.	Have capacity to produce; money will elicit performance, though variability in production levels is likely.	Grants-in-aid to governmental agencies, private-sector organizations, individuals
Capacity-building	Money (investment)	Lack of longer-term investment in needed skills and valued goods.	Lack capacity, but investment will mobilize it. Incentives will shift to longer-range goals. Payoff is less likely than for other instruments.	Funding for basic research, training, historic preservation
System-changing	Authority	Existing institutional arrangements are not producing desired results.	New entrants will produce desired results and will motivate established institutions to improve performance. However, new entrants may generate other problems.	Vouchers Contracting-out governmental services
Hortatory	Information Beliefs and values	Information for remedying a problem or making a choice is incomplete. Some values held strongly, so beyond the control of just incentives or rules.	Targets will mobilize, based on strongly held values, and will act on information. But actions may be diffuse, unpredictable, and varied.	Food labeling Recycling Curriculum and testing policies

their actions, particularly in agencies that provide services to the public (Gormley and Weimer, 1999).

The word "empowerment" is often used in connection with this policy instrument because it is viewed as a way to give individuals the resources to choose which risks and benefits they will accept, rather than leaving the decision to government regulators (Stenzel, 1991). For this policy model to operate as intended, however, people must seek and then comprehend information about potential risks and benefits, and they must have opportunities for choice or action in response to that information (Pease, 1991).

In commenting on the values dimension of hortatory policy, Schneider and Ingram (1990) note that "symbolic and hortatory tools assume that people are motivated from within and decide whether or not to take policy-related actions on the basis of their beliefs and values" (p. 519). They argue that hortatory policies send a signal that particular goals and actions are considered a high priority by government officials, and in calling upon people's values, they rely on positive symbols and images. Hortatory policies thus appeal to policy targets' values and beliefs while simultaneously mobilizing them to act on those values. In distinguishing between the two elements that motivate hortatory policies, Howlett and Ramesh (1995) argue that persuasion through an appeal to values (what they call "exhortation" or "suasion") involves only slightly more governmental activity than information dissemination: "It entails a concerted effort to change the subjects' preferences and actions, rather than just informing them about a situation with the hope of changing their behavior in a desired manner. However, it does not include altering the attractiveness of the choice through offer of rewards or imposition of sanctions" (p. 91).

For assessment policy, the information provided is test scores showing how well students are performing, and the values appealed to range from the rather vague notion that U.S. students should perform as well as the best of their peers internationally to specific ideas about what content students should learn and how they should be taught. The targets are policy elites, educators, parents, and citizens who will use assessment data to identify the strengths and weaknesses of the education system and then promote change consistent with that diagnosis. The policy further assumes that interested parties will deliberate about the appropriate course of action and that assessment data will inform the debate. Subsequent policies resulting from those deliberations may include other instruments, such as mandates, but it is the provision of information that serves as a catalyst to change people's behavior and initiate further action.

The appeal to targets' values can take a variety of forms. For example, mathematics teachers might be told that stressing an understanding of mathematical principles and the application of knowledge to solving unfamiliar problems is endorsed by their national professional association and that teaching consistent with those values will enhance the teachers' own professional stature. The expected result is that teachers will move away from instruction focused primarily on rote memorization and basic arithmetic operations and will instead stress critical thinking skills. In reflecting these values, the assessment will not only identify what level of student performance is expected, but also suggest what kind of teaching is preferred. Similarly, parents and the public might be persuaded that allowing students to construct knowledge for themselves through experimentation and application to unfamiliar situations is the best way to prepare them to be active citizens and productive workers. The assumption here is that if parents and the public accept these values, they will press for schools that reflect them in their teaching and in their assessment of students.

Four causal assumptions must be operative for a hortatory policy to work as intended:

- The information expected under the policy is produced and is understandable to its target audiences.
- The values appealed to are sufficiently strong and broadly accepted so as to prompt widespread action.
- Targets have sufficient incentive and capacity to respond.
- Targets' response will be consistent with the policy's goals.

Two other assumptions are not absolutely necessary, but are ones that policymakers typically assume about hortatory policies and that give them much of their appeal:

- Costs will be relatively small and will be borne primarily by policy targets.
- Links to other policy instruments are crucial if effects are to be more than purely informational and symbolic in the longer term.

This chapter examines each of these assumptions, focusing first on the two dealing with information and values as the motivating mechanisms, then on the two related to policy targets, and finally, on the issues of cost and links to other policy instruments. In each section, several factors are discussed that delimit the conditions in which the six assumptions are likely to operate as intended. (Table 2.2 summarizes the theory underlying hortatory policies.)

Information and Values as Motivators

When we analyze the information dimension of hortatory policy, two aspects stand out. First, the information expected under a particular policy may not

Table 2.2. Information and values as policy tools

Causal Assumptions	Limiting Conditions
• The expected information is produced and understandable to policy targets.	• If information is not voluntarily generated, its production may need to be mandated. • The information must be reliable and useful to those who are to act upon it.
• The values appealed to are strong enough and broadly accepted to prompt widespread action.	• Appeals should be forceful enough to motivate action without being divisive. • The values invoked should be general enough to have broad appeal, but specific enough to guide targets' actions.
• Targets have sufficient incentive and capacity to respond.	• Targets are more likely to respond if the actions required do not deviate significantly from existing beliefs and practices. • Additional incentives and capacity-building strategies may be necessary to enhance targets' willingness and ability to understand and act upon the information provided.
• Targets' responses will be consistent with the policy's goals.	• Because hortatory policies are typically open-ended and lack the rule-based frameworks of mandates and inducements, the resulting actions are likely to be diffuse, unpredictable, and varied. • While hortatory policies can encourage local initiative and creativity, the lack of policy rules makes mobilization difficult for political elites to control, and may prompt actions counter to the policy's goals.
• Costs will be relatively small and will be borne primarily by policy targets.	• Many of the costs of the hortatory policies are not completely visible until a policy is fully operative.
• Hortatory policies need to be linked to other policy instruments if their effects are to be more than purely informational and symbolic in the longer term.	• A hortatory policy starts a process to change targets' behavior, but the effectiveness of the strategy may diminish over time if it is not reinforced by policies with tangible consequences.

be voluntarily generated because its dissemination runs counter to the interests of those who must produce the information. For example, because consumers may be less likely to buy prepared foods if they know they contain many additives or have a high fat content, some manufacturers may not voluntarily release nutritional information. Consequently, hortatory policies rarely operate in a pure form, relying only on information and values to change behavior. Rather, policies that use information as their primary strategy typically mandate its production and dissemination. Prime examples are food labeling and community right-to-know statutes requiring that the presence of hazardous materials be publicly reported. In the case of food labeling, federal law requires that food manufacturers report standardized information on the nutrients found in prepared food. The health claims that manufacturers can make about food products (for example, low in sodium, high in fiber) are also circumscribed by this law, and the Food and Drug Administration (FDA) has the authority to enforce compliance. In the hazardous materials area, a variety of federal and state laws require public disclosure about potential exposure to toxic substances. For example, California's Proposition 65 requires businesses to warn citizens if they might be exposed to significant levels of a chemical known to cause either cancer or reproductive harm; failure to comply with the law carries both civil and criminal penalties.

Although information is the primary element used to prompt action for these policies, they are also part of a regulatory framework. For assessment policy, the mandatory aspect differs because state governments, rather than the private sector, generate student test-score data. Still, there is an element of coercion, in that local schools are required to test all those students enrolled in the grades and subjects that fall within the state's testing program.

Second, the quality and relevance of the information provided to various target audiences is a critical factor in determining whether hortatory policies work as intended. Assessment policy illustrates the challenge of producing information that is reliable, understandable, and useful to those who must act upon it. State assessments have three major audiences, each of which has different information needs. Policymakers and the public need general information about individual schools, or in some cases, data that summarize across all schools in a particular community—how well they are performing, compared with an established standard or with other schools and communities; whether or not their performance is improving; whether performance is comparable across different student groups and geographic regions. Parents and students need to know how well individual students are performing, compared with either some standard or with peers, and what individual students' areas of greatest strength and weakness are. Educators need information telling them not only how well the students in their charge are performing, but also about the curricular implications of the assessment—what kinds of teaching are likely to result in higher student performance. These different information needs require that assessment data are reported in differing detail and levels of aggregation. But accommodating diverse audiences also affects which students are tested, how many items are used to measure their performance, and what levels of reliability and validity are acceptable.

Another dimension of information quality is its credibility to those who must use it. In the case of assessment policy, credibility often comes down to whether the test scores make sense to various target audiences. For example: Is the level of performance associated with a state standard for "proficient" or "exemplary" consistent with parents' and the public's notions of what students should know? Do the scoring criteria appear to be fair, and are the scores expressed on a scale that is understandable to those using the information?

How data are interpreted also affects information quality and usefulness. It is easy for information providers to inundate users with too much data or to present data in an inaccessible format. For example, the data reported under California's Proposition 65 have been described by one analyst as "unwieldy and confusing"; industry reports are typically hundreds of pages long, and the format of the reports means that important contextual data, such as the environmental conditions under which released chemicals pose a hazard, are omitted (Black, 1989, p. 1049). Consequently, the information presented cannot be accurately interpreted. A staggering amount of data with little context for interpreting it represents one dimension of the information problem for public disclosure laws such as Proposition 65. But other analysts have suggested a potentially more serious problem. In requiring the reporting of something as straightforward as a warning that a particular substance has been known to cause cancer, a disclosure policy may mislead the public into believing that there are simple answers to complex questions about assessing risk when, in fact, most risk assessments are only tentative because researchers do not fully understand the causal relationship between exposure to a substance and the incidence of cancer (Stenzel, 1991). This same dilemma arises in the case of student testing policy. In reducing student achievement to a single test score, there is always the danger that parents and the public will assume that this score encompasses the full measure of a student's or a school's performance. In essence, there is a trade-off between making information understandable and accessible and ensuring that it can be validly interpreted.

The question of how information is interpreted and used becomes even more complicated when we consider that its purpose in hortatory policies is to persuade targets to take particular courses of action. Stone (1997) argues that "in political theory, persuasion has two faces, one revered and the other feared" (p. 303). The revered side represents one of the strongest principles in a liberal democracy—that citizens should be given information and be allowed to make up their own minds (Sunstein, 1993). This is the rational ideal that "evokes images of reasoned and informed decision, . . . where individual actions are brought into harmony through the persuasive power of logic and evidence. Government by persuasion brings out the highest human quality—the capacity to deliberate" (Stone, 1997, pp. 303, 305).

However, there is also a less positive side to persuasion: what Stone calls its "ugly face," captured in the words "propaganda" and "indoctrination." In its extreme form, propaganda is intentionally manipulative, robbing people of their capacity to think independently. According to Stone, if indoctrination "relies on appeals to fear, insecurity, or anxiety, it drives out rational thought, and if it relies on rational appeals (for example, visions of a more prosperous future), it distorts and withholds information so that rational deliberation is truncated" (p. 305).

Even most critics would not argue that hortatory policies are propaganda tools intended to manipulate public sentiment. But the "ugly face" of persuasion is relevant to policies such as student assessment because of an important point that Stone makes: "the boundary between the two sides of persuasion is blurry" (p. 307). The rational ideal that infuses the positive side of persuasion assumes the existence of neutral facts. Yet facts are not neutral in the sense that they merely describe the world accurately, or that they are not affected by values and interests. As Stone notes, "the rational ideal not only overstates the purity of information, it also exaggerates the rationality of people using information" (p. 312). As a result, the contrasting qualities of hortatory policy are often framed in terms of the blurred boundary between objective information and value-laden interpretations (or even mild forms of propaganda).

Because many hortatory policies rely on both information and values to motivate action, the boundary between the two is necessarily blurred. In fact, for those policies expected to produce significant change, persuasion may depend less on the information disseminated than on how that information is filtered through the lens of a compelling set of values. Hortatory policies must appeal to values that are both strong enough to motivate action and accepted enough to mobilize a widespread response. In addition, technical information related to the policy needs to be simplified and interpreted within the context of those values. Assessment policy, for example, requires a diverse set of targets or publics, including those whose behavior is intended to be changed (students, parents, teachers) and those who can persuade others to change (business and community leaders, the general public). To appeal to these myriad publics, the values articulated in most assessment policies include goals around which policymakers can assume a broad consensus, such as the "ability to compete internationally," "challenging content for all children," and "accountability to taxpayers."

For those policies expected to produce relatively simple and straightforward action, such vague maxims may be adequate. For example, recycling requires a simple response on the part of targets (separating glass, aluminum, plastic, and newspapers from the rest of their trash), so appealing to altruism and a desire to help improve the environment is typically enough. However, for other policies such as educational standards and assessment, an appeal to abstract values may mobilize people, but it does not tell them what they should do once they are mobilized. Arguing that students should be taught challenging content does not specify what that content is or how it should be taught. However, the more precise the values appealed to, the more difficult it is to achieve a broad consensus. As we will see in subsequent chapters, opposition to state standards and assessments has not emerged over whether there should be standards or if they should be challenging, but rather over who should decide what those standards are and what precise knowledge and skills should be included in the curriculum and measured on the state tests.

The challenge for political leaders in using hortatory instruments is to articulate a set of values that will prompt action consistent with what they hope to achieve. In doing so, they have to craft a strategy that balances a variety of objectives. For example, policymakers need to devise appeals forceful enough to motivate action, but they must also be careful that strong exhortations do not become divisive. Schneider and Ingram (1997) warn of the potential danger of hortatory policies that rely too heavily on value appeals based on symbols portraying preferred behavior in a positive light, while presenting people acting contrary to the policy's goals as "backward, out of the mainstream, or deviant" (p. 95). Like Stone, they warn against appealing to a set of values using symbols that separate policy supporters from those preferring alternative approaches. Hortatory policies can be damaging to democratic principles if they persuade through divisiveness rather than through reason and discussion.

As already noted, the values appealed to must also be general enough to ensure broad-based support, but specific enough to guide targets' actions. Because responses can be expected to differ across targets, the strength of the value appeals made to different audiences may also differ. For example, some policies may be successful even if large segments of the public are unaware of them and take no action, as long as there is an active response from critical target groups (primarily teachers, in the case of assessment policy). Consequently, policymakers may have to craft their persuasive communications to elicit a strong response from some groups and only tacit consent from others. Policymakers must recognize that not all target groups will mobilize with equal intensity, and if some targets are likely to be less supportive of the values embodied in a particular policy, officials may decide that successful implementation requires less powerful appeals to some groups than to others. Whether policymakers are successful with such directed appeals depends on many factors, but one is how a policy is defined or framed by other supporters and opponents of a policy and by the media. The response to a community disclosure law, for example, depends on whether targets view it as a way to protect public health or as a barrier to economic development. Similarly, assessment policy can be framed either as a way to report on the status and quality of public education, or as an infringement on students' and parents' right to privacy. The problem for lawmakers is that their influence over how policy values are portrayed is limited and is shared with other actors over whom they have virtually no control. Consequently, they can neither ensure that policy targets will act according to a policy's goals or even that they will act at all.

How Policy Targets Respond

Hortatory instruments assume that targets not only are critical in the causal logic that produces policy effects, but also that targets act as a catalyst, actually triggering the causal process. The targets of hortatory policies may be individual citizens, organized groups, or other political and economic elites, and the actions they are expected to initiate can be quite diverse, ranging from individual consumer choices to "voice" strategies such as lobbying and on to exit from private or public sector institutions. Unless targets act, the information and persuasive communications that define hortatory policies will have failed.

For some policies, the intended targets include both the producers and the users of information. For example, one of the expected outcomes of the federal Nutrition Labeling and Education Act of 1990 is that food manufacturers will extensively reformulate some of their products, because consumers armed with mandatory nutritional information are more likely to make unfavorable judgments about foods with less-desirable nutritional profiles (Caswell, 1992). The assumption is that manufacturers will anticipate consumer responses and reformulate products even before the public acts on the new information offered. A similar assumption underlies public disclosure laws dealing with toxics: "Manufacturers may withhold or withdraw [toxic] products from the market to avoid public scorn and lawsuits that might arise when the warning alerts the public to its exposure to the risk of cancer or other reproductive harm" (Stenzel, 1991, p. 498).

Empirical data on whether various kinds of hortatory policies actually motivate targets to act are scant. Although there is a substantial body of research on the effects of different kinds of persuasive communications in advertising and political campaigns, that research has not been linked to information dissemination and value appeals within policy frameworks. Part of the reason is that some of the most important hortatory policies are relatively new, having been implemented only within the past decade.

One conclusion that does seem to be emerging from experience with mandatory disclosure laws is that despite design characteristics that limit their effectiveness, a number are producing effects disproportionate to either the scope of the policy or to initial expectations. One example is the Toxics Release Inventory (TRI), a federal mandate requiring that manufacturing programs report their annual emissions of 651 toxic chemicals to the Environmental Protection Agency (EPA). Little enforcement is in place to ensure either the accuracy of the data reported or firms' compliance with the reporting requirement.[5] Yet reports from chemical manufacturers, environmentalists, and regulators, along with limited evaluation data, suggest that the TRI has been more successful in getting companies to reduce their emissions than other EPA programs that rely on more traditional regulatory strategies. Although TRI is a relatively small and inexpensively administered program (costing about $23 million annually), its effects have been magnified because the data are used for a variety of purposes, ranging from community education and mobilization to corporate planning (Fung and O'Rourke, 2000).

Energy conservation is an example of an older, values-based policy on which data are available. But most of the research in this area was conducted more than 20 years ago, when the oil crisis of the 1970s put energy conservation on the national policy agenda. These studies provide a mixed, and perhaps on balance discouraging, picture of the effectiveness of hortatory policies. A large number found no relationship between how strongly respondents believed in the reality and seriousness of the energy problem and the kinds and numbers of energy conservation actions they reported taking. However, several studies found a positive relationship between respondents having either a sense of civic duty or a personal norm that valued conservation and reporting higher levels of energy conservation behavior (Olsen, 1978). These studies suggest that hortatory strategies can be effective if they can tap values that targets already hold and can frame the desired policy action to appear consistent with those values.

In her study of an ideas-based instrument in federal mental health policy, Weiss (1990) found that this approach was quite effective when used in combination with an inducements strategy. She reported that while the inducements stimulated growth in community-based treatment, the ideas component provided direction and logic to that growth by supporting a particular vision of mental health care. It provided a variety of targets—including medical students, state mental health officials, researchers, clinicians, and in-surers—with the information, models, and philosophy to proceed in a new direction. In sum, "ideas can mobilize energy, bestow competence, introduce alternatives, direct attention, even change minds about ultimate goals and preferences" (p. 193).

Weiss also concluded that ideas may be especially useful policy tools in domains, like mental health, that are dominated by professionals. Profes-sionals have formal knowledge, and their work requires informed judgments about appropriate responses to a range of diverse problems. In environments where work cannot always be routinized, ideas embedded in external policies can mobilize energy around testing new approaches on a case-by-case basis without threatening the basic notion of professional control. Hortatory pol-icies may make external political accountability more palatable to profession-als accustomed to self-governance.

Research on policies that rely on persuasive communication has focused on whether targets have a sufficient incentive to act. But there is also the question of whether they have the capacity to do what is expected of them. Like mandates and inducements, hortatory policies assume that targets do have the ability to act in accordance with a particular policy; they only need to be appropriately motivated. But just as other policy instruments can fail if targets lack adequate capacity, hortatory instruments often need capacity-building components if they are to be successful.

At one level, building targets' capacity to understand and to act upon the information provided can be accomplished with careful attention to the qual-ity of that information. However, adequate capacity often requires resources in addition to those contained within the information provided directly by the policy. Consumers cannot use nutritional profiles to advantage if they are unfamiliar with the building blocks of a healthy diet or do not know how to prepare nutritious meals. Teachers cannot teach consistent with the expectations of new standards policies if they lack a conception of how such teaching might actually occur in classrooms like theirs. Like most policies, those that rely on information or an appeal to values depend on targets' willingness to act and on their ability to do so. However, building that capacity typically depends on more than just information dissemination; it also requires a long-term investment in education and support for targets.

The need to ensure adequate capacity is complicated by how hortatory policies mobilize people. Most policy instruments are premised on the no-tion that policy targets will take individual actions consistent with broader civic goals—for example, obey speed limits or participate in job-training programs. Hortatory instruments may also define mobilization in terms of individual actions such as picking up litter or not using illegal drugs. Perhaps more than any other policy instrument, however, hortatory policy also assumes that policy targets will mobilize to take collective action, based on the information presented to them. That information might be about educational achievement, crime rates, or health care costs, and it may prompt individual action, but typically the expectation is that people will also join together to work for change. For example, federal, state, and local disclosure policies dealing with hazardous materials assume that the information in right-to-know reports will serve as a basis for political dialogues about the proper use and regulation of hazardous materials within communities (Black, 1989). Consequently, the federal Emergency Planning Community Right-to-Know Act (EPCRA) requires public participation in the administration of state and local reporting and planning processes.

Whether it is collective or individual, the mobilization of targets through hortatory policy increases the likelihood that the resulting actions will be diffuse, unpredictable, and varied. Unlike mandates or incentives that structure targets' participation through rule-based frameworks that allocate rewards and sanctions, hortatory policies are typically more open-ended. They exhort targets to take action and may suggest possible directions and strategies. However, unless they are linked to other policy instruments, hortatory components typically do not prescribe a clear set of procedures.[6] As a result, hortatory policies may lead to considerable variation in the extent and type of mobilization that results.

The open-ended nature of hortatory instruments is both a strength and a weakness of this policy strategy. A distinct advantage is it encourages creativity and local initiative. It also taps the civic virtues associated with grassroots democracy—citizens banding together to solve problems and to petition government to act on their behalf, rather than passively waiting for elected officials and bureaucrats to do what they think best. Even though hortatory policies stem from official government actions, they can mobilize citizens to take collective actions on their own, outside formal governmental processes. For example, environmental activists hope that one of the side benefits of right-to-know laws will be greater public involvement and a grassroots consensus that will reshape policy debates about environmental health and safety issues (Black, 1989).

However, the lack of precise rules makes mobilization difficult for policy elites to control or even influence. As Schneider and Ingram (1997) note, rules are the procedural aspect of policy design that "circumscribe and channel policy-relevant behavior to serve policy-relevant goals" (p. 97). They list several types associated with hortatory policies: *timing rules*, specifying when and in what sequence actions by targets are to occur, *participation rules*, indicating who is to be included in decision processes, and *decision rules*, specifying the level of approval and voting procedure needed for action. In prescribing the terms of participation, these rules may favor some targets more than others (Schneider and Ingram, 1997; March and Olsen, 1989; Moe, 1990). For that reason, policy rules can reinforce existing political and social inequalities or create new ones that limit who is mobilized and able to act. But rules also have distinct advantages. They make policy responses more predictable by specifying the arenas in which actions can occur, the definition of appropriate actions, and the time frame and scope of those actions. In other words, the rules embedded in a policy framework prescribe who can take what actions, as well as where and when.

As we will see with assessment policy, the lack of precise rules about how targets are mobilized may lead to a variety of situations that work against a policy achieving its intended purpose. For example, without clear rules for participation, some potential targets may be excluded from design decisions or subsequent actions based on the policy's hortatory message. The effect of that exclusion may be either to create inequalities among targets or to prompt those who have been excluded to oppose the policy or to work outside its framework. Even with fairly precise rules, however, hortatory policies may prompt actions that are either outside the policy's framework or that stem from values contradictory to the policy's goals. In fact, policymakers often face a trade-off: if they appeal to values that are so strongly held as to prompt action, they run the risk of catalyzing a counter-mobilization around competing values. In highlighting a particular set of curricular values, for example, standards and assessment policies in some states came to the attention of groups with different views about what should be taught, and the policies then served as rallying points for counter-mobilization. In this case, more precise rules might not have stopped the opposition effort, but they might have blunted it if the policy rules governing participation had been more specific and inclusive.

Policy Costs and Who Bears Them

Policy costs have two dimensions: the extent of monetary and non-monetary costs imposed by a policy, and who bears those costs. The types of costs associated with particular policy instruments range from the direct monetary costs associated with enforcing and complying with mandates to the opportunity costs that targets bear when they attend to activities required as a condition of receiving the financial resources offered by inducement policies, and therefore cannot engage in other activities of importance to them (McDonnell and Elmore, 1987). The question of cost burden focuses on what proportion of total costs accrues to the policy initiators and what proportion to policy targets. One of the reasons that hortatory policies have become more popular as an alternative to mandates and inducements is that policymakers perceive them to be low-cost, with most of that cost borne not by governmental initiators, but by policy targets. That assumption is largely correct, but as with other policy instruments, the cost calculus for most hortatory policies is not a simple one.

Certainly, some of the costs of hortatory policies are visible and direct—for example, designing and administering tests to students, putting new labels on food packages, or inventorying hazardous workplace chemicals. But one of the problems with hortatory policies is that many of the costs are, if not hidden, at least not fully visible. For example, Magat and Viscusi (1992) note that when people consider the monetary costs of hazard warnings, they think of the costs of designing and printing labels and disposing of or relabeling products already in inventory. But a larger share is likely to stem from the costs that targets incur in purchasing protective equipment and from the economic inefficiencies that may result from following recommended precautions.[7] With regard to state assessments, we will see in subsequent chapters that policymakers understood that alternatives to multiple-choice tests would cost more to develop and score, but they greatly underestimated the training costs associated with preparing teachers to teach in a manner consistent with the assessments' goals.

Almost by definition, hortatory policy costs will be borne by targets because, unless other instruments are combined with it, the hortatory element offers no other resources except information and persuasive appeals. Consequently, in responding, targets must usually use their own resources. Some informational policies—such as EPCRA, the federal right-to-know law—are actually unfunded mandates. In this case, the federal law requires that states and localities establish reporting and emergency planning procedures for hazardous materials, but it provides no funds to support program administration. In the case of student assessment policy, states have typically borne some of the costs associated with helping local educators respond to the test. But with only a few notable exceptions, most of the training costs have been borne by local districts and individual teachers who want to prepare themselves and their students to do well. In addition, local schools have had to bear a variety of other costs, such as the opportunity costs imposed when the tests direct instructional time toward some subjects and away from others, and the psychic costs to teachers and students anxious about a new testing format.

It is in the interest of policymakers first to estimate as precisely as possible the costs that targets are willing to bear, and then within those constraints, to minimize their own costs and maximize efficient use of their resources. In the case of hortatory policies, policymakers have been more successful with the latter challenge than the former. They have minimized costs at their level of government by pushing them down into the system through decentralized policy responses by individuals and local groups of consumers, parents, educators, and the like. But they have often failed to recognize that hortatory policies are not always as cheap as they seem and that they usually contain a variety of hidden costs that targets are not always willing to bear.

Links to Other Policy Instruments

Most public policies consist of more than one instrument, with policymakers typically selecting a dominant instrument, and then using others to supplement or enhance the primary one. One of the main reasons that policies typically rely on more than one instrument is that they are intended to address multiple problems and influence a variety of targets. For example, a mandate stands at the core of welfare reform: welfare recipients are required to find employment. However, that mandate cannot be met unless jobs and child care are available, so the federal government and states have offered inducements to public and private agencies to provide training and child care, and tax credits to employers to hire welfare recipients. Often the need for multiple instruments stems from the fact that policy targets include individuals whose behavior is expected to change, as well as entire institutions that need the incentives and capacity to alter their activities if the individual-level changes are to occur. Teachers cannot teach differently, or students learn more effectively, if they lack the authority, materials, and other assistance that only schools as institutions can provide.

The need for multiple instruments to address multiple problems and diverse targets partly explains why hortatory policies are often linked to other policy instruments, but there is another reason unique to informational and persuasive strategies. For a hortatory policy, linkage to another policy is often necessary if its effects are to be sustained in the longer term. Some analysts have even argued that without positive inducements or the ability to impose sanctions, most hortatory policies "have either a low probability of success or a relatively short half life." These analysts recommend that persuasive instruments be used in combination with other instruments whenever they are available (Howlett and Ramesh, 1995, p. 92).

Recycling is a good example of a policy that combines multiple instruments with a strong hortatory dimension. To the extent that individual citizens participate in recycling, they do so almost solely because of hortatory appeals. However, with increasing amounts of waste being generated and the availability of landfill rapidly decreasing, the states have realized that appeals to a common spirit of altruism and a conservation ethic are insufficient. Consequently, they have turned to a variety of other instruments such as mandating that communities recycle a certain proportion of their garbage; requiring that commercial businesses separate recyclables; and providing low-interest loans, grants, or tax credits to the recycling industry and to manufacturers using recycled materials in order to create new markets for these materials (Khator, 1993). In this case, individual and community altruism alone is insufficient unless there are efficient markets for the recycled goods produced.

The trend in state assessment policy has been to move away from low stakes tests that result in few tangible consequences for either students or schools toward a greater reliance on high stakes assessments that distribute rewards and impose sanctions. States may, for example, provide cash awards to schools that improve their performance above a certain level, or require a particular level of performance on the assessment as a condition of a student's high school graduation or promotion to the next grade. On the sanctions side, schools that do not meet expected performance levels may be required to accept outside assistance or even to be managed by the state or a third party. Students who do not perform well may be required to attend summer school or to enroll in tutoring sessions or remedial classes.

But just as recycling still depends on an appeal to values despite a policy framework that has grown more complex, the hortatory component of assessment policy has become more important even as tangible consequences have been attached to state tests. The reasons for this seeming contradiction are twofold. First, assessment generally has assumed greater prominence as an education reform strategy because policymakers recognize that it is one of the few top-down approaches that can significantly shape what happens in individual classrooms. As a result, all the various policy instruments used by states in their assessments have become more influential in efforts to change teaching and learning. Second, as assessments are linked to state standards, the curricular approaches and content they measure have become more precise, and the values underlying the tests more explicit. Consequently, even though the desire for rewards or the fear of sanctions may be critical in motivating educators to change their teaching, the hortatory dimension of testing is now even more important in defining the behavior expected of targets.[8] They must understand the values embodied in the test, accept them at least tacitly, and then act on them if the policy is to succeed.

Matching Hortatory Strategies with Policy Problems and Political Conditions

Policies are designed in a political environment shaped by policymakers' ideology and interests, constituent pressures, and a variety of fiscal and institutional constraints. Nevertheless, despite its highly fluid and politicized nature, policymaking is essentially a problem-solving process. Even in its most ideological and politicized versions, it involves an appraisal of current conditions, an assessment of why the status quo is not working as it should, and a search for causes and potential solutions. Thus it is useful to think of the choice of policy instruments as based, at least partially, on different definitions of the problem to be addressed.

Problems particularly amenable to the use of a hortatory strategy typically have one or more of the following characteristics:

- Markets are not working as they should because of information asymmetries.
- A definite solution is not immediately available.
- Other policy instruments are either insufficient to address the problem, or politically infeasible to implement.

Food labeling and energy conservation strategies that rely on information dissemination are examples of hortatory policies designed to correct market imperfections. In the case of food labels, the overriding majority of consumers are not in a position to ascertain the nutritional value of the foods they buy. In contrast to other attributes (such as taste and freshness) that consumers can learn about directly through experience, nutritional content is an area in which sellers have considerably more information than buyers, thus violating the ideal of a perfect market (Caswell and Mojduszka, 1995). Similarly, consumers often lack sufficient information to make informed decisions about complex but infrequent purchases, such as refrigerators and air conditioners (Magat and Viscusi, 1992). In these instances, information is provided to make the market work more efficiently.

Imperfect markets resulting from information asymmetries may not be the central problem addressed in assessment policy, but it is fast becoming an important one as school choice options expand. Not only do parents choose schools for their children infrequently, but it is often difficult for them to collect useful and comparable information about several different schools with which they have no direct experience. Although test scores provide only a limited picture of any school, they can help parents become more informed consumers as they choose from open enrollment, magnet, charter, and other school options.

Howlett and Ramesh (1995) argue that exhortation is a good starting point when governments must deal with problems for which no definite solutions are available. Such policies are relatively easy to implement, and if a problem is solved through exhortation alone then nothing more needs to be done. However, if a better approach is found, then it can be used either to enhance the hortatory strategy or to replace that strategy.

As we have seen, hortatory policies also encourage decentralized, grass-roots responses. Although such responses are difficult to control, they have the advantage of sparking local creativity and prompting a variety of solutions to a problem. This approach of "letting a thousand flowers bloom" is particularly useful when no single solution has been identified or when multiple solutions are needed to fit different local contexts experiencing the same problem.

In a variety of domains, policy instruments such as mandates and inducements—and even ones designed to build greater capacity or to change who holds authority to perform public functions—are limited in what they can accomplish. Good examples are policy goals that lie in the realm of private behavior, such as the prevention of AIDS and domestic violence. Although government has the authority to regulate behavior that poses a public health risk or that causes harm to others, its ability to enforce such strictures is limited when the behavior occurs within private spaces. In these cases, the policy problem requires a solution that seeks to change behavior, regardless of whether the targets can be observed and sanctioned. Similarly, targets need to be motivated by something stronger than material inducements. Hence, the policy also needs to rely on information dissemination, hoping that people will make informed choices to avoid activities that carry the risk of infection or of harm to themselves and others. It also depends on an appeal to deeply held values and beliefs such as the wish for human survival, personal responsibility, concern for the weak and helpless, and familial love.[9]

The values underlying assessment policy are not as powerful as those underlying AIDS and domestic violence prevention. But assessment policy shares some of the same characteristics as these other policies. Mandates cannot be effectively enforced in individual classrooms, and most inducements aimed at changing teachers' behavior are relatively weak, due to teachers' experience teaching in particular ways and their strong sense of what constitutes appropriate instruction. Consequently, mandates and inducements need to be reinforced with strategies that show teachers how well (or poorly) their students are performing and that appeal to their professional and personal values. In sum, hortatory solutions are needed for problems when information and values count and when money and rules alone will have only a limited effect.

Political conditions that make more forceful governmental intervention infeasible may also lead to the use of a hortatory strategy. If government lacks the political support or the resources to regulate behavior, a hortatory approach becomes an attractive option. In discussing hazard warning programs, Magat and Viscusi (1992) make a point that applies to a variety of hortatory policies: "From a political standpoint this policy option is often viewed as a compromise between taking no action at all and taking an extreme form of action such as a product ban. As an intermediate policy option it has political appeal that is somewhat independent of its merits" (p. 4).[10]

In California, the state assessment was viewed by some policymakers as a way to change curriculum content and instructional methods when such changes could not be mandated. The state has a law barring any mandate that is not fully funded. As a result, the state department of education was not in a position to enforce the state's curriculum frameworks, but it could persuade teachers to teach more consistently with the frameworks by testing students on the content and approach embodied in them. The state assessment became a substitute for a mandate that was politically impossible to implement and that still would have needed an appeal to values, even if the state could have required teachers to teach in accord with the state frameworks.

Hortatory policies can substitute for other, more directive policy instruments, when the alternatives are not politically feasible or when the necessary resources are unavailable. However, in selecting a hortatory instrument, policymakers need to make certain that this strategy fits the policy problem they have defined. Hortatory policies can buy officials time and make it appear that they are doing something when no definite solution is available, or when political constraints prevent more direct intervention. But a hortatory strategy is unlikely to work in the longer term unless an information deficit exists or an appeal to values is needed to reinforce the effects of rules and money.

Conclusions

Information and persuasion are increasingly viewed as effective strategies for accomplishing a variety of policy goals, but we know little about how these hortatory approaches operate. Although empirical studies conducted within a few policy domains have provided useful insights, there is almost no comparative research across policy domains and no attempt has been made to identify generic properties. Consequently, this class of policy instruments lacks a well-developed theoretical framework of the type that the economics and policy analysis literature has refined during the past two decades for analyzing mandates and inducements. This chapter has begun the task of building a conceptual framework for understanding hortatory policies by identifying their underlying causal assumptions and analyzing some basic properties common to most policies that rely on information and values to motivate action.

These properties are best understood in the context of the assumptions that must be true if a hortatory policy is to work as intended. From this perspective, we can see the importance to policy success of clear, easily understood information and strong, broadly accepted values. But we can also see that this policy instrument is difficult for policy elites to control: they have less leverage to ensure that targets actually respond than they do with any other policy instrument, and they have virtually no control over what those actions are or whether they are consistent with the policy's intent. Nevertheless, hortatory policies have considerable appeal because most of their costs are borne by policy targets, and because they can address policy problems in situations in which other instruments are either insufficient or infeasible.

Because so little systematic research has been conducted on hortatory policy, it is possible at this point only to suggest, rather than to specify, the conditions under which its underlying assumptions will be valid and a policy likely to succeed. This chapter has outlined some of the trade-offs involved in relying on hortatory policy, particularly between strong values and potential backlash from those opposed to them, and between policy costs at the top and bottom of the system. But these relationships are portrayed only as testable hypotheses, rather than well-tested principles of policy design. Similarly, while it is clear that hortatory strategies are appropriate for particular types of policy problems, the precise circumstances under which policymakers will decide to combine them with other instruments are less obvious. Additional theoretical and empirical work is needed to develop a more rigorous and nuanced understanding of hortatory policy. Nevertheless, this study starts that process by articulating the policy theory undergirding hortatory policy and by outlining its potential promise and shortcomings.

The next chapter begins our examination of the politics of student testing by focusing on the ideas and values reflected in the three states' assessments, and how those values were contested in California and Kentucky by opponents who shared a different vision of what and how children should learn. In analyzing assessment policy from the state perspective, we will see the appeal of this policy instrument, as well as the challenges it presents for political leaders trying to control its direction and effects.

3

The State Politics of Testing

The enactment and implementation of new assessment policies in California, Kentucky, and North Carolina is a complicated and still-unfolding story. All three states devised policies with strong hortatory elements, but only Kentucky included high stakes inducements from the very beginning, with North Carolina following several years later and California not enacting testing with tangible consequences until 1999. The three states' similarities and differences in their assessment politics illustrate the dynamics of a policy designed to persuade. All three were based on strong curricular values and intended to change classroom teaching, but the responses of targets and the extent of political mobilization varied. A major reason for the differences lies in the degree to which the values embodied in the assessments represented a significant departure from past policy.

In chronicling what happened as officials in the three states changed their assessment systems, this chapter highlights four aspects of hortatory policy: (1) the type of policy goals requiring such a strategy, (2) limiting conditions of values-based policies, (3) technical requirements of policies that rely on the production and use of information, and (4) the reasons hortatory policies are often combined with other policy instruments. The recent history of assessment policy in these states also illustrates the role of resources in hortatory policy—both the low-cost appeal of such policies and the tension between the need to build capacity to use information effectively and policymakers' desire to impose costs as far down in the system as possible.

The analytical and narrative threads of the chapter come together in a story that begins with state policymakers turning to hortatory policies because they wanted to use state assessments as more than just accountability tools. They also expected assessments to infuse classrooms with a set of curricular values as a means of surmounting the long-standing constraint of being unable "to mandate what matters." As a result, testing policies were imbued with powerful ideas about what and how students should learn. But state policymakers

46

defined the targets of these policies as primarily teachers and students, neglecting to consider that parents and the public would also be exposed to the same value appeals and that some would choose to use them as a basis for mobilizing around opposing values. Consequently, in two of the three states, the implementation process exemplified the trade-off between articulating values strong enough to motivate action and precise enough to guide it, while also minimizing opposition to those values.

The nature of a particular policy—the strength of its motivating values and the degree of required change—is a major determinant of how successfully policymakers can balance this trade-off. But the course of implementation always depends on the interaction between policy characteristics and the institutional context into which a policy is introduced. In the case of state assessment policies, one aspect of the institutional context was particularly significant in explaining variation in implementation outcomes: whether elected officials viewed implementation as a largely technical task and delegated it to the state education bureaucracy, or whether they had an incentive to try to maintain political control over the process. State legislators and other elected officials must always decide how much authority to delegate to the bureaucracy and how much time and political capital they want to expend overseeing policy implementation. However, the decision to delegate may have greater political consequences in the case of hortatory policy. With this approach, the response of policy targets is likely to be less predictable, because the policy lacks the more precise rule-based framework common to mandates and inducements.

The first section of this chapter examines the legislative enactment of these policies, with a second section analyzing their implementation by state government. Considering the values embodied in them, it is not surprising that in two states the policies became focal points for interest-group opposition during implementation. What is surprising, particularly in view of subsequent events, is that their enactment was so low-key and uncontroversial. The concluding section returns to elements of the framework presented in the previous chapter, and examines how we can better understand the evolution of state assessments through the theoretical lens of hortatory policy.

The Politics of Enactment

Ideas and Expectations

Even though California, Kentucky, and North Carolina differed in the origins of their assessment policies and in their test formats and uses, three ideas were common to each state's approach. These ideas represented the underlying hortatory values, and as such, articulated a set of beliefs about how educational change and improved student learning should occur. Policymakers and their reformer allies believed that these ideas were so powerful that educators would accept them and would change their classroom behavior accordingly.

The first idea is that the assessment should be linked to a set of standards or to a specific curriculum. In California and North Carolina, the assessment was specifically aligned with the state curriculum frameworks. In the eyes of many educators, the lack of alignment between the earlier CAP and the state frameworks had been a major obstacle to full implementation of the frameworks: they assumed a constructivist approach to instruction, while CAP, with its multiple-choice format, was reinforcing more directive, traditional forms of teaching (Wilson, 2003; Cohen and Peterson, 1990; Marcano, 1990). In North Carolina, a major impetus for the new assessment was closer alignment with the statewide curriculum (the *Standard Course of Study*) than had been possible when the state was relying on a generic, commercial test. Although the state frameworks were not as specific in Kentucky and were not completed until after the first administration of KIRIS, the state assessment was tied to a concrete set of performance standards.

Directly related to this link between curriculum and assessment is a second idea underlying the three state assessments. While also functioning as an accountability mechanism, assessment should influence classroom instruction. State policymakers assumed that the curricular values embodied in the assessment system would persuade teachers to teach differently.

> I see the assessment as accomplishing both accountability and curriculum change. Some people see the assessment as only being about accountability. But if you have a test of this importance, it will drive the curriculum. (Kentucky legislator)

> The General Assembly thinks that the best shot at changing the curriculum is to have a test aligned with the curriculum. The Department of Public Instruction (DPI) has now changed its rhetoric, and is telling teachers to teach to the test. (North Carolina DPI official)

The third idea embodied in these assessments was a particular view of how students learn most effectively. The assumption was that rote memorization of facts does not result in the sustained, worthwhile knowledge that students need. Rather, according to this view, students should learn in a way that will allow them to think critically, solve problems, and apply knowledge in unfamiliar situations.

What the legislature had in mind was designing a system that is performance-based. They want our kids to do things, not just know things. (Kentucky Department of Education official)

I was a math and science teacher before I took this position. The typical student is thinking, "Tell me, I may remember. Show me, I may remember. Involve me, I will understand it." I saw the importance of this as a basketball coach: students with glazed eyes wake up with sports. The performance events will motivate students. Working with other folks, youngsters will be able to see, to be involved, to do experiments. (Kentucky teachers' union official)

According to this view, teaching for understanding is most likely to occur if students have opportunities to construct their own learning through hands-on experiments and projects, interactions with other students, and the application of knowledge and skills to real-world problems. In this model, there is less lecture and teacher-directed instruction, and a greater emphasis on the teacher facilitating students' active learning. Although North Carolina's assessment did not go as far as the other two states in measuring this kind of learning, the curriculum frameworks in all three states reflected this philosophy.

These ideas were embodied in policies designed to meet particular state needs and circumstances, but the policies were also connected to a broader national movement. Academics such as Marshall Smith (later to be undersecretary of education in the Clinton administration) were writing about an education reform strategy whose core is a coherent set of state curriculum standards linked to policies dealing with teacher training and licensure, curricular materials, and student assessment (Smith and O'Day, 1991). Others promoted the idea of changing instruction and learning through the testing process, and stressed the importance of a constructivist approach to student learning (Resnick, 1994). Some of the professional associations, most notably the NCTM, were also developing content and performance standards that outlined what students should know and be able to do (National Council of Teachers of Mathematics, 1989).[1]

In California and Kentucky, the links between the national movement and the design of state assessment policies were quite direct. The initial blueprint for CLAS was conceived by an Assessment Policy Committee (APC), appointed by the State Department of Education (SDE) and chaired by Thomas Payzant, then superintendent of the San Diego city schools.[2] The APC's design was incorporated into SB 662, the CLAS legislation. Its members included policy staff to Hart and Wilson, school superintendents, teachers' union representatives, and a representative of the state's business community.

It also included several academics who were active in the national standards and assessment movement.

Although Kentucky's valued outcomes originated in the work of the in-state Council on School Performance Standards, established before the state supreme court decision, the state's education reform was also influenced by national reform trends. In fact, policymakers acknowledged that they had intentionally modeled KERA on the national reform movement. "Most of the ideas came from national discussions," noted one of the legislators instrumental in the reforms. The governor's education aide indicated that they had "talked to everyone prominent in alternative assessment." Like a number of other states, Kentucky designed its mathematics standards and assessment to be consistent with those recommended by NCTM. North Carolina's assessment was less influenced by national reform trends, but it too revised its mathematics curriculum to be consistent with the principles espoused by NCTM.

Ideas about the link between curriculum and assessment and the role of assessment in leveraging changes in classroom instruction were joined in the three states with the more traditional notion that testing should serve an accountability function. As they described the curricular functions of assessment, state-level respondents also discussed its role as an accountability mechanism. For example, a member of the Kentucky State Board of Education noted that KIRIS "will fix responsibility and accountability," and that "holding schools responsible will put peer pressure on teachers who are not doing well." He went on to describe the state assessment as a way "to sell patience to people whose taxes went up two years ago." Even teachers' union leaders, whose support of the new state assessments had been tepid, acknowledged their accountability function: "There's no question that testing is a quid pro quo for the additional money that came to schools with the Basic Education Program [a program that increased state funding to local districts and guaranteed a base level of support] . . . The philosophy is: 'we've poured all this money into the Basic Education Program, so now we want to make certain that it pays off' " (North Carolina teachers' union official).[3]

Despite their different approaches, the new policies in the three states embodied a clear set of ideas, not only about the ultimate goal of assessment, but also about the theory or causal processes leading to the achievement of that goal. The assessment would be linked to well-defined standards and curricula; the underlying curricular values—combined with the public notification and consequences associated with an accountability system—would prompt changes in teaching; and as a result, students would not only learn more effectively, but would also acquire knowledge of greater worth. Subsequent events demonstrated that these ideas and the expectations they generated were overly ambitious. Nevertheless, the new assessment policies were notable for the powerful values undergirding them. They combined a long-standing assumption that educators would alter their classroom teaching in response to the demands of a public accountability system with a belief that assessment could and should shape the instructional process. Translating these ideas into legislation, and eventually into actual student assessments, depended on a variety of factors, some that were common to the three states and some that were unique to each.

Opportunities for Policy Action

In each of the three states, the new assessment was a product of unique opportunities for policy action. The California and Kentucky cases closely followed Kingdon's (1995) model of agenda-setting. He hypothesizes that policy emerges from the coupling of three independent process streams—problems, policy proposals, and politics: "They are largely independent of one another, and each develops according to its own dynamics and rules. But at some critical junctures the three streams are joined, and the greatest policy changes grow out of that coupling of problems, policy proposals, and politics (p. 19) . . . A problem is recognized, a solution is developed and available in the policy community, a political change makes it the right time for policy change, and potential constraints are not severe" (p. 165). In California and Kentucky, a policy window opened when a solution was joined to a set of problems and both were joined to favorable political forces. In all three states, the solution was a new assessment linked to state curricular standards and relying on a broader range of testing formats than just multiple-choice questions. But the problems and the politics differed in each state.

Three related factors dominated the problem stream in Kentucky: the state's chronically low educational achievement, persistent regional inequities, and the need for greater economic development. Kentucky has traditionally had one of the highest adult illiteracy rates in the nation, and the 1990 census showed that only Mississippi had a lower percentage of adults who had graduated from high school. Related to this low academic achievement is the widespread poverty that has plagued the eastern part of the state for generations. It has led to high levels of migration from the state and the isolation of the Appalachian counties from the more prosperous central Bluegrass region and the western part of the state. Kentucky worked aggressively during the 1980s and 1990s to attract new industries to the state as a way to lessen its reliance on coal mining, tobacco farming, and heavy manufacturing. The symbol of both the state's success at economic development and its as-yet unfulfilled aspirations is the Toyota plant in Georgetown, Kentucky. Policymakers noted the connection between low levels of educational attainment and the need for greater economic development:

> People in this state make the connection between education and economic development. Toyota in Georgetown would only hire high school graduates, and they found that many of the applicants were not qualified. Toyota Georgetown is changing people. (State Board of Education member)

> At heart, KERA is an economic reform to prevent the loss of people. The state needs a viable labor force. The Kentucky education reforms are more tied to the state's economic future than in other states. (State Department of Education official)

In 1988, Governor Wallace Wilkinson sought to address the state's persistently low educational achievement by proposing a series of reforms based on a set of student standards and an alternative assessment to measure progress in those standards, with cash awards for teachers and schools that showed improvement on test scores and attendance, and greater instructional autonomy for individual schools. However, legislators balked at the $75-million-a-year price tag and, based on the state's recent unsuccessful experience with standardized testing, they also questioned whether an appropriate test could be developed to measure student performance. Consequently, Wilkinson's proposals stalled in the legislature.

During the 1988 legislative session, his initiative was passed by the Kentucky Senate, but the legislation never got out of committee in the House. The governor then created the 12-member Council on School Performance Standards to determine what skills and knowledge Kentucky students were to master and how best to measure that learning. When the Kentucky Supreme Court decision was announced in June 1989, the council had completed about two-thirds of its work, and Wilkinson was hoping to call the legislature into a special session in August to try once again to deal with school reform.

The state supreme court decision provided an opportunity that changed the nature of the politics stream, and necessitated an even broader reform than Wilkinson had proposed. In *Rose v. Council for Better Education* (1989), the Kentucky Supreme Court directly addressed the major educational problems facing the state. It agreed with the trial court that each child in the state was entitled to an education that provided:

(i) sufficient oral and written communication skills to enable students to function in a complex and rapidly changing civilization; (ii) sufficient knowledge of economic, social, and political systems to enable the student to make informed choices; (iii) sufficient understanding of governmental processes to enable the student to understand the issues that affect his or her community, state, and nation; (iv) sufficient self-knowledge and knowledge of his or her mental and physical wellness; (v) sufficient grounding in the arts to enable each student to appreciate his or her cultural and historical heritage; (vi) sufficient training or preparation for advanced training in either academic or vocational fields so as to enable each child to choose and pursue life work intelligently; and (vii) sufficient levels of academic or vocational skills to enable public school students to compete favorably with their counterparts in surrounding states, in academics or in the job market. (790 S.W.2d 186, *212)

It also ruled that the maintenance and funding of common schools in Kentucky is the sole responsibility of the general assembly (state legislature), that common schools should be available and free to all Kentucky children, that they should be substantially uniform throughout the state, and that common schools should "provide equal educational opportunity to all Kentucky children, regardless of place of residence or economic circumstance" (790 S.W.2d 186, *212). Having found the state's school system to be constitutionally deficient by these standards, the court directed the general assembly "to recreate and redesign a new system."

The governor and his staff had expected the supreme court decision "to be purely fiscal." But its broader scope gave Wilkinson "an unexpected vehicle." According to one of the governor's aides, "the court decision came down, and we had just come out with our six goals. The decision had seven—it was made for us! The court said that the constitutional solution had to be performance-based. So the court order broke the deadlock with the general assembly."

In the case of Kentucky, then, the assessment was the result of a confluence of clearly articulated problems, the expansion of an existing policy proposal, and a unique set of political circumstances that provided the opportunity for a marked departure from past policies.

The situation in California was considerably less dramatic than in Kentucky. Nevertheless, the same pattern was present—a new form of assessment had been identified as the solution to the problem of a mismatch between the state's new curriculum frameworks and its old, multiple-choice test. In this case, the precipitating political event providing an opportunity for action was Deukmejian's veto of the CAP appropriation, and the election of a new governor interested in providing parents with standardized information about their children's academic performance.

The enactment of a new state assessment in North Carolina followed the Kingdon model of agenda-setting less closely. Still, while the politics stream lacked a single catalytic event like that in each of the other two states, North Carolina faced the same problem as California. The lack of alignment between the state assessment and the curriculum framework was a hindrance to full implementation of the content and pedagogy reflected in the state's *Standard Course of Study*. The original impetus for a new state testing program came from the Public School Forum, a foundation- and business-funded education support group whose board is equally divided among business, members, elected officials, and education representatives. The initiative was then picked up by the Department of Public Instruction, which convinced the legislature that the state needed an assessment that was more closely tied to the statewide curriculum and that demanded more of students. The general assembly authorized the development of such an assessment as part of legislation designed to grant local districts and schools greater autonomy. North Carolina has traditionally had a highly centralized school system, with state government circumscribing local operations through a finance system (which specifies with considerable precision allowable expenditure categories) and through a statewide curriculum. The legislature saw its School Improvement and Accountability Act of 1989 as a way to grant local units greater autonomy by allowing them to apply for waivers from state regulation and to begin to move toward site-based management. The assessment was conceived as an exchange for this decentralization of authority.

What was perhaps most striking in all three states was the lack of any opposition to the new assessments when they were first enacted. The teachers' union in each state was a group likely to oppose the new assessment, or at least to express reservations about it. Because the state assessments were expected to alter curriculum content and instructional strategies and to ensure greater school accountability for student learning, teachers would have to bear much of the cost associated with responding to the new tests. Yet in each state, the teachers' union had a strong reason to support the new assessment, or at least not to oppose it. As noted previously, in North Carolina the assessment was understood to be a quid pro quo for increased state resources for the schools, much of which was spent on teacher salaries, including the hiring of 13,000 additional teachers statewide, according to a teachers' union official. The same motivation helps explain the response of the Kentucky teachers' union: "Kentucky used to be among the worst in terms of level of state funding for education. The reforms meant more money for education, so as far as teachers were concerned, there was little bargaining over the reform package" (Kentucky teachers' union official). The California Teachers' Association (CTA) supported the new state assessment because the CTA viewed the legislation as an improvement over the old system of multiple-choice testing, and because it saw the bill as opening the door to more alternative assessments in the future, including assessments designed by teachers and incorporating student portfolios, according to a teachers' union official.

Disagreements among other participants in the policy process were either minor or involved issues incidental to the state assessment. In Kentucky, disputes about some provisions of KERA arose in the general assembly. Debate centered on the size and method for funding the tax increase needed to support the reforms, provisions to minimize nepotism in local school districts, and limits on the involvement of school employees in school politics. However, the state assessment was never an issue of dispute, and the assumption that schools would be held accountable to a set of standards reflecting the areas outlined in the state supreme court decision was never contested by any of the participants.[4]

Perhaps most notable, considering subsequent developments, was the lack of vocal opposition from the groups that would later oppose the state assessments in California and Kentucky. The absence of their involvement in California is not particularly surprising, because the assessment legislation was essentially developed within the APC by representatives of the state's major education policymakers and then enacted by the legislature with little discussion or debate. Even legislators who later opposed CLAS acknowledged that they had not been paying attention either to the assessment or to the state curriculum frameworks that had preceded the assessment by some five years. The opposition groups' concerns seemed to have stemmed initially from individual test questions that offended them. They then moved from those specific items to the general principles underlying CLAS. Consequently, the opposition did not emerge until after the test had been administered.

In Kentucky, several opposition group leaders reported attending public meetings in Frankfurt when KERA was first being designed and becoming concerned that "only one educational philosophy was reflected" (interview with opposition group leader). Another opposition group leader ran unsuccessfully for state superintendent in 1991—even though the elective post would soon be abolished as a result of KERA—simply as a way to publicize the anti-KERA position. However, even though KERA was highly visible in Kentucky, its individual provisions—and particularly the assessment—

were not well understood by the public, and opposition groups did not become well-organized until after the legislation was enacted and the test actually administered.[5]

Policy Constraints

For the most part, then, the political constraints that would eventually derail CLAS and threaten KIRIS did not exist when the original assessment legislation was enacted. In all three states, a new assessment was perceived as a partial solution to pressing educational problems. Facilitating political conditions then provided an opportunity for placing the new assessment on the state policy agenda. However, even in this positive environment for policy action, political and fiscal factors constrained the clarity and scope of assessment policy.

In California, the political circumstances that created CLAS led to constraints that would eventually hamper its implementation. Behind the consensus among the governor, state superintendent, and senate education committee chairman lay different expectations for what the new assessment should accomplish. Each of these men supported CLAS for different reasons, and they expected it to accomplish very different things.

Governor Wilson wanted CLAS for one major reason: as a condition for his support, he demanded that it include individual student scores that would provide information to parents and would, in his view, allow for the evaluation of individual teachers. Wilson wanted eventually to move to a system of merit pay, in which teachers with high-scoring students would be rewarded. As one of the governor's aides noted, "we could care less about authentic assessment. It costs more money, and we don't know if it is any better. For us, having individual student scores is really powerful: it brings accountability into a system where it isn't there now. It will be possible to assess students, teachers, schools, and districts. Parents can then say they don't want their child in Ms. Smith's classroom because they will have the assessment information."

These expectations contrasted with those of Senator Hart, who also viewed the primary purpose of the new assessment system as accountability—but a very different kind of accountability. Hart saw a more valid form of assessment as the quid pro quo for allowing schools to move to site-based management. For him, the school site, not the individual teacher, was the unit of accountability, and his model was that of an exchange—greater accountability for outcomes in exchange for greater autonomy in the areas of instruction and school operations. Honig's motivation was not inconsistent with either of the other two policy actors, but he emphasized different expectations. He was interested in assessments that are more aligned with a particular kind of curriculum, that measure real world performance, and that influence teaching. Although he too was interested in accountability issues, Honig came to the enactment of CLAS from a different angle—a curricular philosophy, a set of performance standards that flows from that philosophy or framework, and an assessment appropriate for measuring performance on those standards.

The immediate result of these differing expectations was that the SDE agreed to produce individual-level test scores within a time frame that exceeded its technical capability. As early as 1992, one of the governor's aides argued that "Honig probably agreed to things he can't deliver within the Prop. 98 limits" (state constitutional revenue limits for K–14 education funding). After the CLAS continuation had been vetoed, one of the SDE officials responsible for the assessment noted, "it's true that Bill [Honig] wanted the new test so badly that he said we'd do individual student scores— [saying] 'we'll do whatever it takes.' " But the SDE felt that it had no choice but to overpromise, since at the governor's insistence, a sunset provision was included in the original legislation repealing the program after only three years (on January 1, 1995). Time became one of the major constraints imposed as a result of state policymakers' fundamentally different notions about the purposes of assessment.

From the beginning, funding was another significant constraint in all three states. Assessments that include formats in addition to or in place of multiple-choice items cost more. Moving from multiple-choice tests that can be scored by machine to ones that include open-ended or constructed responses, requiring the judgment of a trained scorer, adds substantial costs. In North Carolina, because students in so many grades are tested, items requiring hand-scoring numbered five million. In California, the number was three million. Estimating the total cost of alternative assessments is difficult because the state, local districts, and individual schools all bear those costs. In addition, some costs, such as the distribution and collection of tests, are less visible than the obvious ones for development, teacher training, scoring, and reporting. Picus (1996) estimated that the state share of KIRIS costs averaged about $46 per student tested for each annual administration between 1991 and 1994, while the more traditional format of North Carolina's end-of-grade assessment cost about $7 per student tested for each year between 1992 and 1995.[6] No cost estimates for CLAS are available, but based on state appropriations for the test, it cost at least $30 per student tested. These estimates contrast with $2 to $20 per student for commercially developed, multiple-choice tests.

In all three states, the initial constraints were less about politics than about tradeoffs among time, money, and the technical limitations of a new testing technology. The common response was to concentrate on developing the state-administered accountability assessment at the expense of designing decentralized options that would also be tied to the state standards, but that could be administered and scored by individual teachers in their own classrooms to supplement the once-a-year state tests. Besides their assumed pedagogical benefits to students, these classroom-based, ongoing assessments would have reinforced the curricular values underlying the states' annual assessments. Teachers would be more likely to accept, understand, and act on those values if they were exposed to them more consistently and had to think more systematically about how they would integrate them into their everyday teaching.[7]

Professional development for teachers was another area in which the effects of time constraints and fiscal limitations were most obvious. One of the explicit goals of these assessments was to change teaching, and several decades of implementation research indicated that such change could not occur unless teachers were given sufficient training and time to adapt new approaches to their classroom routines (Fullan, 1991; McLaughlin, 1990). Yet the average teacher in the three states received very little professional development in preparation for the new assessments. Kentucky made the greatest commitment, and by the standards of what states typically spend on such capacity-building, it was substantial. School districts were allowed to use up to nine days a year for professional development and in addition, $400 per teacher was allocated for professional development, with 65 percent of that sum under the control of the local schools. The state and local districts also developed a variety of professional development and technical assistance networks. Still, given the magnitude of changes expected under KERA, such as the transition to an ungraded primary, even this significant resource commitment was inadequate.

In California, no additional resources were allocated for professional development associated with CLAS. State policymakers expected that state-funded subject-matter projects would provide the necessary assistance to teachers. These professional development networks focus on particular subjects, such as mathematics and writing, and are run by the University of California. Although they are highly regarded by practitioners, they can serve only a small fraction of the state's teachers.

North Carolina also did not allocate additional funding for professional development related to the new assessment. The state distributed a booklet to all teachers in the tested grades that explained the purpose of the assessment and that included examples of test items and their scoring rubrics. The state also provided some assistance to district officials through its regional technical assistance centers, and the DPI hoped that because a large number of teachers were involved in scoring the state assessment, they would convey their experience with the scoring rubrics to their colleagues. Despite these attempts to offset the shortfall in professional development, fiscal constraints meant that the goal of changing instruction through the state test was considerably more difficult to achieve.[8] As one teachers' union official noted, "the tests are supposed to deal with thinking skills and call for judgment. But who's prepared the teachers when they have been bombarded for ten years with fixed content and six-step lesson plans?"

In addition to these common responses to the constraints they faced, each state also made some unique accommodations. For example, the major reason that North Carolina did not include performance items on its state assessment is that testing experts in the DPI judged them to be too unstandardized for accountability purposes and too expensive to score. They reasoned as follows: "Multiple-choice gives reliability, is less costly, and means less time is spent on testing. Now it's true that some things are only measured indirectly by multiple-choice items. Therefore, we also included open-ended, constructed responses. The only thing left was whether students could do a task. But performance tests are so expensive, and they're unlikely to be standardized. We decided that they should be kept as classroom exercises."

Kentucky officials, on the other hand, were firmly committed to performance tasks and saw multiple-choice items as sending the wrong instructional message to teachers and students, even though they may be more reliable and cheaper to score. However, Kentucky also had to accommodate competing demands for time and resources. One of its major compromises was to design and administer the assessment before the state curriculum standards were fully developed.

The Kentucky legislation mandated that the SDE develop standards and then test students on those standards, but not promulgate a statewide curriculum. Therefore, the SDE was initially wary of being too prescriptive about curricular content. It also had only a short time before the first administration of the assessment—two years, during which a number of other major reform programs also had to be implemented. In 1993, after the first administration of KIRIS, the SDE published *Transformations*, what SDE officials considered to be a resource document. The document outlined the state learning goals and outcomes, and it provided numerous examples of instructional activities that might be used in teaching concepts related to those goals and outcomes. However, the emphasis was on pedagogy, rather than on the curricular content to be covered. Yet *Transformations* was the only official guide that teachers had for discerning how they needed to change their teaching in response to KIRIS. Without more guidance about content, they reported having to infer from released test items what they needed to teach.

Still, state officials expected that the test should influence what teachers taught as well as how they taught.[9] Eventually, after growing demands from local educators, the SDE issued a second edition of *Transformations* that included content guidelines and suggested course outlines. But this more specific guidance came only after the assessment had been administered for several years. In looking back over its implementation, one respondent involved in developing KIRIS gave this advice to other states considering the design of new assessments: "You need to make certain that the test doesn't lag the curriculum standards and frameworks too much because the test is a measure of how well teachers understand what's expected of them. Giving the test motivates them to change, but they can only do so as they understand the frameworks. If their understanding is 'wrong,' the scores won't improve."

By some measure, the politics of enacting new assessments in the three states was unremarkable. Because of KIRIS's tie to the historic KERA reforms, it garnered greater attention at the time of enactment than either California's or North Carolina's assessment policies. However, none of the three assessments were highly visible or contentious issues. Policymakers saw them as meeting identified problems, and their champions were able to leverage favorable political conditions to secure legislative passage. One goal of these policies was entirely consistent with that of past state assessments. Policymakers assumed that by testing students and then publicly reporting the scores on a school-by-school basis, parents and the general public would use that information to hold the schools accountable. The Kentucky legislature took the notion of accountability one step further, using the test results as a basis for rewarding or sanctioning individual schools. The state assessments were subject to the same kinds of time limits and fiscal constraints as most policies. Policymakers expected the assessments to be developed and ready for administration within a short time frame, and funding was insufficient to implement all the assessment components.

However, two aspects of these assessment policies made their enactment distinctive. First, as hortatory policies, they were premised on a clear set of ideas about what should be taught in each state's public schools, and on an expectation that a particular kind of assessment would lead to teaching reflective of those curricular values. Although there is evidence that some policymakers in California and Kentucky did not understand the full import of either the assessment or its underlying values, and that some supported the new policy for reasons unrelated to its curricular implications, the legislative mandate was clear. The assessment was to measure student learning defined as the ability to think critically, solve problems, and apply knowledge in new situations.

A second factor that made these assessment policies special—though by no means unique among public policies—was their reliance on a testing technology that was unproven on a widespread basis. Some states, including California, had experience with writing assessments that demonstrated that essays and other types of open-ended responses could be scored reliably and that such assessments did positively influence teaching and learning. Nevertheless, with the exception of specialized tests such as the Advanced Placement exams, no large-scale system for testing elementary and secondary students had moved as far away from multiple-choice tests as California and Kentucky were now going. Knowledgeable policymakers understood that they were traveling into uncharted territory and they accepted the cautions of testing experts, but they also assumed that limitations and problems could be addressed simultaneously with the implementation of new assessment strategies (McDonnell, 1994). In sum, while the policy formulation process might not have held any apparent clues about how implementation of the assessments would proceed, the novelty of the assessments' underlying values and the technical challenges they presented did suggest that implementation might not be as smooth as enactment had been.

The Politics of Implementation

Policy implementation is typically viewed as a set of administrative activities, rather than as a political process. The factors traditionally considered to be most important in explaining implementation outcomes are those associated either with the implementing agency (examples include how it communicates policy intent to local practitioners and the level of resources provided) or with the local context (especially the capacity and will of local implementors). However, analysts who focus on policy design variables and those who examine the role of "street-level bureaucrats" such as teachers emphasize that implementation also has a political dimension (e.g., Palumbo and Calista, 1990; Ingram and Schneider, 1993). Other analysts have noted that conflicts or ambiguities about policy intent not resolved during the enactment process will only persist during implementation, and will constrain that process as well (Bardach, 1977).

In addition to the political and bureaucratic challenges associated with all types of policy implementation, limits on hortatory policies present constraints unique to this approach. Assessment policy embodies both values and information as policy tools. As values-based policy, it runs the risk that those values will be either insufficiently powerful or precise to motivate policy targets, or they will lack broad acceptance and become a catalyst for opposing views. For several interest groups in California and Kentucky, CLAS and KIRIS prompted the latter response, thus jeopardizing the implementation process. Although value conflicts were the most significant threats to these policies, the unproven testing technology meant that their function as systems capable of producing reliable information on which policymakers, educators, and the public could act was also compromised.

In California and Kentucky, interest groups were mobilized, the state assessment became a more visible focus of media attention during implementation than it had been during enactment, and policymakers were pressured to reconsider their initial decisions. In California, lawsuits were filed against the SDE and several local districts. By all objective measures, such as numbers of people attending meetings and rallies and the proportion of parents who forbade their children to take the state test, the politics of implementation involved only a small minority of each state's students and parents. Nevertheless, this political activity was largely responsible for the demise of CLAS in California and the intense public scrutiny of KIRIS in Kentucky. In both states, the assessment also became an issue in the gubernatorial election campaign.

This section analyzes the political dimensions of implementing the new assessments in California and Kentucky.[10] It focuses on the debate about the assessments' underlying values by examining the groups that opposed CLAS and KIRIS, and the differing responses of officials in the two states to that opposition. Because technical concerns about the tests eventually became factors in the disputes and called their reliability into question, those issues are also examined.

Opposition Groups and Their Concerns

Opposition to the California and Kentucky assessments was led by a loose coalition of conservative groups that are part of what has become known as the "Religious Right." Several of these state-level groups, such as the Eagle Forum and the Rutherford Institute, are chapters of national organizations, while others, such as the Family Foundation in Kentucky and the Capitol Resource Institute in California, have informal ties with national movements. The groups, particularly those in California, had an informal division of labor during the CLAS controversy, with a few concentrating on lobbying state officials, others filing lawsuits against the SDE and local school districts, and still other groups mobilizing grassroots opposition. In both states, local groups with ties to the state organizations also worked to mobilize parents against CLAS and KERA.

Opposition groups represented a small minority of parents and teachers. The largest group in California had about 2,000 subscribers to its newsletters, and the largest in Kentucky, about 900. The rallies at the state capitol that the groups organized in each state drew no more than several hundred people. Another indicator of the extent of opposition in Kentucky was that a petition to the legislature calling for KERA's repeal was signed by about 11,000 people (May, 1994a). In California, the best indicator was probably the number of students in grades in which the CLAS test was administered who "opted out" of taking it with their parents' permission—a protest tactic recommended to parents by the opposition groups. According to SDE records, that number equaled about 61,000, or about 5 percent of the more than 1.2 million students who were to be tested.

Despite their minority status, however, there is evidence from national public opinion polls that the opposition groups were tapping into concerns shared by a larger segment of parents and the public. An overwhelming majority of the American public supports having local schools conform to a set of national achievement goals and standards and to requiring that standardized tests be used to measure student achievement on those standards (Elam, Rose, and Gallup, 1991, 1992). A majority also sees raised standards as a way to encourage students, even ones from low-income backgrounds, to do better in school (Elam and Rose, 1995, p. 47). Consensus about the need for standards and assessment does not extend, however, to what those standards should be and how students should be taught and tested. Public opinion data indicate that some of the questions raised by opposition groups reflect broader public concerns. For example, surveys about the teaching of mathematics and writing point to fundamental differences between the curricular values of education reformers and those of large segments of the public (Johnson and Immerwahr, 1994).[11] In a Public Agenda survey conducted in August 1994, 86 percent of the respondents in a national sample said that students should learn to do arithmetic "by hand"—including memorizing multiplication tables—before starting to use calculators (Johnson and Immerwahr, 1994). This opinion contrasts with the 82 percent of mathematics educators responding to an earlier survey who said that "early use of calculators will improve children's problem-solving skills and not prevent the learning of arithmetic" (p. 17). This survey also found similar differences in the opinions of educators and the general public about how to teach writing and about the value of teaching students in heterogenous ability groups. It was that concern and seeming inconsistency between reform goals and parental expectations that opposition groups in the two states attempted to mobilize.

In California, six groups led the opposition to CLAS:

- The Traditional Values Coalition (TVC) is a lobbying group that claims 31,000 churches nationwide as part of its network and a $2 million annual budget. It is based in Anaheim, and has lobbied in favor of prayer in the schools and against abortion and gay rights (Zoroya, 1995).
- Capitol Resource Institute (CRI) is "a conservative public policy center focusing on state and local issues impacting families in their communities" (Capitol Resource Institute, 1994). CRI, located in Sacramento, has about 2,000 paid subscribers who receive its materials; it is affiliated with Focus on the Family, a conservative Christian coalition based in Colorado (Colvin, 1995d).[12]
- The Eagle Forum is a national group founded in 1972 by Phyllis Schlafly. Like most of the other groups, its agenda extends beyond education to include minimizing governmental intervention into what it considers to be the purview of families, maintaining a strong national defense, and encouraging private enterprise unfettered by governmental regulations.
- Parents Involved in Education (PIE) is a statewide umbrella organization whose major aim is to "reinstate" parental rights. It provided information and other types of assistance to local organizations with similar goals. PIE's leadership overlapped with that of the state Eagle Forum, and it established networks with similar organizations across the country.
- The Rutherford Institute is a conservative legal foundation based in Virginia, with volunteer lawyers across the country willing to litigate cases in which they believe constitutional liberties have been violated.[13] It has a particular focus on parental rights and the exercise of religious freedom.
- The United States Justice Foundation (USJF) is also a conservative legal foundation. It was founded in 1979 and is based in Escondido. Although it has dealt with other education issues such as school desegregation, its past cases have been wide-ranging and include ones dealing with tax issues, term limits for public officals, union decertification, and health care. Its basic aim in all these cases is to limit the scope of government.

In Kentucky, three major statewide groups opposed KIRIS:

- Parents and Professionals Involved in Education (PPIE) a grassroots organization founded in 1990 specifically to respond to issues related to

KERA. The group held workshops, distributed information, and was involved in various types of lobbying activities. At the height of the KIRIS controversy, with a about 900 subscribers statewide, it was considered "the oldest and largest of citizen groups critical of the reform act" (Associated Press, 1994).

- The Eagle Forum in Kentucky is similar in its goals and strategies to the state chapter in California.
- The Family Foundation is a conservative organization founded in 1989 to deal with issues related to the family. Although it has been a constant critic of KERA, the foundation has also focused on welfare, pornography, health care, and crime issues. It has an annual budget of about $170,000 that comes largely from donors within Kentucky (Schreiner, 1996).[14]

Several other smaller groups also opposed KERA. These included. America Awaken, a Paducah-based organization that circulated the petition calling for the repeal of KERA, and a similar group in Owensboro, Families United for Morals in Education, that regularly criticized KERA in newspaper advertisements (Associated Press, 1994). In October 1994, the three major opposition groups formed an umbrella lobbying group called Campaign for Academic Renewal in Education (CARE), and proposed an alternative to KERA that included standards emphasizing traditional academic content, more reliable state tests, greater local control, and a voluntary nongraded primary program.

Despite some differences in their size and numbers, opposition groups in California and Kentucky had similar concerns about the state assessments that fell into two broad categories: their underlying values and their technical quality. Opposition groups argued that the state assessments embodied inappropriate values because their outcome standards were not sufficiently academic, they represented a social and cultural agenda that was offensive to some parents, and they intruded unnecessarily into family life by asking students personal questions, thus violating parental rights.

Opposition to the state assessment was somewhat stronger in California, and focused primarily on the language arts portion of the test. Most of the reading passages that evoked opposition were from works by authors of color such as Richard Wright, Dick Gregory, and Maxine Hong Kingston. Critics charged that many of the selections on which students were tested promoted inappropriate values such as violence and the questioning of authority.[15] The selection that caused the greatest controversy was "Roselily," a short story by Alice Walker that was included on the tenth-grade CLAS test in 1993. CLAS opponents argued that the story about a black woman's thoughts during her marriage ceremony to a black Muslim was disrespectful of religious people.

The kinds of questions that most upset critics were language arts prompts asking students to discuss family matters (for example, "Why do you think some teenagers and their parents have problems communicating?"—an item on the eighth-grade exam); to question authority ("Think about a rule at your school—on the playground, in the cafeteria, or in the classroom—that you think needs to be changed. Write a letter to the principal about a school rule you want changed."—a fourth-grade item); or to delve into people's psyches (an "open mind" question showing a picture of a head with nothing in it and asking students to read a literature passage and to fill the head in with symbols, images, drawings or words showing what a character was thinking).

Controversy in Kentucky focused less on specific passages and more on the questions asked of students and on what critics perceived as biased scoring rubrics. One example that several opponents cited as an inappropriate question came at the end of what they considered to be a "charming" reading passage for fourth graders titled "Your Dad's a Wimp?" The question asked, "Would you like to be part of Jesse's family? Why or why not?" One of the opposition group leaders described how her ten-year-old daughter reacted to the question: "The open-ended question made my ten-year-old go nuts. She assumed that she wouldn't be in her own family any more when the test asked if she would want to be a part of Jesse's family. I had to ask the school to destroy my daughter's test. When you're testing ten-year-olds, you shouldn't be investigating their attitudes."

Another opposition group leader made the same point about the "Jesse question," but expanded it to argue that the scoring of this and other items reflected a bias:

> The state doesn't make the scoring guide until they get all the answers in. That doesn't give parents any confidence. The state says that whether students answer the question yes or no doesn't make a difference. But then they include on the scoring guide an answer that goes against traditional family arrangements. If a student answers that she wants to be part of Jesse's family, then she is saying that she wants to leave her own family. Also, a student doesn't really know what it would be like to be part of Jesse's family. There's a larger concern that there's a bias in the scoring. That's usually true in reading and social studies.

Similarly, the president of the Kentucky chapter of the Eagle Forum charged in an op-ed article that not only did KIRIS writing prompts require students to choose sides on controversial subjects such as euthanasia and citizens owning firearms, but that the scoring rubrics favored students whose answers reflected pro-multiculturalism, pro-women's rights, and pro-environmental positions (Daniel, 1995). In an *Education Week* article, she was quoted as describing opposition to KERA as a "classic case of cultural warfare" (Harp, 1994).

The following excerpts from interviews with several of the opposition leaders in the two states amplify these broad concerns:

We were opposed to it [CLAS] for two reasons. The first concern was the one that had a tendency to catch the attention of the media. It was that the test seemed to be delving into areas of students' psyches. The types of questions and the types of stories were emotional ones. It appeared that the people making the test had a philosophical agenda. The test was an invasion of student and family privacy. But there was a much deeper concern that we didn't see until we delved into the test much more. CLAS was not challenging enough for kids academically. The standards being tested were unclear and not rigorous. I would define rigorous as testing kids for a knowledge of facts, but more than just a regurgitation of facts. A rigorous test would also challenge students' intellectual abilities . . . There's a tendency for a lot of people involved in education to believe in helping children develop. They want to get kids excited, and one way to do that is to get them writing about their personal feelings . . . In the right circumstances, questions like "What makes you happy?" are all right. But teachers are not trained to be therapists and classrooms aren't meant to be therapy sessions. You need someone who is trained to bring closure to such discussions, and parents have to be involved. I'm not certain that CLAS was intended to be the "great therapy session," but that's how it turned out. (California opposition group leader)

They [the state tests] need to give parents something to evaluate. There was nothing published that would evaluate students' ability in language skills. It didn't test their ability to interpret the author's intent, write grammatically, spell correctly, or to punctuate. It didn't show a concrete level of mastery of reading and writing. This was a test that was supposed to be an individual student assessment that would test their basic skill in language arts. But what the language arts section was really doing was using a situation prompt in order to enlist a student's ability to draw from a personal experience a similar situation. We realized all of the stories that were being used to draw from an experience were from a very negative content. There is nothing concrete being academically measured . . . When asking students to relate to their own personal experience, that could possibly be another way of gathering data on the life of the family. The eyes of our children will become the window of our household. (California opposition group leader)

Our number-one concern with KERA is that it narrows the curriculum. It dumbs-down the curriculum; the less-is-more philosophy ... The outcomes are intentionally vague; they haven't communicated anything to teachers, students, and parents. There's all kinds of leeway for mischief. For example, *Transformations* has as one of the suggested activities for middle school students that students join or contribute to Act Up, NOW, or UNICEF. The department of education heard a lot of noise about that, and Tom Boysen [the former state commissioner of education] labeled it "an unfortunate mistake." Also the vagueness of the outcomes lends itself to mediocrity. (Kentucky opposition group leader)

Most of the groups framed their state-specific concerns in the larger context of opposition to outcomes-based education (OBE). OBE is an education strategy designed to focus instruction on helping students master a specified set of skills or outcomes. It took on political overtones and became a target of conservative groups because the outcomes specified by SDEs and local school districts included not just academic goals, but also ones dealing with students' attitudes and their psychosocial development. The OBE controversy escalated in 1991 when conservative groups protested Pennsylvania's draft "learning outcomes" (Boyd, Lugg, and Zahorchak, 1996). Critics argued that it was inappropriate for government to require that students demonstrate their ability to bring about and adapt to change in their lives, or that they develop personal criteria for making informed moral judgments. The critics maintained that while they strongly supported students developing such skills, they feared that such outcomes would lead to the state specifying what behaviors were ethical and that students might be barred from graduation if they did not demonstrate the right attitudes. The critics distorted the state's intentions, but the vagueness of the outcomes and the implicit political content of some (for example, those dealing with the environment) provided a platform for the opposition (Ravitch, 1995).

A videotape featuring the leader of the Pennsylvania opposition, Peg Luksik, was used by opposition groups in California and Kentucky to argue that what they viewed as the weaknesses of CLAS and KIRIS were specific instances of a larger national problem. In addition, materials such as a publication produced by Focus on the Family, titled *Not with My Child You Don't: A Citizens' Guide to Eradicating OBE and Restoring Education,* was widely available to opponents and their supporters. In Kentucky, the anti-OBE crusade was aimed specifically at two of the state's "valued outcomes" that dealt with self-sufficiency and responsible group membership. A number of the outcomes specified under these two goals resembled the ones that had become controversial in Pennsylvania, and critics were particularly concerned about ones requiring students to demonstrate "an understanding of, appreciation for, and sensitivity to a multicultural and world view" and to demonstrate "an open mind to alternative perspectives." In talking about her group's opposition to OBE and its link to CLAS, Carolyn Steinke, the president of PIE, noted that OBE "is something that is difficult to explain, yet so dangerous" (Walsh, 1994).

Although most of opposition groups' concerns centered on the assessments' underlying values, they also raised questions about the technical adequacy of the tests. They argued that the performance levels were vague and not understandable to laypeople. There was also a widespread perception among opponents that the scoring of the state tests was subjective and unreliable:

> CLAS couldn't give individual-level scores because the tests take too long to score. We didn't believe the SDE when they said they could produce individual-level scores, because those scores are just too subjective. (Opposition group leader)

> The test is all subjective; the department of education and the testing contractor can do whatever they want. The scores were all higher just before the [1994] election, but I don't think that will take the edge off. (Kentucky opposition leader)

Some of the opponents' concerns about the technical adequacy of the state tests evidenced a misunderstanding of how large-scale assessments are scored, but as the technical reviews of CLAS and KIRIS would show, some of the weaknesses identified by assessment critics were confirmed by testing experts.

How Valid Were the Opposition's Criticisms?

One of the issues raised in California and Kentucky by those in the policy community who had to respond to the opposition groups was the extent to which the groups' concerns were sincere or were part of a strategic move to advance a broader political agenda.[16] A number of policymakers argued that criticisms of CLAS and KERA were merely a component of a larger strategy to promote school vouchers. In California, Proposition 174, a ballot initiative to fund vouchers that was supported by many of the same groups opposed to CLAS, had been rejected by the voters the previous year. Similarly, in Kentucky, groups such as the Eagle Forum had discussed voucher legislation with members of the general assembly. When confronted with a public charge by former Governor Wilkinson that they were criticizing KERA as a way to get tax money for private school tuition, Martin Cothran of the Family Foundation and Donna Shedd of the Eagle Forum argued that the two issues were separate. Shedd maintained that although she likes the idea of school choice, that did not mean that she did not care about public education. Cothran noted that while the Family Foundation would probably be in favor of vouchers, it had not taken an official position on the issue (May, 1995a). However, both Shedd and another leader of the KERA opposition were active in the homeschool movement in Kentucky. The situation was similar in California, where opposition group leaders acknowledged that they were active in the voucher movement, but saw their opposition to CLAS as a separate issue.

The question of sincere versus strategic motives raises a related question that also cannot be answered unequivocally—whether the criticisms made against CLAS and KIRIS were valid. Answering that question is difficult because so much depends on the religious, political, and cultural values one holds. Clearly, political and cultural conservatives, whether or not they are religious, will arrive at a different judgment than will those who are more liberal in their beliefs. Nevertheless, it is possible to sort out some of the criticisms and separate those that are clearly false or exaggerated from those that have merit. For example, some claims, such as the one made by a KERA opponent charging that the education reform act promotes the teaching of witchcraft, bordered on the preposterous (Ward, 1993).[17]

Other claims were exaggerated or distorted, although it is not clear whether the misrepresentation was intentional or not. One example was the claim by CLAS opponents that offensive test items were on the assessment when they were not.[18] A particularly egregious example was used in literature distributed by the Capitol Resource Institute and in a special radio broadcast that CRI lobbyist Natalie Williams did with James Dobson. This item was never on the CLAS test, but was presented as such in a CRI publication:

> One math question goes like this: There are seventeen apples and four students. How would you divide the apples and explain why. The state-desired response that would score the highest (6 on a scale of 1 to 6) was this: Four apples go to three students and five apples go to the fourth, because the fourth student was the most needy. This clearly reflects a value judgment that has no basis in mathematical problem solving, unless that is what they mean by "the new math." (Capitol Resource Institute, 1994)

Opponents admitted that some items that got into the "pot" of public debate were not official CLAS items, but they argued that even if an item were only a sample from a field test or a locally developed one to prepare students for the CLAS test, it should be included as part of the CLAS system.[19]

Another particularly distorted criticism of the test was the charge that students' responses would be computerized and made available to other government agencies, businesses, and individuals. In California, assurances from the SDE that information about students' ethnicity, family income, and responses to test questions would be kept completely confidential were not believed by opposition leaders. Rumors circulated that students who had written negatively about their parents had prompted calls to their homes by child protective services workers. Although it is difficult to identify the source of such rumors, it appears that in a few cases the teachers who were scoring the exams suspected possible child abuse based on students' answers. Since teachers are legally required to report such abuse, they told their SDE supervisors, and SDE staff then reported it to the principals at the students' schools. The assumption was that the local site administrator would investigate and decide whether legal authorities should be contacted. To the best of the SDE's knowledge, very few cases were ever reported to principals, and Child Protective Services never intervened as a result of the CLAS test. But as an SDE official noted, even if principals were contacted about responses on only one-hundredth of 1 percent of the CLAS exams, that represented more than 100 students. As we will see in subsequent sections, this rumor, unique to California, might have been avoided if the test development and administration had been more open to public participation and understanding.

Despite these examples of opposition concerns that either exaggerated or distorted the actual situation, the tests did appear to highlight a set of social values in addition to measuring academic skills. In a few cases, scoring judgments were also made that seemed to contradict parents' sense of what constituted an appropriate answer.[20]

A review of the first edition of *Transformations* (Kentucky Department of Education, 1993) indicates that joining Act Up was not a suggested activity for middle school students, contrary to what one opposition leader charged. Most of the community activities proposed were ones that the majority of the public would view as commendable (participating in community service projects such as Habitat for Humanity or a Red Cross blood drive; producing a video to explain school rules). However, the political groups listed as "learning links" or community resources were all liberal groups such as the ACLU, the NAACP, labor unions, the Sierra Club, and Amnesty International. None of the political organizations with which the opposition groups were affiliated were included in the original edition of *Transformations*. Similarly, many of the activities listed would likely be acceptable to people of different social and political beliefs, but the examples reflected only a liberal viewpoint. For example, a high school activity involving a debate over rights gave as examples animal rights and the right to die. Such an activity might be more acceptable to conservatives if the list of examples also included a right valued by them, such as property rights. Likewise, a middle school activity that had students interviewing people whose lives were affected by a social movement listed as examples the Equal Rights Amendment and civil rights movements. A more inclusive list might also include religious fundamentalism as an example of a social and political movement that has transformed the lives of its adherents.

Achieving a balance among diverse perspectives was also an issue for CLAS. As a number of commentators have noted, the literature selections and test items that opponents found offensive represented only a small proportion of all the content included in CLAS (Wilgoren, 1994). Nevertheless, even CLAS's strongest supporters understood in retrospect that the language arts portion appeared to reflect a narrow range of lifestyles and human emotions. One language arts assessment consultant noted, "I had never read through the entire body of [language arts] tests until I had to meet with the legislature, so I sat down and read all of the tests . . . My response when I sat down and looked through all of them was, 'Oh my God, they are all so much about serious problems.' It was all good literature, and I believed in all the readings that we had. But the whole collection seemed so dark. I thought it was a shame. I don't know if anyone looked at all of them."

Perhaps more significantly, CLAS also represented pedagogical approaches being questioned by a much broader segment of the public than just religious conservatives. That questioning was most evident in the debate about the use of "whole language" pedagogy, which de-emphasizes the teaching of phonics and emphasizes the use of literature in reading instruction. Although conservatives argued against the de-emphasis on phonics in the state curriculum frameworks, it was Marion Joseph, a top aide to the liberal former state superintendent of public instruction Wilson Riles, who was the most influential voice in arguing that the state's move to whole language instruction had gone too far and was not working (Colvin, 1995e). Joseph's efforts—combined with low reading scores on CLAS and the National Assessment of Educational Progress (NAEP) and arguments from classroom teachers that a balance had to be struck between traditional methods and whole language—led to a change in the state's recommended approach to reading instruction (California Department of Education, 1995).[21]

Like the findings from the Public Agenda survey, the debate about whole language in California suggests that the opposition groups were tapping into concerns shared by a broader segment of parents and the general public. There is no question that debates over CLAS and KIRIS were infused with misinformation, but when all the exaggerations and distortions are stripped away, there still remains a core of concerns that were viewed as legitimate by people outside the small group of vocal opponents.

Opposition Group Tactics

The substance of their concerns helped advance the opponents' cause, but their tactics were also instrumental in ensuring that their influence exceeded what might have been predicted considering their numbers. In Kentucky and California, opposition groups relied on lobbying and grassroots mobilization to promote their agendas. In Califonia, the Rutherford Institute and the United States Justice Foundation added a third tactic: filing lawsuits.

Opposition groups in both states testified before legislative committees and the state board of education, organized rallies at the state capitol, and lobbied individual legislators. In California, CRI and the TVC were the two opposition groups most focused on lobbying, while in Kentucky, all the opposition groups were involved in lobbying activities. The opposition groups worked primarily with Republican legislators in both states, and some endorsed electoral candidates.

In California, opposition groups worked closely with one another, but did not coalesce with any traditional education interest groups. In Kentucky, however, the Family Foundation joined with the Kentucky School Boards Association, the Kentucky Congress of Teachers and Parents, the Kentucky Association of School Administrators, and the Kentucky Association of School Superintendents in sending a letter outlining their concerns about KIRIS to the state board of education. The letter listed three major issues: a lack of public confidence and ownership in the testing system; the need to ensure that KIRIS is fair and that the state is providing incentives to improve teaching and learning; and a resolution to the technical problems related to KIRIS's design, administration, and scoring. In explaining why the four groups representing key segments of the education establishment had joined the Family Foundation in writing the letter, they noted that their recommendation to have an open process for making decisions about the test would not have been credible if they had excluded a group that agreed with their position on this particular issue (May, 1995b).

Grassroots mobilization took a variety of forms. Representatives of opposition groups spoke in churches, community forums, and at "coffees" in individual homes. One leader of a Kentucky opposition group reported that she had logged 100,000 miles on her van traveling around the state. One of the most effective tactics that groups used to publicize their position to audiences beyond their traditional constituents was use of the media. The Kentucky groups were particularly effective in gaining visibility through the general news media. Martin Cothran of the Family Foundation wrote op-ed articles that were printed in several of the state's major newspapers.[22] A number of daily and weekly newspapers printed opinion pieces written by Donna Shedd, vice president of the state Eagle Forum. Cothran and Shedd became the opposition spokespersons that journalists contacted when they needed critical responses to KERA developments. Consequently, they and the positions they represented became quite visible across the state. In addition, other opponents wrote letters to the editor reiterating the groups' position in response to specific incidents or the comments of KERA supporters.

Probably because CLAS was a considerably less visible policy than KERA, and because CLAS was the subject of intense controversy for only a year, there was significantly less media coverage in California than in Kentucky.[23] Nevertheless, opponents used some of the same tactics as in Kentucky, particularly the use of local letters to the editor. A few opposition leaders, such as Gary Kreep of USJF, Carolyn Steinke of PIE, and Rev. Louis P. Sheldon and his wife Beverly of TVC, became the spokespersons whom the media quoted in CLAS stories.

Although the California groups may have been less successful in using the secular media than were their counterparts in Kentucky, the CLAS opponents had an additional tactic in the form of legal challenges.[24] The USJF filed lawsuits against 19 school districts seeking to block administration of the 1994 test, and the Rutherford Institute filed a similar number. These suits argued that at least some of the items on the CLAS test were covered by the California Education Code, which stated:

> No test, questionnaire, survey, or examination containing any questions about the pupil's personal beliefs or practices in sex, family life, morality and religion, or any questions about his parents' or guardians' beliefs or practices in sex, family life, morality and religion, shall be administered to any kindergarten or grade 1 through 12 inclusive, unless the parent or guardian of the pupil is notified in writing that such test, questionnaire, survey, or examination is to be administered and the parent or guardian of the pupil gives written permission for the pupil to take such test, questionnaire, survey, or examination.

Consequently, according to the lawsuits, if school districts did not obtain permission from all parents prior to administering CLAS, they were violating the law. Parents who could serve as named plaintiffs were recruited by local opposition groups with the promise that either USJF or Rutherford would provide pro bono legal assistance. School boards that wished to oppose the state were also offered such assistance. In addition, parents who contacted CRI or PIE and who wanted to take legal action were referred to the two legal aid foundations.

The CLAS opponents lost their cases in court, with the first ruling coming in a suit brought by two parents with children attending school in a suburban area of the Los Angeles Unified School District. The judge in that case ruled that the CLAS materials "are obviously designed to elicit analytical comprehension and writing abilities . . . The questions are not designed to elicit the prohibited information. More importantly, they, in fact, do not call for a revelation of the pupil's parents' or guardians' beliefs and practices on the prohibited subjects" (Merl, 1994). That ruling set a precedent that allowed districts to avoid having to obtain permission from all parents before the CLAS test was administered.[25] However, several weeks before this ruling, a San Bernardino Superior Court judge had ruled that individual parents could have their children excused from, or "opted out" of, taking the CLAS test. The SDE subsequently agreed to such an option, allowing districts to excuse students from taking the test if their parents objected to its content. As indicated, that option was exercised by about 5 percent of parents of students in the tested grades. Various opposition groups provided many of those parents with the forms to opt their children out of the exam.

The States Respond

For a variety of reasons, primarily related to different political incentives, officials in California and Kentucky responded to the opposition in different ways.

THE CALIFORNIA RESPONSE.   Because of the sunset provisions in the original CLAS legislation, the assessment had to be reauthorized during the height of the controversy. Gary Hart, the chairman of the senate education committee, was responsible for guiding the reauthorization through the legislature. He made a number of changes in the reauthorizing legislation (SB 1273) in response to the demands of the opposition groups and their legislative allies. For example, SB 1273 contained a prohibition against asking students about their sexual, moral, and religious beliefs and those of their families. It also added parents and other members of the public to the teams that would develop the assessments and it established a citizens' committee, appointed by the legislature, to review the final test. SB 1273 also required that the CLAS test contain a mix of performance assessments, multiple-choice, and short-answer items that measured "building block" skills as well as higher-order skills. In addition, the bill required that the SDE distribute sample exams as broadly as possible so the public would know what types of questions had been asked.

After the bill had passed the senate and was awaiting passage in the assembly, Governor Wilson used his power of the line-item veto to veto CLAS's 1995 appropriations, arguing that the testing program had to be reformed and that SB 1273 did not meet his criteria. In September 1994, after SB 1273 had passed both houses despite opposition from conservative Republican legislators, Wilson vetoed the measure. In his veto message, Wilson argued that SB 1273 departed from the vision of CLAS embodied in the original legislation. Rather than making the generation of individual student scores the first priority of CLAS,

> SB 1273 takes a different approach. Instead of mandating individual student scores first, with performance-based assessment incorporated into such scores as this method is proven valid and reliable, it mandates performance-based assessment now and treats the production of individual student scores as if it were the experimental technology—which it clearly is not. In short, SB 1273 stands the priority for individual student scores on its head.
>
> Performance-based assessment—if well-designed—can play an important role in a system in which multiple measures are used to accurately assess *each student's* academic achievement. But under SB 1273 it remains only a too-long deferred good intention—only a "goal," and one not to be achieved until "the spring of 1999." That's not good enough. It's too long to wait. (September 27, 1994)

Wilson then reaffirmed his commitment to a testing program that produced "valid, reliable individual-level student scores; objective world-class performance standards; and an appropriate mix of questions designed to assess students' mastery of basic skills, as well as more sophisticated abilities to apply knowledge." He urged the legislature to give its highest priority to enacting such a program.

Several months after the governor's veto, the 1994 CLAS results were released, showing extremely poor achievement among those students who were tested. For example, more than 40 percent of the tenth graders tested in mathematics scored at the lowest of the six performance levels, meaning that they had "little or no mathematical thinking and understanding of mathematical ideas." In fact, the overwhelming majority of tested students scored at one of the three lowest levels in mathematics; the reading scores were only slightly better, with 60 percent scoring in the three lowest levels. The newly elected state superintendent of public instruction, Delaine Eastin, immediately appointed two task forces to examine the mathematics and reading curricula and to recommend how they might be improved. Debate continued not only over the most productive way to teach mathematics and reading, but also over whether the curriculum embodied in the state frameworks and CLAS had ever really been implemented in classrooms and thus given a fair test of its effectiveness (Colvin, 1995b). Both task forces determined that a more balanced approach to instruction was necessary. During this same period, two liberal Democratic and one Republican member of the state assembly introduced legislation requiring that spelling, phonics, and basic computation be taught in the state's schools. As one news report noted at the time, "the fact that legislators believe it necessary to make such pronouncements is probably more significant than the pronouncements themselves" (Colvin, 1995c).

Early in 1995, the state legislature passed AB 265 authorizing the Commission for the Establishment of Academic Content and Performance Standards. It was to have 21 members, with 12 appointed by the governor, six by the superintendent of public instruction (SPI), one by the senate rules committee, and one by the speaker of the state assembly, and was also to include the SPI or his designee. The commission was charged with developing content and performance standards in mathematics, language arts, social studies, and science, and then submitting them to the state board of education for its consideration and final approval.

Included throughout AB 265 and related legislation were provisions requiring that parents, educators, and the public be involved "in an active and ongoing basis" in assessment design. Both the commission and the state board were required to hold hearings throughout the state as they deliberated about the standards. The legislation also prohibited the standards from including any "personal behavioral standards or skills," and the subsequent assessment was not to include any items that would elicit personal information about a student or his or her family.

Key state policymakers decided that one reason for CLAS's failure was a lack of clear, measurable content standards (Olson, 1998). Although CLAS had been linked to the state's curriculum frameworks, critics argued that the frameworks focused more on a particular pedagogy than on what content should be taught. Consequently, the commission was charged with developing "academically rigorous content standards and performance standards" that were "measurable and objective."

In July 1998, the commission completed its work and submitted the last of the four sets of content standards to the state board. But once again, the process highlighted strong value conflicts among educators, university academics, parents, and the public about what should be taught in the state's schools. Somewhat surprisingly, the language arts standards were developed without controversy, and reflected a skillful integration of phonics and whole language approaches. Some participants attributed this shift away from CLAS-era conflict to the fact that the "language arts wars" had been fought three years earlier and common ground had already begun to emerge as the commission began its work. Others argued that it was the deliberative process the commission's language arts task force used that led to such a productive synthesis. In any event, the language arts standards were approved by the state board, all of whose members had been appointed by Governor Wilson. The commission also developed social studies standards without any significant problems.

The mathematics and science standards were another matter, however. Their development prompted profound intellectual disagreements over the balance between basic skills and conceptual learning and between direct instruction and discovery-based learning, and over the degree to which traditionally separate subdisciplines within mathematics (such as algebra and geometry) and science (such as earth science and life science) should be integrated in student coursework. Further disagreement ensued about the amount and specificity of the content that students should be expected to learn.

The commission's deliberations in establishing standards for these two subjects warrant a separate analysis (for an examination of the California standards-setting process, see McDonnell and Weatherford, 1999). But, in brief, despite the commission's efforts to produce a consensus document in mathematics that largely reflected the NCTM standards, the state board rejected the commission's version and rewrote the standards in a more traditional vein, consistent with a minority report submitted by one of the commissioners. In science, the commission produced a document representing what it believed was a compromise between the two views of science presented to it by scientists and science educators (for a description of the standards-setting process in science, see Olson, 1998). However, a dozen U.S. scientific societies, including the American Association for the Advancement of Science, criticized the standards for being so "overstuffed" with facts that students would not gain any understanding of scientific concepts, and they urged the state board not to adopt them (*Chronicle of Higher Education,* 1998). Nevertheless, the state board unanimously adopted the standards.

For three years, California had no statewide student assessment.[26] In the spring of 1998, the state administered a commercially published multiple-choice test, the Stanford-9, to all students in grades 2–11. The test administration was controversial because of the state's requirement that all students, including those with limited English proficiency, take the test in English, and because of the lack of alignment between the Stanford-9 and the state's academic content standards, which were still in development. The plan was to augment the Stanford-9 with additional test items once the state board adopted the content standards. However, the state board continued to be wary of including open-ended and performance items and remained committed to a largely multiple-choice test.

The state seemed to have learned critical lessons from CLAS: the standards development process was more open and publicly accessible than it had been for CLAS, and those charged with developing the standards were a more diverse group that included—in addition to classroom teachers and university academics—several businesspeople and a mother who schools her children at home. Nevertheless, the standards-setting process demonstrated that disputes about what should be taught in the public schools had not been resolved. In this round, the opposition was spearheaded by well-educated parents questioning academic priorities rather than cultural and political values (Sommerfeld, 1996). Although some of the proponents of more traditional mathematics and science standards were political conservatives, others characterized themselves as moderates and even liberals.[27] But some of the same themes continued to characterize public discourse: whether there is sufficient evidence in support of new curricular approaches; what the appropriate balance is between a traditional and a more progressive curriculum; and how much weight should be accorded to professional judgment, compared with parental and community preferences.

WHAT EXPLAINS THE CALIFORNIA RESPONSE? The obvious question that emerges after a review of the California case is, How could an assessment, heralded by education reformers and curriculum experts as the most innovative in the country, be decimated so quickly by groups representing a minority of the state's parents and voters? Six factors shaped the state's response to the CLAS opposition and help to explain the policy's eventual fate. What is perhaps most surprising is that these factors relate primarily to the process by which the assessment was developed and monitored by political authorities. It is always easy to argue in hindsight, "Things might have been different if only . . ." However, in this case, a different process might very well have diffused the worst controversies associated with CLAS and allowed it to continue with its basic features intact.

The first factor relates to the process by which the CLAS test was developed and to the types of participants in that process. The strong desire of

SDE officials to use the test as a lever to shape the curriculum led to a development process dominated by curriculum experts, psychometricians, and teachers who favored a constructivist mode of pedagogy. It was an insular process with no public involvement. Those involved in the development process acknowledged that:

> There was a strong bias [among the members of the language arts test development committee]. First of all, we didn't select anybody who didn't have a good understanding of what current thinking is in the field, who wasn't an exemplary teacher. Remember the point of the test was to drive instruction in the direction of the framework. The framework represents a particular take on what it means to read and write, for work in the language arts. We only wanted on the development team teachers who understood that framework and as practitioners exemplified what the frameworks stood for. In so far as it represents a particular bias, the test is mandated to support a particular bias. Bias as to the best current state of knowledge in the field. In that sense it is bias. (language arts assessment consultant)

Talking several months after the CLAS reauthorization had been vetoed, one SDE official suggested that perhaps the test developers had overestimated the ability of the test to drive the curriculum. He characterized the curriculum experts involved in the test development as "the true believers who wrote the curriculum frameworks" and noted the "significant gap in expectations between the curriculum and the measurement people." He continued,

> At the time, we just didn't realize the gap between what we were doing curriculum-wise and what we could do measurement-wise. [A psychometrician] was one of the members of the technical advisory committee least sympathetic to the curriculum people. He'd say, "Why should we measure it when you're not even teaching it?" [The curriculum experts on the committee] would say, "As soon as you test it, it will get taught." I now realize that it was unfair to put the burden on the testing system to change teaching.

However, this debate over CLAS' potential occurred at a purely technical level among experts. Until the controversy erupted in 1994, no one considered broadening the group responsible for developing and reviewing CLAS:

> Almost nowhere in discussions about the frameworks was there any consideration of where public involvement should enter into it. There had been such a battle among the experts and the academic community

about the social studies frameworks, that public involvement would probably have caused even greater disagreements . . . I watched other states with citizens' commissions writing educational goals and the like. But the members of those commissions are typically leaders from business and other sectors; they're not really representative of the general public. If we had involved the public, we would probably have involved the wrong people—they probably would have been the "gung-ho" reform activists. (SDE official)

A second factor, time and budgetary constraints, has already been discussed. One manifestation was the SDE's refusal to release test items that had become the subject of dispute. The department believed that the release of test items might advantage some test-takers at the expense of others, and that unless some items could be used for more than one year, costs would increase and trends would be more difficult to discern. However, the SDE persisted in requiring test secrecy even in the face of outrageous rumors about what was on the test. Only belatedly did the SDE allow legislators to view the test. The general public was allowed to see the literature portion of the test at 41 sites statewide for one month after it had been administered to students, but no copies could be made of it.

Although there were clear bureaucratic reasons for the secrecy surrounding the test, the effect was to undermine the SDE's credibility. Opposition leaders could play upon the refusal to release test items, saying, "It makes you wonder what people are doing to your children if you have no right to see the test." After the controversy was over, an SDE official acknowledged the negative effect of the department's secrecy: "Where we really lost it is that the more we said, 'You can't see the test,' the more we fed mainstream fears."[28]

The limited information from the SDE about CLAS also meant that technical problems with the test were exaggerated, and that the SDE could do little to counter erroneous accounts. One prominent example related to the scoring of the tests. Because of the high cost of scoring, the SDE decided to score only a sample of the 1993 tests (about 42 percent). However, according to the expert review of CLAS, that decision was never adequately communicated to parents or even to local superintendents (Cronbach, Bradburn, and Horvitz, 1994). The SDE's failure to communicate how it was dealing with fiscal constraints permitted opponents to overstate those constraints by making incorrect assertions, such as, "Less than one percent were even scored of the students who took the test."

A third factor explaining the California outcome was the lack of scrutiny by elected officials. Just as there was no public involvement in the development of CLAS, there was little political oversight until after the controversy erupted. Two mechanisms existed for political oversight of CLAS: the traditional one of legislative hearings, and the APC which served as an advisory committee to the SDE and included representatives of all the relevant elected officials. However, legislative hearings on CLAS were few, and the APC never saw a copy of the CLAS test. One legislative staffer who was a member of the APC explained the situation:

> The lack of oversight on SB 662 was no different than for most legislation. There's really no mechanism for [oversight] to happen. The legislature operates on a contingency basis; if there's some kind of crisis, then there's oversight. The checkpoints are really in the budgetary process—how much money is included for an activity in the governor's budget and then the legislative hearing on the budget. But there was never a hearing that focused on issues such as what the result of the CLAS pilots showed or what the SDE was communicating to parents. The oversight for SB 662 was supposed to be through the policy committee, but that was like "singing to the choir." The SDE basically did a "show and tell" for us and we thought everything was fine because we believed in what the SDE was doing. We assumed (incorrectly perhaps) that the SDE was checking with different constituencies. We only started to hear later that there were concerns about the frameworks; Honig was such a cheerleader for the frameworks.

Another member representing a more conservative elected official confirmed this limited role of the APC: "We were repeatedly reassured by [SDE officials] that the whole issue was being blown out of proportion by the conservative right wing. I don't know why the policy committee didn't become concerned, but the SDE was saying everything was all right . . . I guess it's pretty surprising, but the policy committee never got involved in test content. We relied on the expertise of the SDE. The test was 'by teachers, for teachers.' The committee was going by the agenda of the SDE; we were an advisory group."

This limited political oversight was coupled with a fourth factor, a lack of political leadership. Bill Honig had been the state official most committed to CLAS. He was an articulate and passionate advocate for the state frameworks, and he understood that although the state could not mandate such a curriculum in local schools, the CLAS test would move classroom teaching closer to that goal. However, by the time of the CLAS controversy, Honig had resigned his position because he had been indicted on conflict-of-interest charges involving consulting fees paid to his wife. His replacement as acting state superintendent, William D. Dawson, was a career civil servant who by all accounts did not have Honig's political skills.

Several policymakers involved with CLAS argued that if Honig had still been in office, the CLAS debacle could have been avoided. That sentiment was expressed by both legislative and gubernatorial staff:

> Dave Dawson did a remarkable job under the chaos and the pressure. The poor soul was like the character in the Peanuts cartoon carrying around the cloth. He was in there as a pinch hitter for Honig who was a wheeler and a dealer. The SDE just wasn't geared up to respond. A lot of people said that the whole thing wouldn't have happened if Honig had still been in office. I would vote with that sentiment. The battle would have been different because Honig would have been in the forefront of the battle. (legislative staffer)

> It was Dawson's naiveté that fanned it more than anything else. If the first ripple had been handled right, it [the controversy] would have gone away . . . I think they [the CLAS tests] stink; they're instructionally horrible. They got that way because the curriculum Nazis—the content folks in the SDE and the people they used on committees—had an agenda. These people are a very insular, inbred group. That wasn't a problem when Bill [Honig] was there. I'm convinced that *Black Boy* and the open-mind question would not have been on the test if he had been there. I know I sound like I'm saying, "If only Bill, if only Bill . . ." But it's true, it would have been different if he had been there. (member of the governor's staff)

An SDE official disagreed with the notion that Honig's presence would have changed the CLAS outcome: "I'm almost certain that it wouldn't have made a difference if Honig had been here and had read the test. He wouldn't have seen the problems, and when the opposition emerged, he would have seen them as the enemies of education reform and there would have been a battle. We were psychologically incapable of putting ourselves in the critics' shoes. Most people aren't empathetic enough to do that."

Clearly, participants had different perceptions about the role that Honig might have played if he had remained in office, with some seeing him as a moderating influence and others assuming that he would have escalated the controversy by fighting in a spirited, visible way. It is also unlikely that one person, no matter how committed and skilled, could have reversed a political movement with such momentum. Nevertheless, Honig's absence meant that once the CLAS controversy began, there was no visible political leader strongly defending the testing concept. Among the three officials who had initially supported CLAS, only Honig had stressed its underlying curricular values as the dominant rationale for the test. Gary Hart tried to save CLAS because he saw its worth as a curricular and school accountability tool, but he lacked Honig's visibility and had other items on his policy agenda, notably charter schools and teacher training. Pete Wilson had never been a strong supporter of CLAS's content and format; his only interest was in individual-level student scores that could be obtained in a number of different ways, including traditional multiple-choice tests. Consequently, it is reasonable to assume that had Honig still been in office, CLAS would have received a more vigorous and skilled defense when it ran into trouble.

A fifth factor explaining the CLAS outcome was timing: the controversy occurred in an election year. Democrats argued that Wilson's veto of the CLAS reauthorization could be explained by the fact that he was running for re-election. Further complicating the picture was the campaign for state superintendent of public instruction. Delaine Eastin, the Democratic chair of the assembly education committee, was running against Maureen Di-Marco, a Democrat who was Wilson's appointed secretary of child development and education. DiMarco was in a particularly difficult position because she had opposed Proposition 174, the state voucher initiative that was supported by many of the CLAS opposition groups, and she was viewed as part of the education establishment by those groups and their supporters. At the same time, her affiliation with Wilson made traditional Democrats less likely to support her, so opposing CLAS would distinguish her from Eastin and increase her chances of gaining support from those planning to vote for Wilson. It is difficult to know exactly how great an effect the election campaign had on the CLAS outcome. Still, most study respondents assumed that there was some relationship. Even an opposition group leader said that considering Wilson's past support for CLAS, "if it was not an election year, I don't know if he would have vetoed that re-authorization."[29]

In contrast to the closed process by which it was developed, the controversy surrounding CLAS caused it to become publicly visible, largely through media coverage. Although the effect of this final factor on the demise of CLAS is difficult to estimate, the media certainly helped focus public attention on what had been a relatively obscure education reform. Furthermore, for the large majority of Californians who did not have school-aged children at the time, and therefore lacked firsthand knowledge of the schools, the media presented them with an image of CLAS as problematic and controversial.

In 1991 and 1992, articles appearing in the *Los Angeles Times* about the state assessment had averaged approximately twenty each year, with the total falling to only three in 1993. However, in 1994, during the height of the CLAS controversy, the *Los Angeles Times* ran 171 articles about the state assessment. Of these, 75 percent focused on aspects of the controversy, compared with the remainder that either described the test or reported on its results. Although the *Los Angeles Times* was instrumental in calling public attention to the technical problems with CLAS's scoring and reporting, most of the newspaper's coverage focused on the cultural criticisms that opposition groups were making (for example, that CLAS was an invasion of family privacy, that test items reflected a particular social agenda), and on the actions they were taking to stop administration of the test. About 40 percent of the articles also identified specific groups, thus making them more visible to the public than they previously had been.

Although the CLAS controversy led to a huge increase in media coverage, it is important to note that the *Los Angeles Times* coverage was balanced. About one-third of the entries dealing with CLAS were op-ed pieces, editorials, or opinion columns, and in their tone, one-third of these were critical of CLAS, one-third supportive, and one-third neutral in their portrayal. Similarly, about 12 percent of the 1994 entries were letters to the editor, with two-thirds discussing CLAS in neutral tones. The news articles that represented over half the entries were overwhelmingly neutral in tone. So the issue was not that the media coverage was biased and unbalanced. Rather, it was that CLAS came to the attention of the California public only once it had become controversial, and that controversy meant that those who learned about CLAS through the media were far more likely to hear about its weaknesses than its potential benefits. CLAS's low visibility during its enactment and the closed development process gave the media little incentive to report on it when it was still a viable policy. By covering the state assessment only when it became controversial, the media inevitably portrayed CLAS to the public as a problematic policy with vocal critics.

Suggesting that the CLAS controversy would not have occurred if there had been a more open, inclusive development process is only speculation. One might argue that such a controversy was inevitable in a state as culturally and politically diverse as California. Nevertheless, there is some evidence that a different process might have led to a different outcome. For example, an SDE official reported that after the CLAS controversy began, the department convened a panel of parents and members of the public expressly chosen to represent disparate viewpoints. The purpose was to see if the panel could agree on an appropriate set of reading passages and other items to include on CLAS. Although the group reached consensus on only a small subset of passages and items, the exercise did demonstrate that people with diverse cultural, religious, and political beliefs could agree on curricular content that they all thought was appropriate and worthwhile. Unfortunately, by the time the panel was convened, CLAS was already facing extinction.

A second piece of evidence comes from Kentucky's experience. Like California's, Kentucky's development process was dominated by testing experts, curriculum specialists, and classroom teachers. Also like California, it encountered serious opposition. However, the state response in Kentucky differed significantly from California's, with the result that the basic underlying principles continue to be implemented, albeit in a modified form. The Kentucky case suggests that while controversy might be difficult to avoid, political leadership and oversight can be effective in minimizing such conflicts.

THE KENTUCKY RESPONSE. During the 1994 legislative session, the political and business elites who supported KERA mobilized to blunt the opposition and to ensure the reform act's continued implementation. One strategy involved the legislature and the state commissioner of education making some "midcourse corrections" to protect KERA from further assault and to ensure that it would remain basically intact. They eliminated two of the state's six learning goals—dealing with individual self-sufficiency and responsible group membership—that were targets of the most intense criticism; they delayed the imposition of sanctions on under-performing schools until 1996; and they shifted the on-demand high school assessment from the twelfth to the eleventh grade.[30] The state's 75 "valued outcomes" were reduced to 57 "academic expectations" with an emphasis on goals that were academic and could be measured by the assessment. All references to "emotions," "feelings," "evolution," and "environment" were eliminated from the standards. In addition, the commissioner of education announced that any adult who was willing to sign a non-disclosure agreement would be allowed to see all the KIRIS test items.

KERA, and particularly KIRIS, became an issue in the 1995 gubernatorial campaign. The Republican candidate, Larry Forgy, argued that the state should be using a national, standardized test that would allow Kentucky's scores to be compared with those in other states, and that less emphasis should be placed on writing portfolios, because they consumed too much time and the grading was too subjective. Forgy's opposition to KERA became a highlight of his campaign commercials, with him saying that KERA was "failing us in the classroom" and that it was "putting our children at risk." In focusing on this issue, he was capitalizing on voter sentiment. A state poll conducted during the campaign showed that about 42 percent of likely voters who had read or heard about KERA approved of the changes it was bringing about, while 45 percent disapproved (Cross, 1995a). The Democratic candidate, Paul Patton, largely defended KERA during the campaign. However, in response to Forgy's criticisms, Patton agreed that the state assessment had problems and suggested that the number of performance levels be increased and that more fact-based questions that everyone could agree upon be included on KIRIS. In his campaign commercials, Patton promised to undertake "a comprehensive review of KERA—keep the programs that work, get rid of those that don't" (Cross, 1995b). Patton won the governorship with 51 percent of the vote. Most political commentators agreed that KERA had been one of the major issues in the campaign and that it was likely to be modified further during the 1996 legislative session, but that the essence of KERA and KIRIS would continue intact. In fact, during the 1996 legislative session, the general assembly made few changes to KERA, while the governor fulfilled his campaign promise to appoint a task force to study KERA. The 18-member task force, with members appointed by the governor, the state senate, and the house, was to take 18 months to study KERA and make recommendations for the 1998 legislative session.

In the months leading up to the 1998 legislative session, however, it became clear even to KIRIS supporters that major modifications would be necessary if the assessment were to survive politically. The state reported in 1997 that students' average test scores had improved in a majority of the state's schools, including eight of the nine schools that had been declared "in crisis" by the state. Nevertheless, a number of developments had further undermined KIRIS's credibility. Earlier in the year, the SDE had announced that the 1996 test scores for almost all the elementary and middle schools in the state—more than 1,000—had been miscalculated in two subjects by the state's testing contractor. As a result, the state fired the contractor and quickly had to hire another testing company. During the same period, several cases of cheating by school officials came to light. While instances of teachers reviewing test questions with students in advance or inappropriately assisting them in preparing their portfolios were few, they gained statewide and even national attention (see Stecklow, 1997) and further jeopardized political support for KIRIS.

In December 1997, the public education task force recommended changes in the state assessment system to include, along with the state-designed test, a national norm-referenced one so that Kentucky students could be compared with those across the country; multiple-choice items in addition to open-ended ones and portfolios; less time spent on testing; and a different way to measure schools for rewards and sanctions that would give monetary awards to school programs rather than to teachers. In April 1998, the governor signed a bill authorizing a new state assessment, the Commonwealth Accountability Testing System (CATS), to replace KIRIS. It required that CATS include: a national norm-referenced test that matched the state's core curriculum, fewer constructed responses (open-ended items), individual scores recorded on student transcripts, and the ability to make longitudinal comparisons within the same group of students. Rewards and sanctions were revamped, with rewards now allocated to schools rather than to individuals, and low-performing schools subject to a broader range of assistance and sanctions, including mandatory audits, school improvement funding, and the services of state staff, as well as the option for students at these schools to transfer to more effective ones. The law also established three testing advisory panels appointed by the governor and the legislature, including a panel of national testing experts; a legislative oversight committee; and a public committee consisting of educators, parents, and public representatives.

Although there was no question during the 1998 legislative session that Kentucky would continue to administer some kind of state test, the original bill passed by the state senate would have represented a more significant departure from KIRIS. This bill would have suspended the high stakes test until 2002, and divided the funds for rewarding schools among all the state's schools. In addition, portfolio scores would not count, and a legislative agency, the Office of Educational Accountability, would have had primary oversight of the state assessment. However, the senate was pressured to compromise with the house on a bill that modified KIRIS and changed its name, but preserved its emphasis on accountability through a system of rewards and sanctions. That pressure came from the coalition of business leaders and reformers who had supported KERA and who continued to see accountability as a quid pro quo for the new resources KERA had pumped into the state's schools; from editorial writers around the state; and from the Kentucky Education Association. The coalition prevailed, and after a three-month stalemate, the CATS legislation was agreed to by both houses. Consequently, KERA and the accompanying state assessment were given something rare in education reform—more than a decade to be implemented and to show results with only modest revisions and a firm political commitment to "stay the course."

WHAT EXPLAINS THE KENTUCKY RESPONSE? Two strategies characterized the state response in Kentucky and distinguished it from California's. The first is that key state officials quickly responded to opponents' criticisms. Thomas Boysen, then commissioner of education, moved promptly to meet with KIRIS opponents. For example, he met with 180 members of the Greater Lexington Ministerial Fellowship, whose members had been among those most critical of KERA. Boysen admitted that "it was extremely unfortunate, in bad taste" for *Transformations* to have included as a recommended activity that students join two liberal organizations. In speaking to the group, Boysen also promised to work with the ministers to change KIRIS items that they found objectionable and to consider ways that churches might participate in the character education of students (White, 1994). The SDE began to include anti-KERA leaders on SDE committees and advisory groups that were revising the state standards and previewing KIRIS.

The KERA opponents argued in public that the midcourse adjustments did not go far enough. Donna Shedd of the Eagle Forum called the adjustments "back fires": "They're burning off some vegetation to stop the fire coming along the prairie. But the fire is too big. The back fires won't work" (as quoted in May, 1994c). Nevertheless, opponents like Shedd participated in the state-level advisory groups and regularly met with Boysen and his staff, even as they continued to seek major changes in KERA.

A second factor that distinguished the Kentucky response from California's is that groups and prominent individuals mobilized in support of KERA. The Prichard Committee, a statewide group that had promoted education reform for over a decade, launched a campaign to counteract criticism of KERA. As one activity, it sent letters to the editors of Kentucky newspapers citing inaccuracies in the op-ed articles and letters written by KERA opponents. The Partnership for Kentucky School Reform, an organization of business leaders affiliated with the Prichard Committee and the national Business Roundtable, sent letters to all state legislators affirming its support for KERA.[31] It also placed advertisements in the state's newspapers countering charges made by KERA opponents. When KERA became an issue in the 1995 gubernatorial campaign, the Partnership spent more than $100,000 on a television advertising campaign defending the state reforms (Associated Press, 1995). In 1998, the Partnership was focused on higher-education issues and was alerted to the senate revisions to KIRIS only after the bill had been passed. But its members quickly made their position clear, distributing a position paper in support of school accountability to all legislators, and making clear in statements to the press that they favored the house version of the bill, which continued accountability through a system of rewards and sanctions (Blackford, 1998). So, unlike in California, political and business elites were willing to speak out in favor of the state assessment and the principles underlying it.

One critical difference between Kentucky and California largely explains the two states' differing responses to the similar opposition each faced. The scope of KERA, including its visibility and cost, meant that the political leaders who endorsed the reform program had to be active and visible in their support to get it enacted and funded. Several respondents noted that the core of legislators who were in leadership positions when KERA was enacted had "basically staked their careers on education reform" (interview with legislative staffer). As a result, they had no alternative but to ensure that "objections to it [were] met very energetically" (interview with Kentucky Department of Education official).

One of the elected officials most involved in enacting KERA further attributed politicians' active support to the development process: "There were three viewpoints at the time of the supreme court decision about how the legislature would react. One was that the legislature would be involved in responding to the decision and devising a remedy. The second was that the legislature would stonewall, and the third was that we would form a blue ribbon commission composed of business leaders and the like. The first option prevailed. As a result, it gave members of the legislature pride of ownership. If the leadership is stable, we should be able to support and maintain KERA." Consequently, even though KERA was developed by a small group, it was more directly a legislative product than was the case in California, where the APC was responsible for the basic structure of CLAS, with elected officials' involvement limited to ratifying what their representatives had designed. Not only was there a greater policy incentive for elected officials to take a strong stand in Kentucky, but the deliberations that had occurred during the enactment process meant that at least a few political leaders understood, accepted, and could defend the ideas behind KERA and KIRIS.[32]

It is unclear what effect the media coverage of KIRIS and KERA had on state officials' response to public criticism of the test. Certainly the media devoted considerably more attention to the state assessment in Kentucky than in California. Not only did the *Lexington Herald-Leader* run almost twice as many articles than did the *Los Angeles Times* in 1994, but in the years before that, when the *Los Angeles Times* was averaging fewer than 20 items a year, the *Herald-Leader* had run 54 in 1992 and 154 in 1993. There are probably two major reasons for the difference. California is a much larger, more diverse state with many more issues competing for space in the state's newspapers, and unlike CLAS, KIRIS was essential to the most profound change in the state's education system since the founding of the Kentucky commonwealth. In that light, the high level of media coverage is not surprising. However, despite the greater prominence of KIRIS in the Kentucky media, the pattern of coverage in the *Herald-Leader* was virtually identical to that in the *Los Angeles Times*. Straight news articles represented slightly more than half (55 percent) of the entries, and these were overwhelmingly neutral in tone. Like those in the *Los Angeles Times,* opinion pieces (op-ed pieces, editorials, letters to the editor) were evenly split between those opposing and those supporting KIRIS (at about 40 percent each), with the remainder neutral in their position. Considering that half the respondents in a 1994 statewide poll reported little or no knowledge of KERA, one might argue that the additional newspaper coverage in Kentucky had little impact. However, it is probably reasonable to conclude that KIRIS's and KERA's greater prominence in the media further motivated those public officials who supported the reforms to defend them in the face of opposition, and to address problems quickly.

The Technical Becomes Political

From the very beginning, policymakers had to contend with the technical limitations of CLAS and KIRIS, and the fact that policy expectations had exceeded what test developers could produce within a limited time frame. Testing experts warned that while performance assessments potentially could be vastly superior to multiple-choice tests, they were not without their problems. In an analysis of performance assessments, Linn (1993) focused particularly on the generalizability problems associated with new forms of assessments. He noted that one of the major stumbling blocks to the implementation of performance-based assessment systems is "the limited degree of generalizability of performance from one task to another" (p. 9). Citing evidence from performance assessments in history, mathematics, science, and even licensure examinations in law and medicine, Linn concluded that because performance on one task has only a weak to modest relationship to performance on another, a large number of tasks (or increased testing time for more complex tasks) would be necessary to ensure that assessments produce comparable information and fair results. However, the remedy of increasing the number of tasks creates its own feasibility problems in terms of cost and time burden.

Limitations on the ability to make valid generalizations, and the reliability of a scoring process requiring considerable judgment on the part of multiple scorers, are the major technical problems associated with performance assessments. These problems are exacerbated when parents and politicians expect individual-level student scores, which require a different and more-expensive design than the matrix design typically used in assessing schools. When assessments are used for high stakes purposes, reliability and validity problems also become more serious.

The assessment systems in Kentucky and California were evaluated by panels of testing and measurement experts, who found both systems to have serious flaws. The first report about Kentucky found that KIRIS was not reliable enough to use as the basis for rewarding or sanctioning schools. The panel concluded that the performance standards for deciding students' level of proficiency were based on too few items; that the scoring of portfolios was too subjective and inconsistent for a high stakes system; that errors in equating across assessments made year-to-year comparisons of KIRIS results of questionable validity; and that at least for fourth-grade reading, student gains on KIRIS were not matched by the scores of Kentucky students on the NAEP (Hambleton et al., 1995).[33] The panel agreed with the Kentucky Department of Education's 1994 evaluation that concluded: "The content being assessed is not well enough defined and the relationship among the learning goals, academic expectations, the curriculum frameworks, the program of studies, course outlines, released items and performance standards is not clearly described. This makes it difficult for teachers to focus their instructional efforts and to explain to parents what is being taught and assessed" (p. 10).

The panel recommended that portfolios not be used for accountability purposes; that validation work be expanded; that the performance standards be reestablished and full documentation of the process be provided; that public reports be clear about limits on generalizability of findings to a new set of tasks; that multiple-choice items be added to increase content validity and scoring reliability; and that the state reconsider its shift toward instructional process at the expense of curriculum content.

SDE officials accepted the majority of the panel's recommendations, and moved to make changes in the assessment. Among the changes were the inclusion of multiple-choice items beginning in 1997; greater attention to the technical quality of the test through more extensive equating and validation; greater emphasis on the testing of content knowledge; and the administration of national norm-referenced tests in reading and mathematics in grades 6 and 9. The major disagreement with the panel was the SDE's decision, with legislative support, to continue to include writing portfolios in schools' accountability scores. However, the state implemented routine audits to ensure reliable scoring of the portfolios by teachers. The state also decided to continue KIRIS as a high stakes assessment, with rewards and sanctions attached to test scores.

A second technical review of KIRIS was commissioned in 1997, with a report issued in early 1998. This review, conducted as part of a legislative audit after the state fired its testing contractor, evaluated the extent to which the SDE had responded to the recommendations of the earlier expert panel. It concluded that "the KIRIS cognitive assessments as presently constituted and implemented are marginally adequate for reporting back to schools — although portions such as the KIRIS writing portfolios are somewhat suspect with respect to psychometric characteristics" (Catterall et al., 1998, p. 14). These experts also found that the accountability index that served as the basis for rewarding and sanctioning schools was flawed, and tended to inflate actual gains in student achievement. It singled out as particularly suspect the 60.7 percent increase in the average school reading score between the 1995–96 base year and 1997.[34] This second group of experts recommended that Kentucky needed a more consistently structured and administered testing program, and that the best way to accomplish that would be to begin a new accountability cycle with a new baseline. It also recommended that if writing portfolios were to remain in the accountability index, they would have to be audited more frequently to minimize score inflation, and that multiple-choice items continue to be included on the test and that they be included in the accountability index (Catterall et al., 1998).

The committee evaluating the California assessment identified fewer fundamental problems with the test and in fact, argued in its report that all the shortcomings of CLAS could be remedied and that as CLAS matured, it should be able to deliver "a highly useful product" (Cronbach, Bradburn, and Horvitz, 1994, transmittal letter). Some of the technical problems with CLAS were logistical—for example, lost test booklets, errors in matching student identification sheets to test booklets. The most serious problem the committee found was that because of resource constraints, the SDE and its test contractor did not score all the test booklets. As a result, few school-level reports in 1993 were reliable. The level of standard error was also unacceptably high as a result of "allowing no more than one or two hours of testing time per area for examining on a range of complex intellectual tasks" (p. 4). The select committee recommended that the state not distribute individual-level scores until the technical problems could be resolved.

In California and Kentucky, assessment designers had to balance daunting technical challenges against the political reality that elected officials expected to see performance assessments on-line very quickly. There is no question that SDE officials in both states promised more than they could deliver. Considering that they had to generate individual student scores, limit testing time, report student performance in terms of a set of absolute curriculum standards, keep scoring costs within reasonable time limits—and in the case of Kentucky, make high stakes decisions based on assessment results—considerably more time was needed for test development. However, in both states, SDE officials calculated that a flawed assessment was less costly than waiting until it met higher technical standards and risking diminished political support.

In both states, opponents used the technical reviews to bolster their cases, and the reports became part of the political debate. But in neither state were they a deciding factor in how the assessment controversy was resolved. In California, the report on the technical quality of CLAS was issued after political controversy had overwhelmed the assessment. Consequently, the report's assumption that technical problems could be remedied over time was never verified, since CLAS was discontinued several months later. Because officials moved quickly in Kentucky to implement most of the first panel's recommendations, and because the legislature reaffirmed its support for KIRIS, the technical report became only temporary fodder in the debate. However, the second technical review came at a time when KIRIS supporters had already recognized that substantial changes were necessary. Although the test's critics used parts of the report to argue for more drastic changes or for eliminating KIRIS, its central recommendation that the test be fixed and not abandoned strengthened the position of those who sought to preserve the assessment's core elements in a new guise.

The Move to High Stakes Testing

Although some policies may rely on values and information as motivators to change targets' behavior, most combine hortatory strategies with other policy instruments. The previous chapter argued that without links to other policies, the effectiveness of hortatory policies is likely to diminish. Elected officials have typically assumed that policy targets need material incentives if they are to make substantial changes and sustain them. The history of testing policy in North Carolina, California, and a number of other states fits this model exactly. The state assessments in North Carolina and California were for many years low stakes, relying on a variety of appeals to curricular and accountability values, and assuming that assessment information alone would mobilize school publics. However, by the late 1990s, the two states had attached tangible consequences to their testing systems, even exceeding those in Kentucky, by imposing them on both schools and individual students. The progression from low to high stakes testing in North Carolina and California not only demonstrates the evolution of hortatory policies,[35] but also shows how the shift from a solely values-based policy to one that imposes rewards and sanctions can change the terms of the policy debate. Although discussions of curricular values still permeate the public discourse about testing, particularly in California, the move to high stakes testing has shifted the focus of policy debate to questions of equity and appropriate test use.

In 1995, North Carolina enacted the ABCs of Public Education to impose greater accountability on schools, while at the same time increasing local flexibility and control. The acronym ABC reflected these goals: a strong focus on accountability (A), an emphasis on basic skills (B), and maximum local control (C). The end-of-grade test, tied to the state's *Standard Course of Study,* continues to be administered, but its results now have consequences for schools, individual educators, and students. Teachers at schools that improve their test scores beyond their "expected growth" can receive bonuses of up to $1,500, but those in the very lowest-performing schools in the state must work with state-sponsored assistance teams and (in rare circumstances) can even lose their jobs.

In April 1999, the state board moved to end social promotion by requiring students in the third, fifth, and eighth grades to pass the end-of-grade tests before they can be promoted. The state also requires that high school students pass an exit exam in order to graduate. At the time the policy to end social promotion was passed, the state estimated that 2 to 4 percent of the students in the relevant grades would be retained because of low test scores.

The reasoning behind the move to high stakes testing was state policy-makers' belief that school-level accountability was a reasonable quid pro quo for increased state funding and for greater local flexibility in fiscal and curricular decisions. But the change also stemmed from frustration that North Carolina's students continued to score "at the bottom of the bottom" on standardized tests. One former legislative staffer described the bipartisan legislative and gubernatorial consensus that emerged around high stakes testing by saying that politicians saw the state as a "sinking ship": "[Their attitude was:] '[We] don't care if the captain of the *Titanic* was asleep in his cabin or at the helm, the ship hit an iceberg and sank.'" With such an analogy framing their definition of the policy problem, more drastic action seemed necessary. The change in North Carolina was also part of a larger trend throughout the South to improve student performance through high stakes measures, prompted by a belief that, compared with other regions, improvement had been insufficient and needed to be ratcheted up.

Although North Carolina escaped political controversy about the curricular values underlying its state assessment, the move to high stakes testing led to two major controversies, both resolved in ways that maintained the core of the state policy. The first related to a provision in the original ABC legislation that required all teachers working at low-performing schools where state assistance teams had intervened to take a general knowledge test.[36] As noted in Chapter 1, the approximately 250 educators who were initially required to take the exam planned to boycott it, and the North Carolina Association of Educators (NCAE) threatened to sue the state. However, just days before the test was to be administered, the legislature changed the policy, requiring that only those teachers who received poor evaluations due to a lack of general content knowledge would be required to take the exam.[37]

Despite the few teachers who are now affected by the policy, it has continued to engender controversy even as North Carolina has moved to raise teacher salaries and to provide incentives for them to obtain certification from the National Board for Professional Teaching Standards and earn master's degrees. Considering that two-thirds of the state's elementary and middle schools were rated "exemplary" based on their 1998 test scores (with the proportion rising to 80 percent the next year) and that the state awarded $116 million in bonuses to teachers in those schools, any given teacher was more likely to be rewarded than tested or fired.

Nevertheless, teachers view the high stakes testing system with considerable skepticism for several reasons. Unlike Kentucky, where state officials have "stayed the course" in their reform strategies, North Carolina has implemented five major reforms since the early 1980s. State policymakers have viewed these reforms as connected and representing a steady progression in efforts to improve student achievement. Teachers, however, have questioned whether officials are giving each round of reform policies sufficient time to be implemented and assessed before moving to greater state direction and intervention (interview with NCAE official, Simmons, 1997). A 1998 statewide poll found that more than half of North Carolina's teachers did not believe that the ABCs program would improve education; they were especially critical of the state test's emphasis on reading, writing, and mathematics to the exclusion of other subjects such as social studies, science, and art (Simmons, 1998).

A second source of controversy has revolved around the equity implications of a high stakes testing system. The issue of equity led to a lawsuit filed in federal district court against the Johnston County school district by a group of parents represented by the NAACP. Johnston County, an 18,000-student school district south of Raleigh, instituted a social promotion policy in 1996, prior to enactment of the state policy. Students who do not score at the proficient level on the end-of-grade exams are given intensive remediation (including tutoring and Saturday programs), and then retained in their grades if they continue to perform below grade level on the state assessment. At the time the lawsuit was filed, about 500 students, or 6 percent of those in grades 3 through 8, had been retained after remediation and three attempts to pass the test.

The plaintiffs argued that using the end-of-grade test to make promotion decisions about individual students was not a valid use because the test was designed primarily to assess how well a school is covering the state curriculum standards. Additionally, they charged that the policy was having a disparate impact on minority students, because while only 4 percent of the district's white elementary students were retained, 11 percent of African-American students and 10 percent of Hispanic students were not promoted. District and state officials countered that the end-of-course exams were well-aligned with the curriculum and a good measure of what students should have learned, and that the possibility of retention made students more accountable and focused teaching on the curriculum and on students' mastery of that curriculum (Manzo, 1997).[38]

The Johnston County lawsuit was settled out of court. The district did not change its policy, but it agreed to codify it and to communicate it more clearly to parents. Teachers are now required to review each student's record at the beginning of the school year, and to designate as "at risk" those students whose grades, test scores, and attendance make it likely that they will fail the end-of-grade test. Teachers are then required to prepare plans for those students (similar to the individualized education program [IEP] prepared for special education students); meet with the parents, who must sign the plans; and then provide quarterly progress reports to the parents, according to a district official.

This lawsuit highlights a major problem that continues to challenge the implementation of North Carolina's high stakes assessment policy, as well as school systems in most other states—the persistent achievement gap between minority and white students. In 1999, 79 percent of the state's white students performed at grade level on North Carolina's mathematics and reading tests, compared with 49 percent of African Americans, 52 percent of Hispanics, and 50 percent of Native American students. As the proportion of students performing at grade level has increased, these racial and ethnic disparities have continued (Viadero, 2000).

Politicians, testing experts, educators, and the public will continue to debate whether and under what conditions standardized tests should be used to make high stakes decisions about schools, teachers, and individual students. But most would agree that the distribution of scores on state assessments is not the root of the problem. Rather, it reflects underlying societal inequalities, some of which stem from differences in the school experiences afforded different groups of students. Highly visible test results point to disparities among students that were often overlooked in the past. But they do not validate any particular solutions, and those now in vogue, such as ending social promotion and requiring exit exams for high school graduation, are often controversial (Heubert and Hauser, 1999). North Carolina officials have acknowledged the persistence of the achievement gap, and have set about to address it. The state is requiring that every district prepare a plan for narrowing racial and ethnic achievement gaps, increasing funding for programs that serve students performing below grade level, publishing a report card that tracks achievement by race, and launching a pilot program in five districts that will reward schools if test scores improve for every racial, ethnic, and socioeconomic group (Manzo, 2000; Viadero, 2000).

Although California officials moved to high stakes testing later than North Carolina, their reasons and policy choices were quite similar. The shift began with the 1998 election of Gray Davis, who had campaigned on the promise of making education his top priority and improving the state's schools through a series of reform initiatives. Shortly after taking office, he called a special session of the legislature to enact four major education policies. The first established a peer review and assistance program for teachers, and the second focused on reading instruction in the primary grades, providing funding for intensive summer reading programs for K–4 students and professional development institutes to train beginning teachers in reading instruction. The third and fourth initiatives proposed developing for the first time a high stakes statewide testing and accountability program for schools, educators, and students. The school accountability initiative would establish an academic performance index (API) that would rank all the schools in the state, with scores on the state assessment constituting 60 percent of the index and other factors, such as attendance and graduation rates, the remainder. About 5 percent of the state's schools that fell below the 50th percentile on the API would be selected for special assistance from the state. If they failed to improve for several years, they would be subject to state intervention and reorganization. Schools that met or exceeded student performance goals would be eligible for financial rewards.

The fourth initiative established a statewide high school exit exam that all students would be required to pass before graduation. A year earlier, the state legislature had passed legislation requiring that all school districts in the state develop policies governing grade-to-grade promotion and retention for second through fifth graders and for those students moving on to middle and high school. Local districts have the discretion to use either the results of the state test or indicators of academic achievement designated by the district to determine which students should be retained or are at risk of being retained. By giving districts the option of using the state assessment in promotion decisions, California officials made the test less high stakes than it had become in North Carolina and a number of other states. Nevertheless, the prospect of a statewide high school exit exam and the possibility that the state assessment could be used as part of district promotion policies were major changes in the potential consequences of state tests for individual students.

Although they were modified somewhat during the legislative process, all four of Governor Davis's bills were passed by the legislature within 10 weeks of being introduced. In a state with complex and often divisive politics, the swiftness of the legislative enactment was extraordinary and due to unusual circumstances. Not only had Davis won the governorship by a wide margin with 58 percent of the vote, but the Democrats also had strong majorities in both houses of the legislature. Although the Republicans in the legislature introduced reform measures of their own and were critical of Davis's proposals, arguing that they did not go far enough in ensuring accountability, they were in a position to secure only minor modifications in the bills. On the other side of the political spectrum, members of the governor's electoral coalition, most notably the state's two teachers' unions, were unhappy with some aspects of his proposals, but were uncomfortable publicly opposing someone whom they had supported with significant campaign contributions.[39] Other Democrats, such as the elected state superintendent of public instruction and key legislators, were also in the position of not wanting to criticize a fellow Democrat publicly. Consequently, if they made their concerns public, various interest groups and elected officials did so by suggesting modifications to the governor's basic framework.

As a result, the bills were modified somewhat. The cost of the entire reform package increased from the governor's original proposal of $444 million to $470 million. Republican legislators were able to include a provision in the reading initiative that phonics be required as part of intensive reading instruction. The teachers' unions got the peer review and assistance bill modified so that the program was subject to the local collective bargaining process. If districts failed to implement peer review, they stood to lose funds targeted for the teacher assistance program, rather than those designated for cost-of-living increases.[40]

The accountability measures were also modified. Democratic legislators concerned about the fairness of ranking schools with significantly different student populations required that school rankings include a separate indicator that compares a school's score with other schools that have similar rates of student mobility, ethnicity, fluency in English, family income, and parental education. In addition, instead of all the state's 8,000 schools being arrayed in a single group in the general ranking, they are grouped in deciles, so that the public knows if a school is in the top 10 percent, 20 percent, and so on. The legislators also decided that instead of allocating a disproportionate amount to reward high performing schools, the funds would be divided equally between the rewards and the assistance program. In deference to local school boards, the legislature decided that the boards, instead of the state, would be authorized to impose sanctions on schools that did not improve sufficiently after two years of assistance. Finally, the legislature made the exit exam first applicable to the graduating class of 2004, rather than the class of 2003, as the governor had proposed. It also ordered the state board of education and the superintendent of public instruction to study whether other criteria would be appropriate for students "who are regarded as highly proficient but unable to pass the high school exit examination." If the SBE finds other criteria, such as an exemplary academic record or an alternative test of equal rigor (appropriate and consistent with the goals of the exit exam), it can then recommend changes to the legislature.

Unlike the initial enactment of CLAS, California's move to high stakes testing was highly visible. The media reported on it and portrayed it as the central plank in the campaign platform of a newly elected governor, who then went on to stake his 2002 reelection on a promise that these reforms would produce a significant improvement in academic achievement. Like the passage of CLAS, however, the enactment of these latest reforms occurred with no major controversy or serious criticism of the basic assumptions underlying the governor's proposals. A few civil rights lawyers argued against the high school exit exam, and an Oakland advocacy research organization placed an ad in the *New York Times* contending that exit exams in other states had led to higher dropout rates among minority students. However, criticisms by other groups were muted, seeking changes in specific details of the governor's proposals without challenging the notion that the state should move to high stakes testing. It also appeared that the concept of high stakes testing had considerable public support. A February 1998 statewide poll, conducted by Policy Analysis for California Education and the Field Institute, found that almost two-thirds of the public (62 percent) favored setting uniform statewide student promotion requirements "based on students passing an achievement test, rather than leaving this up to teachers." Support was quite consistent across the political spectrum, and black respondents were the only ethnic group with less than a majority (42 percent) supporting the proposal (Fuller, Hayward, and Kirst, 1998).

Implementation of the state's high stakes testing system is ongoing, and parts of the process have been troublesome. Although most of the problems have been technical ones, they have stemmed from the political imperative that the program be implemented quickly. California students in grades 2–11 now participate in the Standardized Testing and Reporting (STAR) program that consists of the Stanford-9 test—which tests them in mathematics and language arts, with students in grades 2–8 also tested in spelling and high school students in science and history/social studies—and an "augmented" assessment that measures performance on the state's academic standards. The majority of the two assessments consists of multiple-choice items, but the state has added a writing assessment in two grades. Because the state lacked reliable data on measures such as graduation rates and teacher attendance, the API currently consists of only a school's assessment scores.

Schools that fall below the state mean on the API are part of the Immediate Intervention/Underperforming School Program (II/USP), with each school receiving $200 per student to implement an improvement program. These schools are expected to increase their test scores by 5 percent each year or face sanctions after four years. Because they had not improved sufficiently, 13 schools in the state (10 of them in the Los Angeles Unified School District) were targeted in 2001 for state intervention. The state also awarded bonuses of about $600 per teacher to several thousand schools that increased their API scores by 5 percent.[41] In addition, about 12,000 staff in 300 schools that showed exceptionally high test score gains received rewards ranging from $5,000 to $25,000 per certificated staff member. This $100 million program represented the largest monetary award ever attached to a single test (Groves and Ritsch, 2001). However, the advent of a state budget crisis in 2002 limited the likelihood that rewards could continue at this level.

Implementation of the high school exit exam, with its high stakes for individual students, has been particularly problematic. The major concern has been whether all students will have an adequate opportunity to learn the content being tested. There are several reasons for such a lack of opportunity: some schools have not yet completely aligned their curricula with the state standards; traditionally, not all students have taken algebra, a subject included on the exit exam; and students still learning English may lack sufficient familiarity to pass the language arts portion. When the assessment was field-tested in 2000, the independent evaluator for the state found that half or more of the state's tenth graders would fail either or both the mathematics and language arts sections of the test (Wise et al., 2000).

Fearful of potential legal action, the state reduced by half the number of algebra items on the mathematics portion, and also shortened the language arts section by about 20 percent. Like some other states, California initially set a low passing score, with students required to answer correctly only 60 percent of the language arts questions and 55 percent of the math questions. In the spring of 2001, about 40 percent of the ninth graders who took the exam on a voluntary basis passed both sections, but the proportion was considerably lower (about 25 percent) for Latinos and African Americans.[42] No lawsuits have been filed against what appears to be the exam's potentially disparate impact. However, civil rights organizations are monitoring the exam's implementation, and are prepared to take action if the same pattern continues once the exam's actual consequences become evident. Concerned about high failure rates and threatened legal action, the state board of education decided in July 2003 to postpone full implementation of the exam, making it mandatory for the class of 2006 rather than 2004.

Thus the testing policies that dominated education reform agendas during the 1990s continue to define the states' efforts to hold schools accountable and to shape classroom instruction. Disputes over curricular values are more muted now, as these testing policies are no longer purely hortatory, but now also rely on material rewards and sanctions. Yet the academic standards that defined the assessments of 10 years ago still stand at the core of this next generation of state tests. The difference is that now the debates revolve less around what is most important for students to learn, and more around what constitutes acceptable mastery of the state standards and what role tests should play in rewarding and sanctioning schools, educators, and students.

Conclusions

The story of student testing policy in California, Kentucky, and North Carolina during the 1990s can be interpreted and understood from a variety of perspectives. At one level, it continues the saga of America's long search for ways to improve the quality of schooling in a diverse and often fragmented educational system. New forms of assessments, grounded in clear academic standards, held out the promise of reshaping classroom instruction and making the educational experience more coherent across geographic regions, ethnic groups, and social classes. We do not yet know how this particular reform will turn out, but the history of American education suggests that like other innovations before them, recent testing policies will bring about some of their expected results, but will fall short of meeting the hopes of their champions.

At another level, the story of these new state assessments adds another chapter to our understanding of the determinants of successful policy implementation. One might conclude that North Carolina's program was less problematic than that of the other two states because it relied heavily on proven testing technology, and the resulting assessment represented only an incremental step toward an alternative format. Some of California's problems might very well have been due to the competing goals that key policymakers had for CLAS, with unresolved priorities likely to constrain the implementation process. The broad scope of Kentucky's reforms meant that even a thoughtful, well-coordinated implementation strategy would tax state and local staff and would generate some backlash. All three states labored under the traditional implementation constraints of little time, limited resources, and the need to communicate complicated new routines through the governmental system to street-level bureaucrats in local schools and classrooms. Each of these conclusions is reasonable, and suggest a variety of implications for other states considering the implementation of new forms of assessment.

However, to view the politics of assessment policy as either just another search by politicians for the "magic bullet" of education reform, or as their failure to understand the requirements of successful implementation, is to miss a much larger story with implications beyond education policy. The state assessment policies of the 1990s attest to policymakers' belief in the power of ideas as policy tools for persuading people to change their behavior. As such, the history of these policies can help us advance our theoretical understanding of hortatory policy, a strategy that currently lacks the precisely specified and well-tested assumptions that characterize the analysis of mandates and inducements. Consequently, while the politics of state assessment policies chronicled in this chapter is only suggestive, it does help us understand why officials use information and values to motivate policy action, and it illuminates several of the causal assumptions and limiting conditions outlined in the previous chapter.

Chapter 2 identified several kinds of policy problems that are particularly amenable to the use of hortatory instruments. One of these is situations in which other instruments are insufficient. Policymakers' recognition that they have a limited ability to "mandate what matters" (McLaughlin, 1987) in individual classrooms fits this condition. State assessment policies have two goals: to ensure greater accountability and to change classroom instruction. The first goal can be pursued within a framework of rules and sanctions, as the states' move to high stakes testing demonstrates. In fact, half the states in the nation have now decided that information alone is insufficient to ensure that educators are held accountable for the instruction they provide. Without a rule-based structure that assigns responsibility for who is accountable to whom for what, information can serve as a wake-up call, but it does not ensure that any action will result. If there is sufficient political support for a strategy that relies on sanctions and inducements, this approach is likely to be more appealing to policymakers than a strictly hortatory one because the rule-based framework gives them greater control over the process, and the use of tangible consequences allows them to demonstrate to their constituents that "something is happening."

However, 30 years of research on attempts at policy-induced change indicate that mandates and even well-crafted inducements have only limited effectiveness in reshaping classroom instruction. Two related reasons suggest why policymakers, having absorbed the lessons of past policies, might see relying on ideas as a promising strategy. First, because teachers view themselves as professionals, an ideas-based approach is appealing because it can suggest an alternative vision of good practice without threatening notions of professional control. As Weiss (1990) argues, in environments where work is not easily routinized, ideas embedded in external policies can mobilize people to try new approaches on a case-by-case basis. Such policies allow professionals to maintain a measure of control because they can decide how to adapt the new ideas to their workplaces. State assessment policies were linked to a set of curricular ideas that even in their most detailed forms gave teachers some flexibility in translating the standards into instructional practice. For that reason, hortatory policies may be more likely to change classroom behavior than mandates may.

A second reason hortatory policies might be seen as a more effective way to change classroom instruction is the nature of schools as institutions. In Wilson's (2000) parlance, schools are "coping" institutions in which neither outputs (day-to-day activities) nor outcomes are readily observable to outsiders. Therefore, mandates and inducement policies are difficult to enforce in schools. As a result, it is understandable that state officials decided that a hortatory, values-based approach was necessary.

Powerful ideas about what should be taught and how children can learn best stood at the core of the three states' assessment policies. All were linked to state curriculum standards that not only specified what knowledge and skills were most important, but also assumed that knowledge would be conveyed to students through a pedagogy that gave them opportunities to construct their own learning through projects, experiments, work with other students, and real-world applications. What most distinguished these assessments from earlier ones that focused only on accountability was the strong belief that they should influence classroom instruction. Not only would their content motivate what was taught, but the test format would lead teachers to emphasize writing, group work, problem-solving strategies, and hands-on activities. In order to influence instructional strategies as well as content, the assessment format had to include more than multiple-choice items, introducing greater scorer judgment, and hence variability, than in the machine-scored, multiple-choice tests.

Thus the assessments were premised on a strong belief that the state standards embodied what was most worthwhile for students to know, that the state assessment could move instruction in that direction, and that the product would be higher student achievement. The expected changes in North Carolina were relatively modest—more student writing and stricter adherence to the state *Standard Course of Study*, which had been a fixture in the state for close to a century. In contrast, what is remarkable about California and Kentucky is that not only was the state specifying a more precise curriculum through its framework and assessment than it had traditionally, but the curriculum was unfamiliar to most adults in the state.

As outlined in Chapter 2, hortatory policies make a number of causal assumptions about how policy targets will respond and the process by which change will occur. In all three states, policymakers assumed that teachers (and in turn, their students) were the primary targets of the assessment policies, and that they were the group that needed to be convinced to accept the policies' underlying values. In North Carolina, that assumption was essentially correct. The state assessment was only a modest deviation from past tests, and was tied to a long-standing (though recently updated) curriculum. The end-of-grade tests were not very visible to the public; media coverage was limited and primarily focused on reporting local schools' test scores. In essence, the policy was essentially directed at the professionals who would implement it, and whose classroom behavior was expected to change.

For California and Kentucky, however, the assumption that teachers were the only or even the primary target proved incorrect. In Kentucky, KERA and KIRIS were such major, visible, and expensive changes that they became a focus for organized interests. In California, CLAS was a less comprehensive and visible policy, but its curricular values represented a marked departure from what many members of the public expected schools to teach, and they were not well explained or defended to the public. Consequently, interest groups could mobilize at least limited opposition, claiming that CLAS did not reflect widely accepted values. As a result, implementation of the new assessments was unlikely to be simply a technical, administrative task taking place mainly within schools. If mobilized elements of the public did not support the test's underlying values, the policy would become weakened and incapable of moving those values inside classrooms.

To some extent, the vocal protests against CLAS and KIRIS can be dismissed as the views of a small minority representing the "radical right," as several policymaker respondents in both states called them. It is true that opposition leaders in California and Kentucky resisted the state assessments because they viewed them as symptomatic of aspects of secular life that they found to be hostile to the traditional religious and cultural values they espoused. In that sense, the opposition to CLAS and KIRIS could be interpreted as another chapter in the continuing debate over the state interest in schooling versus the right of a small minority of religious parents to protect their children from what they consider to be alien and harmful influences (Gutmann, 1995; Macedo, 1995; McCarthy, 1996). The courts found that the tests did not intrude into students' religious beliefs or family life because students were not required to reveal information from those domains. Rather, the test items were designed to elicit analytical, comprehension, and writing abilities.

Even if the CLAS and KIRIS controversies are seen as merely the attempts of a small minority of religious parents to protect their children from what they perceived to be public harm, these cases are significant because they illustrate the competing interests of home and state that the courts and the larger political system have attempted to balance throughout most of the nation's history. But to see these controversies as only a minority protest is to miss some important points. The available opinion data strongly suggest that the larger public is skeptical of new curricular approaches in reading, writing, and mathematics. In addition, the controversy over whole language and phonics in reading instruction that dominated the education agenda in California and other states suggested that there was considerable merit to parents' commonsensical concerns that their children were not learning the "building block" skills needed to read well, and that "invented spelling" and a lack of knowledge of grammar rules would hinder their writing ability.

Clearly, parts of the opposition leaders' agenda were not endorsed by most parents, but the opponents were also tapping into critical concerns shared by a broader group of secular parents and the general public. The Kentucky opinion polls showing relatively low awareness of KERA even after several years of implementation suggest that concerns about the early use of calculators and inattention to rules of grammar expressed in the national Public Agenda surveys are representative of a widespread unease, though it may not be directly linked to judgments about specific policies. But it may also be the case that particular issues, such as the push for greater attention to phonics in California, represent the concerns of those parents who are most attentive to their children's education and whose support is particularly important to the public schools. Whether these concerns come from uninvolved parents or from those who are better informed and more active is less important than the fact that apprehension about new curricular approaches extended beyond the religious conservatives who spearheaded the opposition to CLAS and KIRIS.

It is certainly the case that the targets of some hortatory policies can be narrowly defined, but as officials in California and Kentucky learned, values-based education policies are likely to engage a broader range of targets than just the professionals charged with implementing them. Because they tap into basic beliefs about what role the schools should play in children's education, hortatory policies often need to consider multiple policy targets beyond just those whose behavior is expected to change. Particularly in California's failure to consider these multiple targets, assessment policy illustrated a major limiting condition on hortatory policy: it is difficult to craft a set of values sufficiently compelling to motivate action without being divisive.

The state politics of assessment policy during the 1990s illuminate several other characteristics of hortatory policy. The transition from a purely hortatory policy to one that also embodies other elements, such as mandates, inducements, and capacity-building instruments, has already been mentioned. Hortatory mechanisms are often linked with other instruments from the very inception of a particular policy, but in those cases where a policy starts as purely hortatory, additional instruments are likely to be added. Nevertheless, even when tangible rewards and sanctions come to dominate a policy as they do in high stakes testing, the hortatory elements remain important in motivating policy action.

Another causal assumption outlined in Chapter 2 relates to the role of information in prompting targets to act. Hortatory policies that rely on information expect targets to act on it. However, a prior condition must be met: the information produced must be reliable and useful to those who are to act on it. In the case of the California and Kentucky assessments, technical problems undercut the quality of the information generated. When questions arose about the technical quality of the assessments, the values-based component also became less credible. It was difficult to convince the public that new forms of assessment better reflected what students should know if the reliability of the scoring was in doubt. In this way, the information and values elements became intertwined, and allowed opponents to call the legitimacy of both into question.

The next two chapters move from the state to the local level, and examine how various targets responded to the assessment policies. As with the state-level data, the local case studies illustrate both the potential of hortatory policies and the possible threats to the causal assumptions that should be operative if such policies are to work as intended.

4

Local Testing Controversies: The Case of CLAS

In California and Kentucky, opposition to the state tests included a grass-roots component. However, it was considerably stronger in California, where those opposed to the test mobilized parents to file suit to block administration of CLAS, not to allow their children to take the test, and to lobby state and local officials against the reauthorization of CLAS. As indicated in the previous chapter, these opponents never persuaded more than a small minority of parents to withdraw their children from taking the test or to participate in a lawsuit. In a few districts and schools, however, opposition was much stronger and more vocal. In those areas, lawsuits were filed, school boards considered not participating in the test, and opt-out rates in a few of the tested grades were as high as 50 percent. The districts where opposition was strongest are not representative of California school districts; they tended to be suburban and in the southern part of the state, with small minority enrollments.

Nevertheless, the anti-CLAS mobilization process in these communities can help explain what happens when a small minority sees its beliefs threatened by an education policy that itself is based on values about what children should learn and how they should be taught. Most education research on parents focuses on their involvement at home with their children and in related school activities. But that involvement is usually defined in terms of how it is sanctioned and structured by the school—primarily through parental assistance with homework, and participation in the PTA and other school support activities such as classroom volunteering. Rarely do researchers study parents who oppose established policies or who actively question educators' decisions.[1] At one level, then, this is a study of outliers. It tries to understand why some parents felt so strongly about CLAS that they were willing to devote considerable time and energy to its opposition and to allow their children to be singled out from their classmates.

Yet this research has implications beyond just the conservative parents who opposed CLAS. National opinion data suggest that a majority of parents

108

and the public disagree with some of the pedagogical values embodied in new approaches to curriculum and assessment, and it is this inconsistency between reform goals and parental attitudes that opposition groups tried to mobilize. Furthermore, at a time when close to half the parents in a national survey indicate that they support using public funds to allow parents to exit the public schools through the use of vouchers (Rose and Gallup, 2000), it is important to examine the concerns and strategies of those who choose to remain and express their dissatisfaction. Not only can such an analysis inform the design and implementation of future assessments, but it can also help in developing a better understanding of the cultural and value conflicts that continue to shape the politics of public education.

In examining the anti-CLAS movement at the local level, this chapter illustrates the limiting conditions on two causal assumptions associated with hortatory policy. If this strategy is to work as intended: (1) value appeals should be strong and widely accepted, and (2) targets' responses should be consistent with the policy's goals. The local CLAS controversies vividly demonstrate how the first assumption can be violated if a values-based policy prompts responses that divide target populations and include actions that run counter to the policy's intended goals. Because hortatory policies lack the well-defined framework of rules that typically govern mandates and inducements, political leaders may be less able to control or influence how targets respond to the values they are being asked to accept—thus weakening the second assumption.

While illustrating the downside of hortatory policy, the data in this chapter also suggest a possible solution to the problem of its limiting conditions. Since most social policies must be implemented through multiple governmental levels and among varied constituencies, the likelihood of diffuse and counterproductive responses can be reduced if officials initially work to develop common understandings of a policy's goals. That process should begin during the enactment process, and requires that policymakers anticipate responses and allow sufficient time for informed deliberation and recognition of diverse perspectives—something that did not occur in California.

The chapter analyzes seven schools in which opposition to CLAS was particularly strong, focusing on three questions: What issues defined the CLAS controversy at the local level? How were opponents mobilized? How did district and school officials respond to the controversy? Because we were interested in districts and schools where CLAS opposition was especially intense, we used a reputational method to select the schools. We identified a group of schools through a systematic canvass of several large-circulation California newspapers (the *Los Angeles Times, Orange County Register, San Diego Union-Tribune,* and the *San Francisco Chronicle*), through interviews with education reporters at these newspapers, and through interviews with the leaders of statewide opposition groups. Since most of the schools in which opposition was most intense are in suburban areas, we selected six within that category—two in a district in San Diego county, two in Orange County, and two in the suburbs of a small city in central coastal California. The seventh school is in a small city in the agricultural central valley, where opposition was intense in several communities.

These schools are not representative of California schools. For example, there was virtually no opposition to CLAS either in schools in the state's largest cities or in schools where students of color constitute a majority of the enrollment. However, all our reading about the controversy—as well as our interviews with reporters, opposition group leaders, and state officials— suggest that these schools are typical of those in which opposition was the most intense. Table 4.1 summarizes the characteristics of the study sample.

During February and March 1995, we conducted face-to-face interviews with the principal at each of the seven schools, teachers in the tested grades, one or more district officials responsible for curriculum and testing, several

Table 4.1. California school sample

School	Level	Total Enrollment	Student Composition (percent)	Percent of Students in Tested Grades Exempted from CLAS
1	Elementary	437	White: 87 Latino: 6 Asian-American: 6 African-American: 1	15
2	Elementary	408	Majority white Minorities are mostly Latino	34
3	Middle	570	White: 45 Minority (mostly Latino): 55	8
4	Elementary	700	White: 80 Asian-American: 11 Latino: 4 African-American: 2	10
5	Middle	1,200	White: 60 Latino: 30 Asian-American: 10	33
6	K–8	1,150	Majority white	>50
7	K–8	1,037	White: 90 Minority: 10	50 (4th and 8th graders) 33 (5th graders)

Table 4.2. Number of respondents by category

Category	Number
District Administrators	6
School Board Members	9
Opposition Group Leaders	9
Newspaper Reporters	4
School Administrators	9
Teachers	18
"Knowledgeable" Parents	30
Opposition Parents	31
Total	116

school board members, leaders of local opposition groups, and a newspaper reporter.[2] In addition, we interviewed from three to five parents at each school who had opposed CLAS and had opted their children out of taking the test, as well as an equal number of parents who were knowledgeable about the school, but who did not actively support or oppose CLAS. The opposition parents were identified through newspaper articles and by opposition leaders and school officials. The knowledgeable-but-neutral parents were selected by the school principals.

The major difference between the opposition and the knowledgeable parents was that 80 percent of the opposition parents identified themselves as politically conservative, and the remainder as "middle-of-the-road." In contrast, only 20 percent of the knowledgeables characterized themselves as conservative, with 43 percent saying they were middle-of-the-road and 37 percent liberal. However, in both groups, more than 70 percent reported volunteering at their children's school on a regular basis, and about the same proportion indicated that they attended PTA meetings. Both groups, then, consisted of involved parents who had close relationships with their children's school.

The interviews were conducted using a structured, open-ended protocol, with each interview lasting about one hour. (A copy of the protocol used in interviewing the parent sample is included in the appendix.) Table 4.2 summarizes the number of respondents by category. A site summary was prepared for each of the seven schools and the four districts in which they are located; it aggregated the interview data according to several key variables—respondents' attitudes toward CLAS, reasons for opposition, mobilization strategies, district and school responses to the controversy, and effects of the controversy. In addition, the parent interview data were entered into a computer database so that responses could be coded and counts made for the major variables. Both these procedures allowed us to make systematic comparisons across the seven schools.[3]

The next section examines the nature of the controversy, focusing on who was involved, why they opposed CLAS, how they mobilized allies, and how successful they were. The third section analyzes school and district responses, and discusses how knowledgeable parents viewed CLAS and the controversy. The final two sections explore the effects of the controversy, and suggest that it has broader implications for policies based on value appeals.

The Controversy

In analyzing the CLAS controversy in the seven schools within the four districts, one is immediately struck by strong similarities in how the dispute unfolded in each case and in the reasons behind it. The schools are all in communities with strong civic infrastructures, high parental involvement and support for the schools, and widespread perception that the schools and their districts are good ones. Several schools, however, had initiated reforms such as heterogeneous grouping of students and curricula consistent with the state frameworks, prompting parental opposition even before CLAS. In these cases, CLAS only exacerbated the frustrations and concerns already present among a small group of parents.

A combination of local grassroots organizations, assisted by statewide and national organizations, led the opposition in these districts. The groups are culturally and politically conservative, some with religious ties. Although the print and electronic media played a role in publicizing the dispute, the groups relied on a variety of mobilization techniques that could be used only in communities where parents were tightly linked to the schools and had long-standing personal relationships with one another. In effect, strong civic infrastructures and high parental involvement facilitated mobilization, a process that probably could not have occurred in communities with apathetic parents or weak civic ties.

The Participants

Although the basic characteristics of the opposition were common to each community, there were also some differences. In one community, a local grassroots organization formed before CLAS was instrumental in leading the opposition. This organization had a county-wide membership base and had been active in trying to pass Proposition 174, the statewide voucher initiative, the year before the CLAS controversy. In a second community, a new grassroots organization was formed during the CLAS controversy to lobby against CLAS in Sacramento and then to work to expand parental rights and to move the district curriculum "back to basics" (for example, through the teaching of phonics in the primary grades). In the third district, the leaders of the CLAS opposition were a conservative member of the school board and the regional president of Concerned Women of America (CWA), a conservative organization headquartered in Washington, D.C., that was originally formed in opposition to the ERA. In these three districts, both the opposition leaders and school district officials estimated the number of parents actively opposed to CLAS to have been between 100 and 400. In the fourth district, there was no formal opposition group. One parent, who had been a candidate for the school board, led an informal opposition campaign that included about 100 parents.

The opposition in all four districts received some kind of outside assistance. In two districts, lawsuits were filed on behalf of several parents—in one case by the USJF and in the other by the Rutherford Institute. In addition, other groups such as the Eagle Forum, PIE, and Focus on the Family provided information and outside speakers. For example, in one district, a group affiliated with the Eagle Forum brought in a psychologist opposed to OBE who spoke to 200 people in a high school auditorium as part of efforts to mobilize parents against CLAS. PIE and Focus on the Family provided copies of what were purported to be CLAS test items and a widely distributed videotape against OBE that originated in Pennsylvania.

An obvious question that arises in examining the interaction between the local groups and state and national organizations is whether opposition efforts were truly grassroots, initiated by local groups, or whether the locals were simply mobilized by outsiders needing a local constituency to make their state-level opposition more credible. It is certainly the case that the Rutherford Institute and USJF actively solicited plaintiffs and offered their services to local school boards and individual parents. However, two pieces of evidence suggest that although the state and national groups were an important resource, local opposition would have been mobilized even without their assistance. First, the speed with which the opposition mobilized was remarkable and probably could not have been accomplished so quickly if the facilitating conditions and local infrastructure were not already in place. The longest period was about two months, but in several schools, the controversy came and went within two and a half weeks. Second, the statewide organizations have good informal networks, but our state and local interviews suggest that those networks extended upward to the state level as much as downward to the locals. The statewide organizations reported that they first heard about the CLAS issue and originally received copies of supposed CLAS items from local groups. These locals were also a source of intelligence about who was supporting and opposing the test among state representatives, school board members, and other local notables. This network also had a strong horizontal component, with groups in one community communicating informally with their counterparts in other areas. Therefore, it seems reasonable to conclude that the CLAS opposition did have a strong grassroots component that probably could have been sustained even without outside assistance.

Part of the grassroots component common to the four districts was the involvement of several conservative Protestant churches in each community. The nature of their involvement and whether the churches played leadership roles in the controversy is not entirely clear. District and school respondents all assumed that the churches were involved. In some cases, they were uncertain about exactly which churches and in others, they identified specific local congregations as venues from which the opposition forces mobilized. In one community, however, the pastors identified by district officials denied that their churches had any formal involvement. In two other districts, pastors were publicly identified with the opposition; in one case, the pastor's son attended one of the schools where the clergyman was actively involved in encouraging other parents to withdraw their children from taking the test.

An unresolved question is how formal the churches' involvement was in each community. It might simply have been, as one local opposition leader argued, that "people who are concerned about their kids' education tend to go to church."[4] We do know, however, that church-related media—such as Focus on the Family broadcasts and a regional Christian newspaper distributed in churches and Christian bookstores—presented arguments against CLAS. In addition, flyers were placed on car windows during church services, and after-church socializing was used as an opportunity to enlist additional parents. At the same time, not all CLAS opponents were church members, and a number of parents were upset that opposition to CLAS was depicted by local educators and the media as a campaign by solely the Religious Right.

Reasons for Opposition

Reasons for opposing CLAS focused on several aspects of the test: the content of the language arts portion, the SDE's refusal to allow parents to see the test, scoring criteria and procedures, costs, and student and family privacy issues. But opposition to CLAS was also tied to broader concerns about the curricula at particular schools, the OBE controversy, and dissatisfaction with the perceived direction and quality of the state's public schools. These concerns were similar to those voiced by state-level opponents of CLAS. However, at the local level, they were often grounded in the classroom experiences and homework assignments of the opponents' children.

Excerpts from six of the 31 interviews with opposition parents in our sample amplify these concerns:

I have a combination of reasons. Our educational system doesn't have that much money. I questioned the amount of money that was going to be used. I don't think it is a good measuring tool of children. The scoring process had a lot of problems. They didn't even get the results back for a year, and they weren't a good measuring tool. It took teachers' accountability away. The stories were negative, if the samples were true. I think it is important to encourage critical thinking, but I don't think it is the end-all. Our children have a difficult time in math, reading, spelling, and grammar. Elementary school is a time to learn the basics. We need to make sure our children are learning. The secrecy involved was another issue for me. Our legislators started to form laws that were taking away parental rights. My right to make decisions over my own child was being taken away by the government. I understand they wanted to protect the integrity of the test, but they went too far . . . At [school], they spent a lot of time preparing for this test. Teachers weren't trained for this. They were giving kids an emotional story and then they wanted kids to read it and relate it to their own lives. I just don't think that teachers are trained in psychology. I have friends who say that their children were having nightmares. They were recalling feelings from the fires [that had burned near the school several years before] and having trouble sleeping at night. They would have discussion circles where the children would talk about their problems. Parents were feeling out of control, the school wanted to take over the family and it made us feel uncomfortable.

I think a lot of the reasons that a lot of the people were skeptical about the test was that there has been a general loss of faith in the education systems in this state . . . When I taught my daughter at home in fifth grade I became very aware of some of the stories in the reading books and the social studies books that were really trying to shape her thinking to oppose the values that we've been teaching her. And that really bothered me . . . And I found that my older children couldn't add in fifth and sixth grade. So I had to do immediate work with them at home. And they're all A students — every one of them. And it's amazing that a person can get A's and not add. Mediocrity is rewarded and even encouraged. It doesn't matter if it's grammatically correct as long as you get it on paper. . . . With the concept-based education and the constant push of think, think, think, and these wonderful rosy idealistic ideas . . . we're turning out a bunch of thinkers who have nothing to think with. And the CLAS test was looking to assess those thinking skills, not facts that they had to think with. It didn't matter whether they had any facts in those thoughts at all, and that's a total waste. That's not education.

How can they be telling us there's not enough money for books and desks and . . . [saying] "we can't do a good job educating your child because we only have *x* number of dollars for students," but yet where does this $50 million [for CLAS] come from? I started contacting my legislators and finding out that the $50 million seems to be there if that's what you want to spend it on.

I didn't like it. I thought it was more politically correct than truthful. I don't like anything given by the state of California or the federal government . . . that is given to children and we don't get to review what they are getting. I don't think that's good parenting. Other reasons, I don't like taking animals and giving them human qualities . . . for the things I reviewed, they were giving human qualities to animals, and they didn't deserve those qualities. And they were making value judgments that weren't accurate. The big thing was, . . . I wasn't paranoid about what children might say; that didn't bother me. But what did is I don't believe that it was an actual objective test . . . that it was more politically correct. I think that education should be objective. One other thing I didn't like the language that was used in some instances. I didn't think it was proper. I didn't like the way it talked about minorities. We don't talk about them that way in our house. I thought it was very stereotyped.

As more and more examples came out in the media and parents got more chances to see more glimpses of it through other sources, I was getting more from [the media] than from the district. That is why I opposed the CLAS testing. Not because of anything in the CLAS test, but because of the way it was managed. At that point, I became of the opinion that the creators of the CLAS testing and the educational system were at war with the parents of these children, and the children were the pawns in this. It became a power struggle over who had access to our children and by what right would they have access to what our children had to learn. The parents would have had no access to understanding what was in the test, how were they graded [and] assessed, how were they measured and what they meant, and how were they able to respond to the test. Basically, the parents had no access to any of that. It was like they were [the state's] children and they belonged to [the state] at school. [It seemed as if the test developers were thinking] "We are going to explore everything in their mind."

I opposed it for some of the content and the controversial nature of the content. I did see a sample of the test. They didn't have samples of the fourth-grade test, but they did have samples of the eighth-grade test that was given on the literature portion. And some of the information that was . . . just the stories that were on the actual test . . . I would not have felt were appropriate even in my home. I do censor what my kids read. And even for an eighth grader . . . I have a seventh grader now and I would not have wanted her reading that the following year.

These six excerpts represent views typical of other opposition parents. The picture that emerges is of a group of parents who do not trust government—particularly at the state and federal levels—to do what is best for their children; who have faith in a type of education and testing that they perceive to be objective and which they believe was absent from CLAS; and who have conservative views about what knowledge and skills should be emphasized in classroom teaching. At the same time, these were also parents who are actively involved in their children's education and who have clear visions of what their children need from school to be happy and successful.

As noted in Chapter 3, some of their views were based on incorrect information about the purpose and content of CLAS and about the procedures by which it was scored. Nevertheless, several studies, based on nationally- and state-representative samples, suggest that the curricular values of the CLAS opposition parents were quite consistent with mainstream preferences. Other studies show that parents want schools to stress the basics—computational skills in mathematics, reading comprehension, grammar and spelling—not as ends in themselves ("basics only"), but as a foundation for becoming more broadly educated ("basics first") (Johnson, 1995).[5] That was also the message of the CLAS opposition parents. The issue is whether CLAS truly was a threat to those curricular values, or whether it actually embodied these values, but the state and local districts failed to communicate that to parents. This question is considered in a later section on local and state responses to the controversy, but the answer depends on what one believes to be the appropriate balance in teaching mastery of basic skills and critical thinking abilities.

The reasons given by local opposition leaders for opposing CLAS were essentially the same as those offered by rank-and-file parents. However, the leaders were more likely to tie CLAS to larger philosophical issues, such as the appropriate size and orientation of government, and the need for parents to exercise greater control over their children's schooling through choice and the decentralization of authority to local boards. Their opposition to CLAS, while also based on their children's experience, tended to be more ideologically grounded. For example:

Why do we have to have a state assessment and state frameworks? Parents care about their kids and know what's best for them, not the state. Just wait and see. CLAS will come back. We'd have a much better quality of education if there was less state involvement. The state doesn't have the right to tell me where to get my hair cut or buy a car. If I don't like my haircut or car, I don't have to do business with those people again. Sure there are safety standards with cars, but the government doesn't tell the manufacturers how to build them. During the controversy, we had a saying, "GM makes a better car today because of Toyota." In other words, competition raises the standard for everyone. By giving parents greater control and letting them choose where to send their children, education would be better. Let parents decide what's best on a local level and by local, I mean my own living room. It's okay to have a little guidance or a central plan, but the state doesn't have to be so involved. Sure there's chaos at the beginning of any deregulation, but after a while things work out. I'm in my mid 30's and I took the SAT. It was a very broad-based way of assessing what we learned. We didn't have frameworks 20 to 30 years ago.

You know what was the biggest thing for me? I don't know how many times I went to bed at night and told my husband, me, who has worked in government all my life, what an eye-opener it was for me when it came to my child and education. For some reason, I put education [above] all government and all the tax money and all the issues that government deals with. I put education for some reason in this little group of people who are so noble and wonderful and certainly they wouldn't be wasting my tax money. After all, they're educating children. Our future is in their hands. Why would they squander our money? Why would they have bad policies? And what an eye-opener it was for me to realize that they are another agency of the federal government and of the state government and truly, they aren't any different than all the other agencies . . . So I would like to see some restructuring and let's have a state department of education that's answerable to the legislature and the governor and then our local school board that hires and fires our administrators and superintendents and teachers, and let's get this control back in the hands of taxpayers because it is truly the bottom line. It truly is a fiduciary responsibility that the state has. We give you our tax money; you educate our children. And if you can't do a good job, then we want our money back to take somewhere else. Because to me it's really just a fiscal issue. They're doing a bad job, I want my money back to provide it somewhere else.

Opposition Strategies

Because local CLAS opponents had multiple objectives, they used a variety of strategies. Their short-term goal was to stop the 1994 administration of CLAS and barring that, to get the state and local districts to allow parents to exempt their children from taking the test. Their longer-term objective was either to get the state to abolish CLAS or to pass legislation to reauthorize it in a modified form. Accomplishing these objectives required filing lawsuits to obtain injunctions against administering the test; lobbying local school boards to suspend administration of CLAS; encouraging parents to sign opt-out forms; and in one district, mounting a lobbying and public-relations campaign focused on state policymakers. As a result, opposition strategies ranged from telephone trees and informational "coffees" in private homes to press conferences and sophisticated fax networks.

As one district official noted, the telephone trees allowed a small group of people to influence hundreds of parents. A parent would call several other parents whom she knew and who had children attending her children's school. She would ask if they had heard about CLAS, explain what it was and what her concerns were, then ask the other parents to attend either an informational meeting sponsored by an individual school or the school board, or a coffee to be held in another parent's home. In one district, the opponents made extensive use of the coffees. Ten to 20 parents would gather in a home and receive information about CLAS prepared by groups such as the Eagle Forum. Often the anti-OBE videotape would be shown, and forms recruiting plaintiffs for a local lawsuit would be distributed. Parents would also be instructed about how to exempt their children from taking the test. In other districts, similar meetings were held in church halls, though not under direct church sponsorship. In several instances, school board members sympathetic to the anti-CLAS forces attended these meetings.

Other grassroots strategies included attending school board meetings at which CLAS was discussed, and meeting one-on-one with school board members, principals, and district officials. One assistant superintendent, for example, estimated that she met with 50 parents individually. In another district, the assistant superintendent reported that about the same number of parents either called or went to the district office to talk about CLAS.

Opponents also distributed anti-CLAS literature in front of some schools and talked with parents when they dropped off their children in the mornings. At one of the schools with the highest opt-out rates, opponents stood outside the school and asked children as they were leaving if they were in the fourth or fifth grades. If they were, they gave them flyers and asked them to have their parents send letters to the school. When told by the school that they could not distribute materials to students, the opponents would move on to other schools until they were also stopped there. In several districts, opponents went door-to-door, leaving packets of anti-CLAS materials. In one school district, opponents held a news conference outside one of the high schools at the invitation of the principal, who was also opposed to CLAS. Opponents also reported writing letters to the editors of local newspapers and participating in local radio talk shows.[6]

In one of the four districts, opponents used all of the strategies described above to mobilize within their community. At the same time, they also lobbied Sacramento policymakers to modify the pending CLAS legislation. At one point, for example, they concentrated on getting the scoring criteria for CLAS revised so that they would more closely resemble the rubrics used on the University of California's Subject A examination, which assesses the writing skills of incoming freshmen. The local opponents sent copies of the Subject A criteria to every member of the senate education committee. They also worked very closely with the Republican staff in both houses. In addition, they reported undertaking, in the words of one opponent, "a complete bombardment of the governor's office, completely, constantly. I don't know if you know, the governor has a recording-type thing. We kept it full, full." Several parents also reported that they met with the local state senator and member of the assembly to express their concerns about CLAS. In other districts, parents telephoned their representatives' offices and contacted the SDE.

The opposition strategies met with mixed success. No court issued an injunction to stop administration of the test universally, but the state agreed to allow individual students to be exempted if their parents requested it. The CLAS reauthorization passed the legislature, but was vetoed by the governor. As the final section details, the effect of the CLAS controversy on local school politics and curricular practice was also mixed. Nevertheless, the controversy and the opponents' arguments against CLAS had the effect of putting the state educational establishment on the defensive and forcing it to justify its policies to an extent rarely seen before.

For state officials, CLAS embodied two policy goals: (1) obtaining information about how well students performed on test items designed to reflect the state's approach to curriculum, and (2) motivating educators to teach consistently with that curricular approach. The views and strategies of opponents illustrate the power of the ideas underlying CLAS, since they were strong enough to prompt decisive action. However, for some parents, that action was mobilization in opposition to CLAS, rather than in support of it. Not only did CLAS exemplify values they opposed, but it also symbolized the reasons for their discontent with public schooling and more broadly, with government. So, in this instance, although strong values prompted acceptance and compliance by the majority, these values were less widely accepted than their proponents assumed, and for a vocal minority, they were another reason for dissent.

The Response

The Districts Respond

Even though most of the local opposition to CLAS was directed to school board members and district officials, these people were highly constrained by the state in how they could address opponents' concerns and arguments. Not only did the SDE tell local districts that they would be in violation of state law if they did not administer CLAS, but they forbade district officials to show the test to parents or even review it themselves. Excerpts from interviews with a district official and an opposition parent who met with the official illustrate the dilemma that districts faced:

> I truly believe had I had the opportunity, as the person responsible for the testing, to have seen the actual documents it would have been far easier to deal with parents who said, "If you tell me that you have seen them and they are fine, my child will take the test." I couldn't do that. I could guarantee them that there was nothing offensive or a problem for the student in the documents. But I could not be honest and say I had seen the actual test.

> I was coming in and just asking about the test and [the district official] was telling me that it was a very fine test and nothing that I should be worried about and then I asked her, "Well, may I see the test?" And she said, "No, you may not." And I said, "Okay, well if I can't see the test, could you at least tell me what's on the test? What is it?" She said . . . she hadn't seen the test. And I said, "Well, now wait a minute. You just told me there was nothing here that I should be objecting to and you yourself have never even seen it. How did you base your opinion that I shouldn't be concerned about this if you've never seen it yourself?" She didn't have any answers.

In most instances, the districts in our sample attempted to respond to the controversy within the boundaries established by the state. However, there were exceptions. The most serious was a district in which the school board decided to suspend student testing until it could review the CLAS documents. After the review, most board members reported that they had found nothing wrong with the test and voted to continue its use. But they wanted to be able to assure their constituents that they were not inflicting any harm on the students for whom they were accountable, and they felt they could not do that if they had not seen the test. As the president of the school board noted, "What I was looking for was if the test was harmful for our students. Will it cause psychological damage? The answer for me is no. The more we can find out about everything, the better. The more open the process is, the better it will be for everybody. School board members were put in the position of having to defend something we had not seen, and people thought there was something to hide." One of her fellow board members echoed this sentiment, saying, "Ultimately we are responsible for what we do in the district, irrespective of what the state says."[7] Although the state did not impose any sanctions on the district, SDE staff told district officials that they were in "big trouble" because at that point, even members of the state legislature had not been allowed to see the test.

One strategy that several districts used to persuade the SDE to be more flexible was to work through the California School Boards Association (CSBA). CSBA, in the locals' view, was effective in presenting their case to the SDE (for example, arguing that boards should be trusted to see copies of the CLAS test), and in ensuring that districts across the state acted consistently. Several respondents mentioned that consistency of response was particularly important for those districts involved in lawsuits. One district, for example, was concerned that unless the lawsuits were defended in a way that would encourage a narrow ruling, parents might be able to opt their children out of all kinds of tests. In addition to working through CSBA, several superintendents sent letters to the acting state superintendent of public instruction expressing their concerns and requesting greater flexibility in how they could respond to opposition.

District officials' inability to see what was on the test and the requirement of nondisclosure of its contents made it difficult for officials to squelch some outrageous rumors circulated by opponents. Even in the case of those rumors that could be addressed without breaching test security (for example, about the scoring process), there was no systematic way to get answers from the SDE until late in the controversy. Three examples from interviews with opposition group leaders show not only the nature of these rumors, but also their persistence:

I had an actual test. There were a number of stories in the literature section that were unacceptable. For example, there was a story about a man who accidentally puts his wife through a meat grinder and makes sausages. He eats his wife and it tastes so good that he starts killing people. This was for fourth graders. I don't want to read such a thing and I certainly wouldn't want my children reading anything like that.

My understanding is that there was a panel of four to five readers who were paid $100 an hour and given lots of training on how to score the test, but the test required subjective grading. Even a representative of the teachers' union didn't have an answer on how the test was going to be scored.

They manipulated the scoring so terribly . . . the administrator from [a district] told me that they didn't even grade [one low-income school]. Now there's our Hispanic community—the scoring. Those scores finally showed up months later. We had documented cases where in some areas they only graded Asian students, or they left out whole districts. I don't know if that was fiscally driven or if it was truly malicious reasoning for only scoring certain groups of people and not scoring others.

In addition to being constrained by the SDE in their responses, local districts had to react quickly to a controversy that was largely unexpected and that emerged with lightning speed. Administrators in the four districts had briefed board members on the CLAS test the previous year when it was first administered, explaining its goals of assessing student performance more validly and testing students on their mastery of the state frameworks. They also handed out copies of the few CLAS items from the pilot tests that had been released by the state. One board member who described her vague impression of CLAS before the controversy erupted was typical in her level of knowledge:

It came as a big surprise when all of this started to unfold. We knew that [the state assessment] was being redesigned and that it was an assessment on how to better test our students. But we really hadn't gotten any true information nor were we requested to get any kind of reaction or input into the process that I can recall. [We knew] only in a generic fashion that they were looking for some better ways to test the kids that was not done well with multiple-choice; I can't recall the term they used for it. But it was relatively brief in nature, in terms of having some open dialogue about it. Most of the dialogue occurred once the controversy started, once it was in the papers.

Not only did most board members know very little about CLAS, but they were forced to deal with the controversy in a crisis mode, since in some districts testing had already begun when the protests reached a crescendo. Once testing began, rumors increased. In addition to copies of the CLAS exam from the previous year that were already circulating, copies of the current exam were leaked by a few teachers. In addition, some students reported to their parents what they remembered from the test, and in districts where lawsuits had been filed, plaintiffs' lawyers were taking depositions from students about the content of the exam.

In all four districts, the board held either an informational meeting or a community forum at which CLAS was discussed. In one district, parents were invited to take the test using the items that had been released by the SDE. In two of the districts, officials reported that a large proportion of the 100–200 people who attended these meetings either were from outside the district or had no school-aged children. However, the superintendent in one of these districts acknowledged that she had also "stacked" the audience by inviting parents whom she knew supported CLAS. Board members also reported meeting with parents individually, talking with them on the telephone, and answering their letters.

As soon as the SDE agreed to allow local boards to opt students out of taking the test, the board in each of the four districts voted to allow this option if parents submitted letters requesting it.[8] The district in which the board had suspended testing while it reviewed the exam went a step further. It sent a letter and a form home to all parents of students in the tested grades, explaining about CLAS and giving them the option to opt out.[9] One of the board members explained why she and her colleagues took this unusual step: "Well, without realizing what we had done, we had taken . . . our morals and values as a standard to measure this test against . . . I started thinking in my own mind, okay, now someone could say to me, 'But that's your value judgment. I don't know whether that's good enough for my child.' So we said as a result of that, we'd vote to administer the test, but we will allow parents to opt out if they can't trust our value judgment. So that's pretty much how we dealt with it."

In this case, the board realized that it may have paid a high price for making the opt-out so easy. In some of the district schools, more than half of the students were opted-out by their parents. Board members feared that this happened not so much because parents opposed the test, but rather because students who "realized that they could get a day off from school waved the form in front of them," as one board member put it, and parents who did not know the difference signed it. Consequently, the district received no scores for the 1994 CLAS test; because so few students were assessed, the state could not generate valid results.

District responses to CLAS opponents illustrate a limitation of hortatory policy: the lack of precise rules regulating the full range of likely responses to a policy's motivating values. The state policy framework provided a set of minimal rules requiring that local districts administer the assessment to all students in the tested grades. But there was nothing in either that set of policy rules or in the SDE's implementation of CLAS that provided a framework for developing public understanding of the assessment's underlying values. Without a policy framework and implementation plan that explicitly took public understanding into account, the SDE and local districts were caught off-guard as the implementation of CLAS unfolded in unanticipated ways. In assuming that CLAS's values would be strong enough to motivate teachers, yet failing to recognize their power to divide parents, the SDE left those districts facing strong parental opposition with little guidance beyond a general testing mandate and its accompanying non-disclosure requirement. As a result, districts could respond only in *ad hoc* and highly constrained ways.

The Schools Respond

The individual schools in our sample were even more limited in their response to opposition parents than were school board members and district administrators. Not only were they subject to the same state strictures against reviewing the test or showing it to parents, but school personnel also tended to be less knowledgeable about the purpose of CLAS than were district officials, though they were closer to the high emotions that characterized the controversy. Responses varied—at several schools, principals made presentations about CLAS at PTA meetings and then invited parents to answer several of the released items, but at the majority of schools in the sample, principals and teachers either met with opposition parents individually to discuss their concerns or simply accepted opt-out requests without trying to persuade parents to change their opinions about the test.

What is most striking about the schools' responses is the context in which they occurred, as defined by teachers', parents', and students' views of CLAS. Although most of the principals and teachers in our sample were accepting of CLAS, they tended to have only limited information about it, were unclear about its purpose, and skeptical that the assessment would be continued. As one teacher noted, "I don't know what the purpose of the test is. Are they looking for individual results? Are they looking for class results? What type of information is coming back to us from this test? How is it going to be looked at? Is it broken down to passing or failing? It was never clear to the teachers where exactly they were going with CLAS." The lack of information about the test made it difficult for school personnel to talk with parents. One principal described the problem in this way: "The toughest thing for someone who is on the front line with the angry parents is to say, 'Trust me.' Because if they trusted you, they wouldn't be angry. They wouldn't be there. And [not being able to disclose the test contents] just makes us all look like fools. And we all went to school too long to look like fools. So I really believe that we should be trusted with, 'Hey, this is the test, this is why we are doing the test and this is what we're looking for.' That's part of education."

Only one of the 18 teachers we interviewed had been involved in scoring CLAS the first year it was administered and was therefore familiar with its content and format, including what constituted good student performance on it. Teachers at two other schools in the sample reported that CLAS reflected much of the content and instructional strategies they had been using as their schools' programs had changed to become more consistent with the state curriculum frameworks.

At the other end of the continuum was a school that had not changed its reading program in response to the state frameworks that served as the basis for CLAS. When teachers tried to adjust their teaching to be more consistent with CLAS, they had no instructional materials with which to work. One teacher explained, "Our reading program was no different last year than it was five years ago. But yet the whole testing procedure was totally different. So it was sort of like a cart before the horse. So we ended up having to teach to the test, but didn't have any materials to do so." Although the disconnect between CLAS and the curriculum was greatest at this school, teachers at other schools reported that CLAS was covering topics (for example, in mathematics) that they were not teaching, and that they had been given little information about the test.

Even though they were generally supportive of CLAS, some teachers and principals criticized the test on grounds similar to those expressed by opposition parents. For example:

I think that we've had a big change both statewide and nationally in terms of the philosophy that seems to be behind electing people . . . and I don't think the state department of education is reflecting necessarily the feeling of the state, at least as expressed by the ballot box, and a lot of the ideas have been somewhat off the wall. A lot of them have been very experimental and now they're coming home to roost, such as the language approach where we are now seeing students at the eighth-grade level who can't spell, who have no idea of the mechanics of English, who feel that anything they put on paper is wonderful. And those of us who are a little bit more traditional are having a hard time trying to say, "No, you have to be understood. No, you have to know how to capitalize." (eighth-grade language arts teacher)

There were some questions and without question—no pun intended—[that] had no business being on that kind of a test . . . If you want students to reflect on literature and write about literature, you don't need to put pieces of literature or to choose selections that are as controversial as some of them were . . . some people did [a] real disservice in terms of writing the test and not having the foresight to see the problems. The process that it was intended to test and measure, which is absolutely a wonderful process that we need to be doing in education, was overshadowed by a lack of good judgment and common sense. (elementary school principal)

I think that two of the selections that I did read dealt with violent themes. And I think that we can find good literature for kids that didn't have to be involved with such stress and conflict. (middle school assistant principal)

For a variety of reasons, a majority of the teachers in our sample portrayed the CLAS controversy as either a frustrating or a stressful experience, especially as it affected their relations with parents and students. At one school, teachers described their frustration with the directive they received not to discuss the CLAS test with parents and to refer all inquiries to the principal or a district official: "One of the things that was really hard for us as teachers was, when the controversy started and people started asking questions, we were told that we couldn't answer their questions, that we had to refer them to [the] administration. It was almost like it became this big top-secret thing. Teachers were really frustrated because we felt like we were under attack and we couldn't even defend the test or defend ourselves since were told that we shouldn't respond to those things."

At other schools, the raw emotions the test engendered in some parents produced very stressful conditions for both principals and teachers. Two schools in particular were the scenes of several angry encounters. At one school, the paint on the cars of several opposition parents was badly scratched; the victims questioned school staff because of their support for the test and they later accused parents who supported CLAS of the vandalism. Although the culprits were never found, the incident was reported in the local newspaper's police blotter, and the school received negative publicity. At this same school, a teacher sent home a story that some parents viewed as controversial as a practice CLAS exercise. The incident was reported in the local newspaper, with the teacher singled out publicly for what most considered to be no more than bad judgment. At the second school, the principal taught the students whose parents had exempted them from the test while CLAS was being administered. She was confronted by a parent who barged into the classroom demanding to know what the principal was doing, and in front of the students, threatened to have her teaching credential revoked. The principal had to request help from the district's assistant superintendent (who happened to be on the campus trying to settle a dispute between a parent who supported CLAS and one who opposed it).

In interpreting these rather extreme actions, it is important to consider that most of these parents were active in their children's schools and had ongoing relationships with the principals and teachers. For example, one of the most vocal opposition leaders at one school was the previous year's PTA president, and at another, one opposition leader was a member of the PTA board. These parents were quick to say that they were not personally angry with the teachers, but the school staff was simply the most immediate target in their efforts to stop the administration of CLAS.

The CLAS controversy also extended to students, even to those as young as fourth graders. At four of the seven schools in our sample, principals and teachers reported some kind of student involvement in the controversy. A few students used the CLAS controversy to question openly their teachers' authority, and some refused to take other standardized tests (such as the CTBS) or to do assignments that they and their parents felt were too much like the CLAS test. Teachers felt that these students were reflecting their parents' views. At one elementary school, the principal reported that children were heard saying to other children, "Your mother must not love you if she is making you take this test." At one of the K–8 schools in our sample, the principal reported that several student leaders effectively persuaded their peers that the test was harmful:

> Our kids are grouped for math only. And that particular class happened to be our algebra class. So that class had all of our strong leaders. So again, it started with two or three kids coming to school and sincerely believing that we were violating their confidentiality, that we were looking for information regarding their personal family situations. And these kids were very vocal. They spent time talking to other kids, trying to convince them of all the negative aspects of the test. And they were highly successful in doing that.[10]

With students directly involved in the controversy, several teachers reported that they felt intimidated. They became more careful about what they said in the classroom, and they avoided "CLAS-like" activities such as the "open-mind" exercise because students and their parents were watching them closely to ensure that CLAS did not reappear in other guises.

The largely *ad hoc* responses of school staff may have been too limited and too late. The seven schools made only modest attempts to persuade dissident parents that CLAS was not the danger they perceived it to be, and at only one school was any countervailing parental support mobilized in favor of CLAS. The schools attempted to ride out the controversy with as little disruption as possible and to ensure that the test was administered to those students whose parents were willing, at least implicitly, to let them take it.

Yet, realistically, the schools probably could not have been expected to do more. The controversy came quickly and unexpectedly in most instances. In fact, one school was already in the middle of testing when the board of education decided to review the test. In this case, the partially completed tests of those students whose parents subsequently exempted them had to be destroyed at the parents' requests. Another principal felt that had administration of CLAS been scheduled at his school earlier in the testing cycle, the ensuing controversy and high opt-out rate might have been avoided. In explaining the schools' responses, the timing of the tests is less important than the schools' place in the policy chain. Simply put, those who were least responsible for the design of CLAS, knew the least about it, and had the least capacity to respond effectively bore the brunt of the controversy.

How Knowledgeable Parents Viewed CLAS

The major factor distinguishing the 30 knowledgeable parents from the parents who actively opposed CLAS in our sample is that the knowledgeables were considerably more trusting of schools and individual teachers. The fact that they had not seen what was on the CLAS test was of less concern to them, because their principals and their children's teachers had assured them that CLAS was not harmful and that it measured the kind of learning the school thought was important.

About half (46 percent) of the knowledgeable sample expressed support for CLAS; 38 percent had no opinion about the test, largely because they had not seen it; and 15 percent had negative opinions of it, offering many of the same reasons that the opposition parents gave. Unlike the opposition parents, the supportive knowledgeables, when giving the reasons they endorsed CLAS, rarely talked about the content of the test. Instead, they focused on its format. They argued that in relying less on multiple-choice items and in requiring students to justify their answers, CLAS was measuring more complex thinking skills. For example:

I was very supportive. I liked that the kids were required to think about what they had read. I have always found that the multiple-choice test was the easiest test to take, because all that you have to do is spit out the facts or try to guess the right answer. Having to actually think about what you write about is much more difficult.

I thought that the math portion of the test not only tested basic math skills, but tested logic and higher thinking skills and required the child to express them in the written form, which is something that they're going to be asked to do over and over again as they move on with their education. No matter what field they go into, they're always going to be required to write, whether they're in a scientific or mathematical field, technical field, or involved in something having to do more with the humanities. The written portion of the test—the reading assignments that were given and then the responses—I thought that those were probably the best portion of the test because they most accurately reflected what the child did in the classroom.

I think it [CLAS] would do a wonderful job in assessing students. Because having to synthesize your own ideas in response to something is a lot harder and a lot better thinking process than just being able to respond to something and answer questions. It's a much harder thing to do and a much more thorough test of the students' thinking . . . Much much better. I think this is the kind of test that we need for students. Not the kind of thing where you fill in the blanks. I think that's a really bad idea. It doesn't require the same kind of thinking.

I felt it was an appropriate way of assessing kids. I think it's a good direction to go. And it's a much better indication of what a student's strengths and weaknesses are. I think it's a better assessment of their ability to problem-solve, to use insight, to sort of look beneath the surface a little bit more in depth. To not just fill in bubbles. To express themselves.

Several of the knowledgeable parents who supported CLAS mentioned that they had spoken out in favor of it at PTA and school board meetings. However, even these vocal supporters suggested that the controversy could have been avoided. As one argued:

During that period of time when the controversy began to escalate, the school district offered work groups or workshops and I attended one. At that point, I did take the test and was convinced more than ever that it was an appropriate testing tool. I thought the presentation was excellent, and I think if they had done that early on and if all or nearly all the parents and community had an opportunity to talk with the teachers and the people who were doing the assessment, most of the controversy for the majority of people who weren't ideologically opposed to it would have been abated.

As much as I disagree with the attitude and approach of the people that were very hostile and critical to the CLAS, I have to support them a hundred percent in that they cared about their child's education, and we have to always remember that most parents care, and those that do care should be commended for that care, even if the direction they want to take the school may be wrong for the bulk of the children, at least we should recognize that it's based on concern . . . Frankly, I think some of the state officials, initially at any rate, tried to discount that.

Although opposition and knowledgeable parents disagreed in their judgments about CLAS, they were largely in agreement in assessing how the controversy was handled. The overwhelming majority of both groups felt that it was not handled well at the state level; 89 percent of the knowledgeables expressed this negative sentiment, as did 77 percent of the opposition parents. Those opposition parents who felt the state handled the controversy well specifically mentioned the governor's veto of the reauthorizing legislation as their reason for this conclusion. The groups split evenly in their judgments about how well local districts handled the controversy, but the knowledgeable parents were more favorable (81 percent) than opposition parents (48 percent) in their assessment of schools' handling of the conflict.

In responding to the CLAS controversy, local officials scrambled to address parental concerns in an emotionally charged atmosphere and within a short time frame, while constrained by SDE mandates that required students to be tested and the assessment's contents not disclosed to parents. School board members tried to balance their legal obligations to the state with the need to be responsive and accountable to the constituents who elected them. For these officials, as well as for school personnel, the waning of trust among a small group of activist parents who had traditionally been supportive of the schools was a major concern. The CLAS controversy was a political conflict, but it was also an estrangement among people who knew each other as colleagues, friends, and neighbors and who shared a common interest in children's education. That personal dimension was evident when opposition parents spoke respectfully about their children's teachers and noted that their anger was not directed at them. It was echoed by knowledgeable parents when they argued that the state needed to consider the views of all parents — including those opposed to the test — and in not doing so, had doomed a worthwhile enterprise. In their responses, local districts and schools were attempting to calm a storm that was not of their making, and that had disrupted well-established patterns of school–parent relations.

Effects of the Controversy

Our sample split evenly in terms of the controversy's effect, with two of the districts and their three schools still feeling the effects almost a year later, while the other two districts and their four schools were largely unaffected. The latter group reported no change in district or school politics, in levels of parental support, or in teacher responses to reform initiatives as a result of the CLAS controversy.

One possible explanation for this difference may lie in the degree to which the CLAS dispute affected a school at the height of the controversy. Two of the schools that experienced no continuing impact had opt-out rates that were only slightly above the state average (at 8 percent and 10 percent). However, the other two schools that were largely unaffected in the longer term had much higher opt-out rates, at 33 percent and 50 percent. The more likely explanation is the extent to which opposition leaders were able to keep their constituents organized and to use CLAS as the basis for mobilizing on other issues. This sustained group activity by opponents then prompted mobilization by those more supportive of the curricular values underlying CLAS.

In two districts, CLAS became a major issue in the next school board election. In one, a woman who had been a long-time school volunteer, but who had never run for public office, decided to run because she felt that the values CLAS embodied represented the direction in which the district ought to be moving. She was careful not to attack the opposition group and its candidates during the campaign, but her position on CLAS was clear. She was elected with the highest number of votes of all the candidates. In this same district, however, opposition leaders campaigned against a school bond measure that was narrowly defeated. These divisions were only beginning to heal almost a year after the controversy, and the opposition group continued to be an informal "watchdog" over the school board's activities. In the other district, a slate of moderate candidates ran for school board positions to ensure that the conservative board member who had been one of the CLAS opposition leaders would not be reelected; he was defeated and the new board became quite cohesive. As in the other district, however, a small number of CLAS opponents continued to be active critics of the district's curriculum.

In the three schools still experiencing the effects of CLAS a year later, CLAS opponents tended to focus their criticisms on related policies. In all the schools, curriculum continued to be an issue. In addition, at one school, opponents worked to have the use of homogenous instructional groups restored, arguing that students were inadequately prepared in mathematics because those of different ability levels were being taught together. At another school, the CLAS controversy strengthened opposition to the school's free breakfast and lunch programs and to its after-school child care program. Opponents argued that these were examples of government encroachment upon family responsibilities.

Several parents took their children out of these schools and placed them in private schools. Principals also reported some decrease in parental support and involvement. Opposition parents at one school felt that they had been unfairly treated, and admitted that they were less active in fund-raising because they believed that their input was no longer valued. Other parents noted that they could not understand how longtime friends could view CLAS and the school's curriculum so differently. But at the two schools that had experienced the greatest divisions because of CLAS, groups of parents emerged as active supporters of the schools and their curricula. One woman even decided to become PTA president so that she could initiate a "year of healing."

In the districts and schools where effects persisted, the CLAS controversy may have served as a catalyst for latent concerns that already existed. Opposition parents were already unhappy with the curriculum and troubled about what they perceived to be a blurring of responsibility between home and school. Perhaps if CLAS had not been implemented or had been administered more skillfully, controversy still would have arisen, simply because opposition groups were organized to tap into latent sentiments. Nevertheless, because the catalyst came from outside, local board members and educators found it more difficult to respond effectively and to limit longer-term damage, especially when established patterns of collaboration and friendship were disrupted.

Conclusions

It is easy to dismiss the experience of these four districts and seven schools as just extreme versions of a unique and unfortunate event in the history of California education. But the responses of outliers have something to teach us because they bring into much sharper focus the different ways that a policy can be interpreted by its targets, and how values-based policies can affect those whose behavior they seek to change. Consequently, this case has broader implications for all kinds of hortatory policies.

The responses to CLAS in these communities nicely illustrate the limiting conditions on two of the causal assumptions underlying hortatory policies. These policies assume that appeals to strong, widely accepted values can change behavior, and that targets will respond to those value appeals by acting consistently with the policy's goals. Yet, as we have seen in the local responses to CLAS, strong values attract responses from both adherents and opponents, and hortatory policies typically lack the framework of rules and procedures needed to structure those responses. Consequently, another limiting condition can result, with political elites unable to control the nature and direction of the countermobilization.

To some extent, the SDE did create a structure for CLAS: school districts were required to administer the test to all students in the appropriate grades during a specific time period, and only those educators directly involved in administering the test were allowed to see its contents on a need-to-know and non-disclosure basis. However, largely because the SDE regarded CLAS as primarily an informational policy grounded in a technical measuring instrument, neither the SDE nor the state legislature adequately considered the politics of local implementation. Consequently, some local boards of education and individual schools were left to deal with a values controversy with neither adequate time to prepare nor the necessary policy tools.

At one level, the major lesson from these intense versions of educational controversy is one that implementation researchers have long known: local context is critical in shaping policy outcomes, and officials at higher levels of government need to give their local counterparts sufficient flexibility to adapt new policies to the local setting (McLaughlin, 1987). In the case of CLAS, the SDE not only gave local educators little flexibility, but it also failed to give them the informational resources needed to explain the test's purpose and to persuade parents of its worth. Again, another lesson from implementation research about building local capacity was forgotten. As a result, local officials were highly constrained and had as their only recourse the parental opt-out—a stopgap measure that eased the immediate pressures, but did little to address the broader issues underlying the controversy.

Clearly, some provision should have been made for parents and teachers (or any interested adults) to review the test before it was administered. In the face of a milder protest, Kentucky instituted such a policy, and it was able to do so with no breach of test security. California could have made a similar accommodation and left it to local testing directors to implement as needed in their own communities. The state also could have provided more thorough information about the test to school board members, educators, parents, the media, and the public—not just when the controversy erupted or test scores were to be released, but throughout the development and piloting process.

At another level, these local CLAS controversies suggest broader lessons about the role of parents in educational decision-making and about the balance between expertise and public responsiveness. One of the ironies of this episode is that the communities in which the controversy was the most intense exemplified what educational leaders in California have been advocating for years—strong community support for the schools and high parental involvement. Opposition parents may have been misinformed about the specifics of CLAS, but most were active in their children's schools and knew what was being taught there. They were not the uninvolved, uninformed group that some CLAS supporters portrayed them to be.

Two conclusions that have implications for other values-based policies flow from this set of circumstances. First, although information about CLAS was needed, a common understanding of that information was also necessary. Not only did opponents and supporters of CLAS interpret its purpose and content differently, but teachers and school board members did not fully understand its intent or share a common vision of what it could accomplish. Developing a common understanding of a policy's goals and operating requirements is necessary before those affected by it can even begin to build a consensus around it. That process takes time and must be done prior to any major policy actions, such as administration of the test. In the case of CLAS, time was in short supply, and local decisions were made in the heat of crisis using a short timetable, with little opportunity for genuine deliberation. It may be the case that had such deliberation occurred, the positions of opponents and supporters would not have changed, because at that point the test could not have been altered to meet objections. Nevertheless, allowing more time for a deliberative process prior to the actual administration of the test probably would have mitigated the worst effects of the controversy. Teachers, principals, and board members would have been less frustrated, and opposition parents would have felt less alienated from the schools. Everyone's position could have been heard and understood—though not necessarily agreed with—by other participants. From the perspective of CLAS supporters, a more deliberative process would have been valuable because opposition group leaders would have had a less fertile environment in which to mobilize allies.

So one implication for other values-based policies is the need for adequate time and informational resources, as well as the need for a structure within which a policy and its values premises can be presented and widely discussed at the point of implementation. This requirement also assumes that those promoting and implementing a hortatory policy understand the full implications of its underlying value premises, and that they can justify the appropriateness and effectiveness of those values.

A second implication relates to who is involved in the policy enactment and implementation processes. Those within the SDE who designed CLAS heeded the lessons of past implementation research that found that involving those who must implement a policy helps develop a sense of ownership, which in turn increases commitment to the enterprise. As a result, the task forces that developed various parts of CLAS included classroom teachers who had reputations for effective instruction and whose teaching aligned with the state curriculum frameworks.

Although this arrangement may have increased the stature of the test among professional educators, it ignored key constituents whose support was needed if CLAS were to be successful: local elected officials, parents, and the public. When confronted with this suggestion after the CLAS controversy was over, several SDE officials argued that such a process would not have been feasible, given the size and diversity of California and the time constraints a legislative sunset provision placed on test development. However, local teachers and parents saw it differently. They argued that even with input from a broader group of constituents, the goals of CLAS could have remained intact as marginal changes were made—for example, in the choice of reading selections, in the balance of multiple-choice and open-ended items, and in the type of prompts used to elicit students' written responses.

Student testing policy, like many other domestic policies, has a strong technical component that in this case draws on expertise in psychometrics and teaching and learning. Consequently, its implementation has traditionally been within the narrow purview of experts, and as we saw in the previous chapter, its enactment was typically uncontroversial and low-key. However, when standardized tests are used to promote particular curricular values, implementation is likely to become a more public, visible activity than it is when testing is viewed primarily as a way to assess student progress, independent of a specific curriculum.

The broader implication is that for many hortatory policies, implementation will likely be a very public process, and policymakers need to prepare for that. By definition, hortatory policies are unlikely to be effective unless they can engage a wide segment of the groups potentially affected by them. So the challenge for policymakers is to construct broad public appeals while also developing a framework that structures the response of various policy targets. The experience with CLAS suggests it is a formidable task, but not an impossible one. Sufficient time and information, flexibility, and an appreciation of the role of those farther down in the implementation chain are key ingredients.

5

Testing and Teaching

The success of any hortatory policy depends on whether the information it produces — or the values it espouses — lead policy targets to change their behavior in ways that are consistent with the policy's goals. In Chapters 3 and 4, we saw that although teachers and their students were the primary targets of the states' assessment policies, some elements of the public mobilized in ways that made their acceptance or rejection critical to whether the policies could even be implemented in local schools. The failure to reauthorize CLAS meant that its potential to change classroom instruction was short-lived. However, Kentucky's KIRIS and North Carolina's end-of-grade tests did continue, allowing their classroom implementation to be studied.

The response of teachers in these two states allows us to explore whether several of the causal assumptions that should be operative if hortatory policies are to accomplish their goals hold true for these assessment policies. These include whether teachers accepted the policy's underlying curricular values; whether they had sufficient incentive and capacity to change their instructional practices; and whether their responses were consistent with the policy's goals.

Kentucky and North Carolina provide a natural experiment through which these assumptions can be tested. At the time of the study, Kentucky's policy linked hortatory elements with a system that allocated rewards and sanctions to schools and teachers, while North Carolina's system was basically hortatory, with no tangible consequences imposed on either schools or students. Although limited in scope, the research presented in this chapter found that despite major differences in the format and policy uses of the two states' assessments, teachers in the two states responded in much the same manner. To the extent that they changed their classroom instruction, teachers did so in similar ways, regardless of whether the motivating factor was only a set of curricular values and the public reporting of test scores or it was augmented by the promise of rewards and the threat of sanctions.

The data on which this chapter is based include 95 interviews with district-level personnel, teachers, principals, and counselors in three districts and six schools each in Kentucky and North Carolina. These interviews were conducted in 1993 and are described in Chapter 1. Sixty of the respondents, of whom 48 were classroom teachers, were interviewed again in 1994. (The appendix outlines how districts and schools were selected, and compares the study sample with the relevant universe of districts and teachers.) In addition to the interviews, 670 regular class assignments, 399 assignments that teachers judged to be similar to the state assessments, and 503 daily logs completed by 23 teachers in Kentucky and the same number in North Carolina were coded and analyzed. (These data are described in the first chapter.)

Because data collection began in both states after implementation of the new assessments had already begun, there are no baseline data on instruction prior to the assessment. Therefore, the analysis cannot determine whether instruction changed in response to KIRIS and the end-of-grade tests. Rather, it relies on teachers' self-reports about the changes they made and on their instructional artifacts to ascertain how consistent teaching was with state goals, though some of that instruction may have preceded the state test. In fact, some teachers, particularly in social studies and language arts, reported that they had always required students to write essay responses and to work on long-term projects.

Additionally, it is not possible to draw inferences from this sample about how all or most schools and educators in Kentucky and North Carolina responded to the new state assessments early in their implementation. Although it mirrors the range of schools and teachers within each of the two states quite well, the sample is small and non-random. Nevertheless, it can still provide useful policy information. At one level, the study represents traditional implementation research, in which comparative case studies are used to understand the interaction among policy design, elements of the implementation process, and local context in shaping implementation outcomes. It is also a policy validation study that seeks to determine whether policymakers' assumptions about the kind of curricular changes they expect state assessments to accomplish are actually valid in practice. The study cannot ascertain the extent to which these assumptions are valid throughout Kentucky and North Carolina, but based on these cases, the research design does allow conclusions about whether policymakers' expectations are reasonable, and about the conditions under which they are likely to be met.

The next section analyzes the process by which the new assessments were implemented in the two states. A second section examines the extent to which teaching in a small sample of Kentucky and North Carolina classrooms reflected the instructional goals of the state assessment. Because this study of local implementation is limited in scope, a third section summarizes other relevant studies, and assesses the extent to which all this research provides a consistent picture of teachers' responses to assessments designed to ensure accountability and to shape instruction. The concluding section discusses what this comparative case study tells us about the conditions under which hortatory policies are likely to operate as intended.

Local Implementation

The State Process

Policy implementation research typically focuses on three categories of factors that shape implementation outcomes: *policy design characteristics*, notably the types of policy instruments used and the level of resources allocated; *the implementation process*, including how resources are invested in building the capacity of those charged with putting a policy in place, the time frame, and the strategies used to communicate a policy's intent; and *the will and capacity* of those at the local level who must translate a policy into everyday practice. Chapter 3 outlined Kentucky's and North Carolina's assessment policies, but the initial policy design is only one factor in determining whether a policy is implemented and produces its expected outcomes. Not only are the process by which that policy moves through the intergovernmental system and the local context also significant determinants, but they are also the factors over which policymakers have only limited influence. This section examines these other factors, mindful that the resource commitments made by elected officials and the time constraints they imposed also shaped the implementation process.

Communication between the state and teachers about the new assessments occurred at two stages: before the assessment, in informing teachers about its purpose, content, and format; and after the assessment was first administered to students, in the types of test score reports returned to schools. Teacher preparation was clearly a higher priority in Kentucky, as reflected both in a more substantial financial commitment and in a more comprehensive communications strategy. The Kentucky Department of Education (KDE) relied on a variety of strategies to inform teachers about KIRIS. About 30 teachers with experience in performance assessment and the use of portfolios were seconded from local districts to the KDE and to eight regional centers to train district assessment coordinators and teachers who would then return to their own districts and schools to train their colleagues. Several programs on assessment were produced for Kentucky Educational Television, with the videos then made available to individual schools. Several editions of the KDE's monthly newsletter were devoted to assessment; other documents were prepared on such topics as how the writing process might be linked to assessment. The state also initiated the KERA Professional Fellows program to include about 150 teachers from across the state who received 20 days of training on the assessment and who agreed to participate in the program for four years.

For most of the teachers in the study sample, however, information about KIRIS came only indirectly from the state. Some did attend workshops at the regional service centers. For example, in one district, the department chairs attended four workshops during the course of a year, with two sessions lasting half a day and two extending for an entire day. But most teachers received information directly from their districts or from county cluster leaders (teachers trained in scoring portfolios who worked with colleagues in several schools in a district). Although most teachers were involved in at least one formal activity that provided information about KIRIS, about a quarter of the sample described a more haphazard process—information about the assessment "just filtered down," "people would talk about it," it came "by word of mouth."

After the tests were administered, the state communicated three types of information. The first was the scores themselves, which told schools how well they were performing and how far their students had to go to meet or exceed the schools' thresholds. The released test items were a second source of information that schools studied to discern what content and instructional activities needed to be emphasized.[1] Finally, the scoring rubrics for the portfolios provided important clues about the state performance standards and about what should be stressed as students prepared their portfolios. In addition, during a two-year period, the state and its testing contractor rescored all the portfolios that had been initially scored by teachers. When they found that teachers had rated a significant proportion of the portfolios too highly, greater attention was devoted to training them to score portfolios. The following year, state-level auditing showed the scores to be considerably less discrepant because teachers were rating portfolios more consistently with the state rubrics.

Part of the implementation process is certainly about communicating the intent of a policy to the "street-level bureaucrats" ultimately responsible for putting it in place, and informing them about how the policy's goals might be translated into ongoing practice. But successful implementation also involves creating a sense of local ownership by convincing those in schools that a top-down policy meets their needs, that their interests are served by endorsing the policy, and that the policy can be adapted to local circumstances (McLaughlin, 1987).

Kentucky's track record on this was mixed. The importance to each school of doing well on KIRIS was clearly communicated. Teachers and principals talked about not becoming "schools in crisis," and the threat of sanctions loomed much larger than the promise of potential rewards. Mutual adaptation by classroom teachers was implied in the *Transformations* document: content and performance standards were specified and suggested activities described, but specific course content and its sequencing was not detailed. However, considering the time constraints, the state's approach was viewed by most at the local level as a lack of guidance, rather than a grant of flexibility. For the first years of KIRIS, the state did little to inform teachers about curricular approaches consistent with KIRIS or about how a state reform strategy might be adapted to local circumstances.

For most of the teachers in the North Carolina sample, the "pink booklet" was the major source of information about the new test. This booklet, describing the purpose of the end-of-grade test and providing examples of test items, was widely distributed by the DPI. In addition, several schools in the study sample had participated in the field tests for the new assessment, so teachers knew what to expect. Some teachers reported attending workshops at the regional service centers, and most received some kind of information or support from their districts. For example, one district used local funds to support a curriculum coordinator at each school. This person was not only responsible for administering the test and informing teachers about it, but she also typically functioned as a resource teacher who went into classrooms for several periods a week to work with students on writing and mathematics. Another small district had several "helping teachers" who functioned in much the same way, holding workshops on new approaches to curriculum and assisting teachers in their classrooms, again usually in writing and mathematics instruction.

It should be noted that the implementation process in North Carolina did not need to be as extensive as Kentucky's. The assessment was based on the existing *Standard Course of Study;* most of the test still consisted of multiple-choice items (although now aligned with the state curriculum); and it was not being implemented in the context of other substantial reforms.

North Carolina's test score data were of mixed usefulness to schools. The state invested considerable resources in scoring and reporting software that allowed each district to score its own multiple-choice items, so that scores were returned to schools within two or three days. In addition, a number of school systems provided each school with a computer file of its scores in a format that allowed principals, curriculum coordinators, and teachers to disaggregate the data by sex, ethnicity, and state competency goals, and to "re-roster" students' scores from their classes in the previous years and add them to the classes in which they were currently enrolled. With such data manipulations, principals could both identify groups that needed extra assistance and inform teachers about the strengths and weaknesses of their classes, based on students' test scores the previous year.

The state was considerably less helpful to schools when providing scores on the open-response items. Because of a series of logistical problems and the need to hand-score such a large number of items, schools did not receive those scores until six to eight months after the test administration. Consequently, schools received score information about the least familiar aspect of the test in the least timely manner.

Local Context

Research has shown that two aspects of the local context are particularly important in shaping implementation outcomes: *will* and *capacity* (McLaughlin, 1987). Will refers to how supportive a local community is of a particular policy; whether it sees the policy as addressing a local problem or need; and whether the policy is consistent with the community's values. Capacity refers to whether local institutions have the necessary organizational resources, expertise, and time to implement the policy. Both factors are necessary for successful implementation: enthusiasm cannot overcome a lack of capacity, and high capacity is of little value if people lack the will to apply it.

It has become a truism in education policy that there is potential for significant variation across local contexts. It is certainly true that in the case of state assessment policy, local will and capacity were important determinants of implementation success. But it also appears that there was little variation across local contexts, particularly in capacity levels. The extent to which local districts and schools saw the assessment as consistent with their priorities varied, and some districts had more experience with the curricular approaches underlying the assessments than others did. Nevertheless, this research (and findings from a number of other studies) suggest that both the newness of the state assessments and their power as policy tools reduced local variation. Particularly in the case of Kentucky, the scope of KERA and KIRIS overwhelmed local priorities and created a substantial need for capacity-building in both high- and low-capacity schools. Even in North Carolina, where assessment policy change was modest, local variation in the ability of districts and schools to respond to the testing requirements seemed smaller than it had during past reforms. In both states, the design of the policies and the implementation process served to reduce local variation. However, they did not overcome the determining effect of teacher capacity in shaping implementation outcomes. In other words, the extent to which the state assessment altered instruction depended on local capacity, but the ways in which teachers responded to the test was less variable across districts and schools than had been the case for past reforms not linked to assessment systems.

LOCAL WILL. No statewide data were available on the attitudes of North Carolina principals and teachers at the time the end-of-grade tests were first implemented. However, there were two such surveys for Kentucky.[2] These surveys provide a general sense of the level of support for KIRIS among those responsible for implementing it at the local level. In the 1994 survey, a majority of principals and teachers (59 percent of each category) expressed support for the KERA reforms. However, a majority (51 percent of the principals and 55 percent of the teachers) also reported that KIRIS was working poorly. No other element of KERA received such a high proportion of low ratings from either of the two groups. When asked why KIRIS was working poorly, most respondents attributed the problem to poor program design, rather than to poor implementation, insufficient time, or a lack of training and technical assistance. Both groups gave the highest marks to local school staffs for the accuracy of information provided and the quality of training. On both measures, teachers ranked the KDE fifth behind their district's central office, their professional association, and institutions of higher education in the area.

Several other findings from this survey are particularly telling with regard to KIRIS. Three-fourths of the principals and two-thirds of the teachers reported experiencing extreme or major stress as a result of the demands of KERA. When asked if they agreed with major tenets underlying KERA and KIRIS, more than half of the teacher respondents either were undecided or declined to give opinions. The beliefs on which no opinions were expressed included: "All children can learn at a relatively high level," "We should set high standards of achievement for all children," and "It is not enough to require that students show their knowledge of the facts—they must also demonstrate that they can apply what they know in real life situations" (68 percent of the teacher sample gave no opinion about that belief). Finally, more than two-thirds of the principals and more than three-fourths of the teachers opposed rewarding and sanctioning schools and teachers based on how well students performed. Their opposition contrasted with the more than 60 percent of the general public and parent samples that supported the idea (Wilkerson, 1994).

The survey that focused just on KIRIS and was administered some eight months later found some of the same attitudes. For example, only 27 percent of the principals and teachers surveyed expressed support for the use of rewards and sanctions. Like the earlier survey, this study found that support for other elements of KERA, such as site-based management and the ungraded primary program, was higher than support for KIRIS. However, a majority of respondents said that they supported the KIRIS program. In this survey, the teachers were evenly divided in whether or not they agreed with the tenet that "all children can learn to a high level." However, an overwhelming majority (83 percent) agreed that regardless of whether or not it is possible for all students to learn to that level, it is an appropriate message to send to Kentucky students.

Related to the instructional improvement goals embedded in KIRIS, Koretz and his colleagues (1996) found that most teachers and principals felt positively about KIRIS's value as an agent of reform. More than half of the sample reported that KIRIS had caused some teachers who were resistant to change to improve their instruction (p. 11). The same proportion acknowledged that KIRIS more closely resembled their instruction than did traditional standardized tests. A majority of respondents also viewed the information produced by KIRIS as accurate and reasonable for drawing conclusions about educational effectiveness.

In the in-depth interviews with Kentucky and North Carolina teachers, they were not asked directly whether they supported or opposed the state assessment. Rather, they were asked what aspects of the assessment evoked the most positive and the most negative reactions from them and from students. Their responses mirror the ambivalence about KIRIS expressed by the survey respondents. Teachers in the study sample saw clear advantages to the new assessments, but they also raised serious questions about the test. Although not generalizable in the way that the survey responses are, the interview data provide context for the survey findings.

The Kentucky teachers identified more negative than positive aspects of KIRIS for teachers, while their assessment of its benefits for students was exactly the opposite. For students, the positive aspects outnumbered the negative by almost two to one. The positive benefit for teachers that was cited most often was that they were beginning to see an improvement in students' writing. Another set of positive benefits was that KIRIS was forcing teachers to look at the curriculum, and it gave them a sense of the direction in which they needed to be heading. Other benefits stemmed from their perception that KIRIS measured students' achievement better and that it was more engaging for students. Several teachers mentioned that KIRIS showed that the people of Kentucky were putting an emphasis on education and that as a result, teachers were getting more attention.

Negative aspects of the assessment for teachers fell into five broad categories. The first was the amount of time students spent completing portfolios and teachers spent scoring them. The second was a concern about whether the test was reliable and valid. A third concern was that the emphasis on writing and preparing portfolios was causing the teaching of subject-matter content to be sacrificed. Fourth, teachers argued that it was unfair to hold them accountable when neither students nor their parents were being held accountable. Finally, a few teachers feared that the accountability pressure would result in teacher burnout.

In terms of the advantages and disadvantages of KIRIS for students, an equal number of teachers viewed the emphasis on writing positively as viewed it negatively. Those teachers who reported that students judged the writing requirements positively noted that students felt pride in what they had written and that they particularly enjoyed writing about their personal experiences. On the negative side, teachers said that students hated writing, even though they knew it was good for them. One high school teacher aptly described this student ambivalence: "The writing is positive in that [students] have written more and they seem to be learning more about it. Some say they don't like writing because they can't write. Even if they have the knowledge, they can't show they know the stuff. It's the devil and the angel all at once."

In the teachers' view, the other positive aspects of KIRIS for students lay in its non-traditional testing format. They reported that their students liked participating in the performance events, working in groups, preparing their portfolios, and doing hands-on activities. The negative aspects were that high school students did not want to waste time on a test that did not count, and the time requirements for both the annual tests administered on a set schedule (too little time allowed) and the portfolios (too much time required, especially out of class) were problems for some students. The time burden was especially acute for elementary students, as one teacher described quite poignantly: "I saw tears in the eyes of some of my students when they were faced with a page of small-type words. And these were the best performers. The passages are so long, and they're not used to reading so much in such a short time."

The North Carolina teachers in the study sample were twice as likely to identify negative aspects of the end-of-grade tests for both teachers and students than they were to identify positive features. The positive aspect of the test most often mentioned by teachers was that, in stressing critical thinking skills, the end-of-grade test represented a better preparation for students' future work than had its predecessor. A third of the teachers mentioned this feature, while an equal number identified the assessment's seeming subjectivity as a negative feature. A seventh-grade mathematics teacher mentioned both these positive and negative perceptions in his response:

The positive for me is that we have been too long on computational skills in the past. In the real world, everything is not laid out. In the long run, it will be useful if students are able to apply knowledge. The new state assessment has also helped keep my own thinking on track. The negative is the scoring of the open-ended items because it involves teacher judgment. After a while, human error comes in. My wife was telling me about a group of teachers at a workshop and they couldn't agree on the scoring. Some items were scored high and some low, even though the same thing was said in each.

The other major positive factors for teachers were that the end-of-grade test allowed them to do a better job of teaching, and that by following the state curriculum, it tested students on skills they were actually learning. As in Kentucky, the positives for students related to the testing format and the kind of teaching that accompanied it: the emphasis on problem-solving, and the use of manipulatives and calculators. The negatives for students were also similar to those mentioned in Kentucky. A third of the teachers reported that students were overwhelmed by the amount of writing required. Other problems for students were the length of the reading passages, the difficult vocabulary, questions that seemed confusing, and insufficient time to complete the test.

What emerged from these data and other surveys is that teachers felt quite ambivalent about the new state assessments. They saw their value for students in that the tests had led them to engage in activities (such as more writing) that they would not have done otherwise, and the assessments measured student achievement more fully than had previous tests. However, teachers remained skeptical about the reliability of the new tests, and they saw them as a source of considerable stress. Consequently, support for the state assessments was truly mixed. They had mobilized local will, but it had been a mobilization of skeptics.

One other measure of local will is whether or not educators saw the assessment as consistent with district and school priorities. As evidence of the power of the assessment in substituting state priorities for purely local ones and hence in reducing local variation, the vast majority of respondents reported that the state assessment fit very well with district priorities because the district was doing what the state had mandated:

I would say that district priorities will become what the state priorities are. I don't know if it makes any difference if our priorities are any different. They'll have to be the same or we'll cease to exist. (Kentucky high school science teacher)

I think the district has changed to fit the goals set forth in KERA and the assessment. The district had to make the change. (Kentucky fourth-grade teacher)

Well, one follows the other, so it coincides—because the state really mandates what should and should not be done at the district level. (North Carolina seventh-grade language arts teacher)

I think it would fit in just as well with the district, because their priorities are the state's priorities. (North Carolina fourth-grade teacher)

Yes, because we're one-in-one—our goal is to do what the state department of public instruction does. (North Carolina fourth-grade teacher)

LOCAL CAPACITY. Like local will, local capacity presents a mixed picture. All but two of the 48 teachers in the study sample reported that they had received some type of formal introduction to KIRIS or the end-of-grade tests. Before the tests were first administered, teachers had at least a general sense that the purpose and format differed from past state tests, and that students would be expected to demonstrate their knowledge at a deeper level and in multiple ways. However, only half of the teachers in each of the state samples received information that extended beyond the specifics of the test's administration and scoring to a discussion of its curricular implications. Furthermore, only six of the Kentucky teachers and two of the North Carolina teachers were participating in any kind of ongoing professional development that allowed them to learn about and work on curricular implications on a sustained basis.

When asked if the SDE, district, and school had been able to provide them with all the support they needed for working on the assessment, two-thirds of the teachers in the sample said that they had received everything they needed or requested. Several teachers in both states noted that the first year had been a problem, but that the level and type of support had greatly improved since then. Again, there are no representative state data for North Carolina, but the Wilkerson (1994) poll data for Kentucky showed a similar pattern. Teachers in that survey were asked whether they had all the information they needed to do their job with regard to KERA. Sixty-five percent reported that they did.

However, in eight focus groups that included a total of 73 teachers, conducted around the state by the Appalachia Educational Laboratory (1995), teachers reported that training opportunities for curriculum development and alignment were limited and of mixed quality. They also indicated that they were uncomfortable developing curriculum at the local level and aligning it with the state standards because they were accustomed to that being done by textbooks. In addition, the teachers in the focus groups reported needing much greater guidance about how to apply the state's academic expectations to specific grade levels. These sentiments were consistent with those expressed by the Kentucky teachers in the study sample. They were provided sufficient information about KIRIS, but half of them had not been given opportunities that would help them take the next steps in changing their instruction. As a high school mathematics teacher explained, "There really hasn't been enough instruction for teachers. The KDE thinks that it is teaching cluster leaders, but all they're doing is giving us examples. They don't show us how to integrate them into the curriculum or how to keep the appropriate pacing." The Kentucky teachers also indicated that they needed more concrete guidance and time to observe other teachers who had changed their instruction in the expected ways.

It is important to note, however, that in the sample of teachers there were no strong complaints about the level and type of support they had received. Both the Kentucky and the North Carolina teachers felt that their respective SDEs could have done more, but the overwhelming majority felt that their own principals and school districts had done as much as they could, both in providing information and in giving them instructional support.

Up to this point, local capacity has been examined as it pertains to teachers' ability to teach consistent with the assessment's curricular goals. But there is another dimension of local capacity related to assessment that is considerably more problematic. It deals with improving students' capacity to do well on the test, and is known as "test preparation." The assessments were designed to encourage teachers to "teach to the test," that is, to focus their ongoing instruction on the skills and knowledge being tested. However, if students are narrowly prepared through the use of practice tests or other devices, the effect may be to distort gains in test scores without appreciably improving either instructional quality or student achievement in the long term.

Koretz et al. (1996) found that 82 percent of the principals in their sample reported encouraging teachers a great deal to use test preparation materials, and 66 percent reported placing a great deal of emphasis on the teaching of test-taking skills. A smaller proportion of teachers reported placing a great deal of emphasis on these strategies (48 percent for test-taking skills and 36 percent for test preparation materials), but the overwhelming majority said that they placed at least a moderate emphasis on them.

These survey data confirm newspaper accounts about widespread test preparation that ranged from a variety of motivational approaches to the teaching of specific test-taking skills. One of the biggest motivational problems was faced by high schools whose progress on the state accountability index largely depended on how well their twelfth graders performed on a test that many students "blew off" because there were no personal consequences for them. As a result, principals and teachers appealed to school spirit, persuaded popular students to convince others to take the test seriously, and offered a variety of rewards, ranging from T-shirts to tardy passes and early lunches.[3] In addition, principals and teachers at all levels stressed test-taking skills relevant to KIRIS—for example, answering short-essay questions, working in groups on problem-solving exercises, and writing more in mathematics and science classes.

The schools in the Kentucky study sample reflected the emphasis on test preparation highlighted in newspaper accounts and documented in the statewide survey. Principals and teachers were very open in talking about what they were doing to improve test scores. Their methods included: providing material incentives for seniors (free days, hamburger barbecues); requiring that all teachers include at least one open-response item on all their tests; requiring that a portfolio piece be prepared in each class, including physical education; and ensuring that all written work follow a model that emphasized audience and purpose. The following examples provide a sense of the range of strategies schools used:

The first year we took the test—which would have been three years ago—we had a high benchmark. The next year, students didn't take the test seriously, and our scores dropped. Everyone said we wouldn't make our benchmark and would be in crisis. We were under a lot of pressure—the teachers more than the students—because every time you saw a state or district official, it was "What are you going to do to raise test scores?" Last year, we had marathon sessions—three weeks where we took the seniors out of class and reviewed with them in each of the four core areas, using questions from previous years—showing them the kind of answers that would get distinguished, proficient, etc. And we did real good last year. (high school mathematics teacher)

I'm working a lot more with the criteria—having students analyze and apply them—more than last year. I'm almost embedding in the students an unconscious evaluative process to internalize those criteria so they focus on those skills and outcomes without really even thinking of them. One thing I've been doing the past six weeks that's different from last year is trying to get them to see the connection between the state curriculum criteria and my content criteria. So, for example, they have to know communication skills and content. It will take 12 weeks for them to apply both sets at the same time. I'm seeing the students become more analytical and more aware of what it takes to make a quality piece of work from both perspectives. (high school English teacher)

The state test has gotten to be more of a priority, and we understand now what we need to do. We're doing open-ended questions every day in all grades . . . Everybody does journals and other writing activities every day. Students work on their portfolios every day. (elementary school principal)

One of the things we do is that we have the kids write open-ended questions or respond to them. This will be on the [school's closed-circuit] TV. Teachers will collect these and give me the test. We call these kids "KERA Scholars," and we give them $5. So we have all these little gimmicks. We'll have about eight scrimmages [practice tests modeled after KIRIS] this year with one adult for every 15 kids—which includes me, the assistant principal, and the guidance counselor—to help go through the trials. (middle school principal)

One of the major changes that occurred in the six fieldwork sample Kentucky schools between the first round of interviews in 1993 and the second round one year later was that whatever response the school made to KIRIS was then extended to both tested and untested grades and subjects. In the first year, most of the test preparation strategies had focused on the fourth- and eighth-grade teachers, and to the extent that anything was happening in the high schools, on the English teachers. During the next year, however, all the schools implemented practices that affected all teachers, so KIRIS's effects were more broadly felt. The argument was that the teachers in the tested grades should not have to carry all the burden for the school's accountability, and that teachers in the other grades could help in the long-term preparation of students. For example, one of the elementary schools in the sample that exceeded its threshold score and earned a financial reward implemented several strategies to involve teachers from all the grades. The second- and third-grade teachers began sharing a joint planning period with the fourth-grade teachers once a week, and there was clear curricular coordination among the grades. In addition, the pieces for the eighth-grade portfolios were collected every year between fifth and seventh grade; that strategy allowed the eighth-grade teacher to work on one long-term piece, with the rest of the pieces being revisions of those done by the students in earlier grades.

Besides the concern that some have expressed about test preparation strategies leading to invalid scores, there is a question of whether such strategies are even effective in raising test scores and whether they lead to long-term improvements in instruction. There is some reason to believe that in the short term, test preparation strategies can increase students' scores. For example, when a state testing official was asked whether schools could use "quick fix" strategies to raise their test scores without fundamentally changing their teaching, he acknowledged that they could:

> For about two to six years schools can get away with that strategy and then they'll hit a wall and be unable to move. Here's one example of a short-term strategy. Forty-one percent of eighth graders' open-ended responses show no evidence of understanding the problem. They were either scored 0 or left blank. To score a 1 [novice—minimal understanding] you have to do more than repeat the question, but if students show any understanding of what's being asked, they get a 1.

However, it may also be the case that for some schools, test preparation strategies were used to start to change the instructional process. Teaching students to answer open-response items and to understand the scoring rubrics were first steps in getting them to think more analytically.

The North Carolina schools in the study sample seemed to stress the motivational "hoopla" less than the Kentucky schools did. Nevertheless, they also focused on a variety of test preparation strategies. For example, one elementary principal reported that the teachers in her school had been practicing all year with sample test items. She went on to note:

> We've looked at the students who scored a 2 [inconsistent mastery] and then asked what will it take to move them to a 3 [consistent mastery—proficient]. We've also looked at each test item and how much weight each carries. We've also looked at teachers' strengths and weaknesses. We're trying to be multi-faceted in analyzing how to move "the twos." Basically, we're looking first at individual student strengths and weaknesses, than at test construction, and then at teacher and class strengths and weaknesses.

The district in which this school is located also brought in a consultant from Ohio to help teachers align the local curriculum with the *Standard Course of Study*. Each elementary school selected five teachers to attend a four-day workshop on alignment. The grade-level team at each school then developed a unit tied to the *Standard Course of Study* that could be used by other teachers in the district.

Like their counterparts in Kentucky, the North Carolina educators acknowledged the advantages and disadvantages of the test preparation strategies they had implemented:

> I hear from the teachers that they are doing overkill on test sophistication. They are having students practice writing so much that it's killing it . . . The end-of-grade test is turning writing into paint-by-numbers.

It's stifling writing, but students' writing has improved incredibly—as measured by the state test . . . We're now playing the game. The writing now starts with a particular kind of sentence. The state test has taken something creative and turned it into alphabet soup. The teachers are saying, "We don't like it, but now we have students who can express themselves in writing. We never had that before." (elementary school principal)

We had as a school goal (before the end-of-grade test) the infusion of critical thinking skills into the curriculum. There are now fewer multiple-choice questions on regular tests, and students are expected to defend their choices. They may not have the right answer, but they need to explain their choice. (middle school principal)

Capacity-building in the schools studied in both states focused on the short term—informing teachers about the purpose and format of the assessment and instructing students in test preparation strategies. Whether this investment translated into the resources needed to make more lasting changes in instruction was uncertain during the early years of the assessment policies.

This section examined two of the causal assumptions that should be true if hortatory policies are to accomplish their purposes: (1) that targets—in this case, teachers—accept the policy's underlying goals, and (2) that they have sufficient will and capacity to act consistently with those goals. To a considerable extent these assumptions were operative, but by no means fully so. Teachers had mixed reactions to the tests, and while they were motivated to act consistently with state assessment goals, their capacity to do so was limited. Teachers in the two state samples perceived the new assessments as representing significant challenges, and they took them equally seriously. They also had similar attitudes about the tests—recognizing their relatively greater benefits for students than for teachers, but questioning their accuracy as measurement tools and finding them to be a source of stress.

Comparing Kentucky's implementation of KIRIS with North Carolina's process for its end-of-grade tests also suggests that in the short term, the two state assessments had similar implementation histories. Teachers responded to the tests in essentially the same way, despite major differences in their policy design. Kentucky's approach differed from North Carolina's in several ways: KIRIS was part of a large systemic reform; the assessment was high stakes for schools and educators, with major consequences attached to its results; KIRIS represented a more marked departure from past practice and it was a more difficult test, as evidenced by its format and the considerably higher performance levels students had to attain. Yet the implementation process for the two assessments was organized in essentially the same way, with teachers receiving about the same capacity-building resources.

Our limited data—and the short time frame that the assessments had been in place when we studied their effects—did not allow us to conclude unequivocally that hortatory approaches to student assessment policy could be as powerful as more regulatory ones. However, the North Carolina experience did strongly suggest that, at least in the short term, relying primarily on curricular values and the power of perceived public scrutiny could effectively motivate educators. At the same time, North Carolina's subsequent move to a high stakes test is consistent with another assumption, outlined in Chapter 2, that hortatory policies need to be linked with other policy instruments if they are to produce longer-term effects.

Did Teaching Look Like the Test?

Teachers' Understanding of Policymakers' Expectations

This section examines another of the assumptions that underlie hortatory policies—that the values appealed to in the policy will motivate targets to act in ways consistent with its goals. In the case of state assessments, policymakers assumed that teachers would change their instructional practices to mirror more closely the curricular values underlying the assessment. As a first step in determining whether classroom behavior was consistent with the state assessments, we needed to analyze teachers' understanding of what policymakers expected the new assessments to accomplish. Considering that legislative intent was relatively clear in both states and that most teachers received some systematic introduction to the tests, we expected most to have a fairly good understanding of policymakers' expectations. Working against that assumption, however, was the low public visibility of the test in North Carolina and the fact that even in Kentucky, where KIRIS was more visible, a small but significant proportion of teachers reported needing more information about KERA and the assessment.

When we first interviewed the sample of teachers in the fall of 1993, we asked them: What do you think state policymakers expected to accomplish with KIRIS (or the end-of-grade tests)? We then asked them if the state assessment was likely to produce the kind of effects at their schools that policymakers intended. The answers given by teachers in the two states were quite similar. Despite policymakers' dual emphasis on accountability and instructional improvement, the overwhelming majority of teacher respondents discussed only one purpose, and most phrased it in terms of improving educational quality, giving students new kinds of skills, or raising test scores (and thus making the state look good). About 20 percent of the respondents specifically mentioned better student preparation for the workforce as a goal, with that objective more pronounced among the North Carolina sample. Here are examples of those responses:

> I think that their first goal is to get the maximum potential from each child if they can—to take him wherever he is and go as far as he can. They want North Carolina's children to be functionally able to compete with any state or any country in the world. Obviously [students] weren't doing that before, but we've continued to pass them anyway. (North Carolina fifth-grade teacher)

> I think the policymakers want to raise the intelligence of our students— and it's a good purpose. They want more emphasis on reasoning and thinking. Students should be able to perform, not just talk about something. We should graduate kids with skills. They're good purposes. (Kentucky middle school social studies teacher)

> I hope they're looking for a student that when they leave, they're self-sufficient and able to function on their own, and also able to be a productive member of society who is able to function with others. To put it in my own words: We're looking for the individual who can be a leader when the time is right and a follower when the time is appropriate. (Kentucky fifth-grade teacher)

> I think they're trying to improve the education of our children and help them to be prepared to be productive individuals, so when they go out to work, they'll have the skills they need to make a living. The reason we emphasize cooperative learning is to teach them to work together in groups and get along and share. (North Carolina fourth-grade teacher)

> Just to make the state look good. They want to say their state is as smart as the others. They want to get kids thinking—they see kids have problems when they go to college. They want to get scores up—everything is the scores. They compare all the counties. They put the scores in the newspaper, and it's big stuff. People say, "Your county is dumber than ours." (North Carolina third-grade teacher)

Only 15 percent of the 48 teachers interviewed specifically mentioned accountability as a policy goal. For example:

> They wanted to make teachers more accountable for what they are doing. We're beginning to feel that we're being held accountable for stu-

dents' grades and scores. Every grading period we get slapped with the distribution of grades and the averages. There's talk about getting test scores that show how each teacher is doing . . . (North Carolina middle school English teacher)

They wanted greater accountability for education. They wanted to know why we had high school graduates who couldn't read. (Kentucky fourth-grade teacher)

Only three teachers in Kentucky mentioned changing instruction as a goal of KIRIS. Similarly, three in North Carolina noted that the purpose of the end-of-grade test was to align the state assessment with the *Standard Course of Study*:

I would guess that their intention is to see that our students are taught a curriculum that is what it should be—adequate. The testing program is a way to evaluate if we've done what they set out to do—which is to teach that curriculum. To me, common sense shows that this is the way to do it. In the past, we had curriculum guides, and we were encouraged to teach from them, then we gave an assessment that didn't really emphasize the important things in that curriculum. If we can make a good curriculum tool and assess it, that would be an improvement. It's kind of getting their act together. (North Carolina middle school science teacher)

From what I understand about the rationale behind the law itself and some of the theory that helped to structure the assessments, I really think they intended assessments to transform the classrooms. By mandating them statewide in such a comprehensive way, they recognized that in order for kids to perform well, the schools had to restructure and change, and in order to provide the assessment needs, they would meet society's needs better. (Kentucky high school English teacher)

Two teachers in the Kentucky sample mentioned equalizing resources and giving all students the opportunity to learn as a goal, and two mentioned policymakers' expectation that "all children will achieve at high levels," but they did not believe that it could be accomplished:

I don't know if this is true or not, but I have been led to believe that policymakers expected all students to achieve at a high level. Some say the average should be 94 percent. Now this may be a misunderstanding on my part, but I can't see how everyone will achieve at a high rate. I use this on students sometimes; I guess you could say it is reverse psychology. But I tell them if everyone comes to the top, there won't be room for all of them. I'm a realist; it just wouldn't work. At the same time, we have to give people the opportunity to try. I don't like to see people down-and-out in our society, but that's the way it is. We've never been able to create a utopia yet, and we won't this time either. (Kentucky high school English teacher)

When asked if policymakers' expectations would be met in their schools, more than one-third of the teacher sample in both states was unequivocal in saying that the assessment policy goals would be met in their schools. An additional group was hopeful that the goals would be met, but uncertain at the time of the first interview whether it would indeed happen. One-third of the Kentucky teachers did not think the expectations embodied in KIRIS would be met, but even the majority of that group felt either that some benefits would result or that the goals would be met, but not for every student. Only three teachers in each of the two states were adamant in saying that the assessment goals would not be met. Interestingly, the reason the three North Carolina teachers gave for the assessment not producing its expected effects was that they feared the state would discontinue the test and implement another one before giving the current assessment sufficient time to work as intended.

The picture that emerged from these responses was of a rather diffuse, shallow understanding of assessment policy goals and guarded optimism about attaining them. All the teachers in the sample identified at least one policy goal or value that state policymakers sought to promote with the assessments. But only a few teachers in each state identified either the dual goals of accountability and curricular change or discussed multiple values underlying the assessment. Still, a sizable number recognized that students were supposed to be taught new kinds of skills. In addition, with only a few exceptions, teachers were confident that eventually at least some of the state policy goals would be met.

Teachers' recognition that they needed to change their approach to instruction emerged more sharply when they were asked in the 1993 interviews whether the state assessment had already affected their teaching, or whether they expected changes in curricular content or instructional strategies at their schools as a result of the state assessment. Again there were both similarities and differences in the responses of the two state samples. In both states, about 20 percent of the teachers reported in 1993 that they were having their students do more writing. The biggest change among the North Carolina teachers was that one-third of them reported modifying their assessment techniques, including more open-ended items on their tests and expecting more in-depth answers from students. Other changes that were prominent among the North Carolina teachers were more "discovery learning" and hands-on activities (six of the 24 teachers), and shifts in curriculum content to align it with the *Standard Course of Study* (five teachers).[4] An equal number of Kentucky teachers reported a greater emphasis on discovery learning and four indicated that they had made changes in their curriculum content to align it better with the state "learner goals." The most widespread change reported by the Kentucky teachers in 1993 was a greater emphasis on having students work in groups, an activity reported by only three of the North Carolina teachers. Similarly, fewer North Carolina teachers (three) than Kentucky teachers (six) reported no longer using textbooks or reducing their reliance on them.[5]

In 1994, we asked teachers whether there had been any other changes in their teaching during the past year. Most reported additional changes, and one aspect is particularly striking. In the second round of interviews, teachers talked more about the changes in their teaching as directly tied to the state assessment than they had the year before. For example:

> I emphasize answering open-ended questions, and I guide them on their portfolios. While we can't help them specifically, we can guide them. I think I go over their tasks more carefully, because I know they'll be assessed. I'm sure there's a difference because of the assessment year — stressing the open-ended questions, and working on the portfolios, and looking for performance events — providing opportunities for them similar to the KERA assessment. We work with a lot of hands-on materials in math. (Kentucky elementary school teacher)

> I have discovered that in science and math both, having a child write what they understand, and why they do something and give a real-life example really lets me understand that they know what they're talking about. Some kids could do it in words and not write it down, so when they saw the same pattern, they couldn't do it. The portfolio pieces have shown me really clearly that they have a deeper understanding when they write it down. So I have them do more writing of explanation and details. That's probably the biggest change that I have made since last year. It's definitely having an impact. I really like what it's doing. (Kentucky high school science and language arts teacher)

> I probably said I always taught the textbook from front to back. Now I move statistics forward. I no longer [teach the whole textbook]. My teaching in the sixth grade has changed drastically, from using the textbook every day to using manipulatives and using partners to be problem-solvers. They have to come up with ideas of how to do things

on their own. Like graphing. They started doing it without knowing what it is. This is an adjustment for me, but I like it. The end-of-grade has influenced my motivation to reorganize the sixth grade. They need to know there's more than one way to solve a problem. They've discovered rules and learned how to graph them. (North Carolina middle school mathematics teacher)

Definitely, the writing test affects what I do in the classroom. Almost all the activities until February are related to persuasive writing. We do projects like an advertising campaign, so it's not just sitting down and writing papers. Now that I have done these projects, I would probably still do them anyway without the test. (North Carolina middle school language arts teacher)

These reported changes might have been quite superficial, reflecting shifts in classroom activities, but not a fundamental alteration in either teachers' or students' understanding of substantive concepts or how one acquires useful knowledge. Nevertheless, the changes were consistent with movement toward the more constructivist approach to teaching assumed in KIRIS and to some extent, in the North Carolina assessment.

Teaching Consistent with State Goals

Teachers' self-reports provided one measure of how consistent their teaching was with the state assessment. Their daily logs allowed a more detailed picture and their class assignments provided both a more nuanced sense of their teaching and independent validation of the teachers' own perceptions.

ASSIGNMENT CHARACTERISTICS.   Because the two states stressed some similar objectives such as more student writing, we first compared assignments from the Kentucky and North Carolina samples. Figures 5.1 and 5.2 compare the assignments collected from teachers in the two states in a two-week period.

Of the 11 assignment characteristics, only two showed statistically significant differences between the two states. The North Carolina teachers relied more heavily on a multiple-choice format, showing evidence of it in 37 percent of the assignments submitted, compared with 22 percent of Kentucky teachers' assignments.[6] This difference may be due to the fact that the North Carolina assessment still relied heavily on multiple-choice questions, while KIRIS did not. If teachers were "teaching to the test," we would expect their assignments to reflect the test. It is not surprising, then, to find that the Kentucky teachers required several-paragraph written responses more often than did the North Carolina teachers (13 percent of assignments compared with 4 percent of assignments).[7] The remainder of the assignment characteristics did not show any significant differences between teachers in the two states. Clearly, writing had a prominent place in teachers' assignments, but other activities, such as group products, peer-reviewed work, and the use of manipulatives, had less significant places than might be expected, based on the teachers' self-reports.

Another change advocated by curriculum reformers, and particularly evident in Kentucky's assessment, was the integration of knowledge across subject areas.[8] Seventy-three percent of the Kentucky teachers had given at least a few assignments that integrated content into two or more disciplines. Despite the high proportion of teachers using this approach, however, on average only 19 percent of the Kentucky assignments were interdisciplinary. In North Carolina, half of the teacher sample made such assignments, with about 20 percent of the assignments evidencing integrated content. The dis-

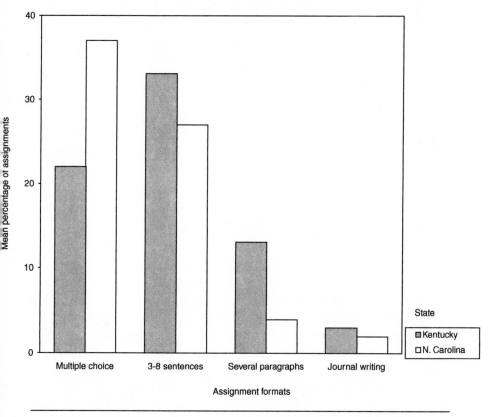

Figure 5.1. Comparison of Kentucky and North Carolina assignment formats

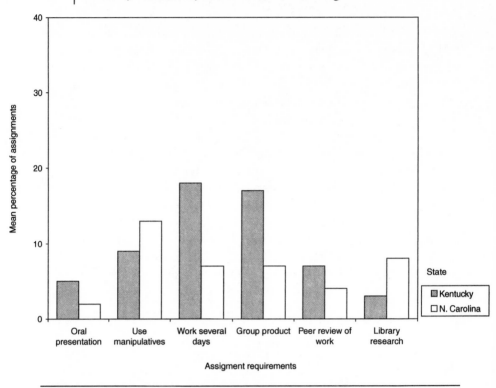

Figure 5.2. Comparison of assignment requirements

crepancy between the proportion of teachers using an interdisciplinary approach and its relatively low incidence across their assignments represents a common pattern. The teachers in the study sample used many instructional strategies consistent with state goals, but these newer approaches were not yet major components of their instructional repertoires.

INSTRUCTIONAL STRATEGIES. On their daily logs, teachers were asked about the modes of instruction they used and the activities in which students engaged during a class period. (A sample log form listing all the instructional strategies and student activities is included in the appendix.) Since the logs were completed by teachers, they do not constitute an external source for validating their interview self-reports. However, the logs do serve as a check on the reliability of the interviews, since they provide greater detail about classroom activities, with the information collected closer in time to the actual events.

Because the Kentucky and North Carolina teachers completed the same log forms, we were again able to make comparisons between the two states. Figures 5.3 and 5.4 present the log data. Instructional strategies and student activities are categorized into those that have been the traditional mainstays of most classrooms, and those that have been advocated in the curriculum reform literature (for a discussion of these categories, see Burstein et al., 1995). Each strategy or activity has two scores, one (duration) indicating how much time was spent on it during any class period and one (frequency) showing how often it occured during the time that log data were collected.

In examining these classroom activities, we find that lecturing, or whole-class instruction, was still the most frequent teaching strategy, occurring

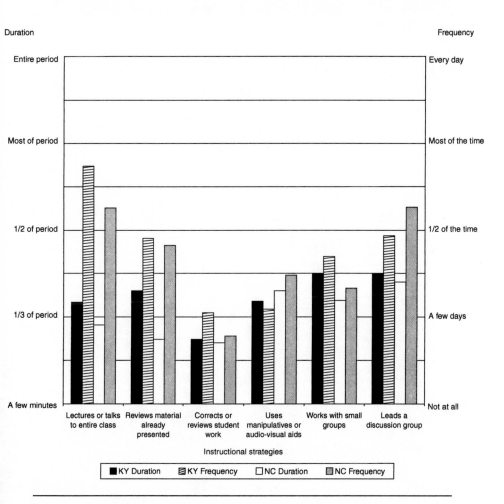

Figure 5.3. Comparison of teachers' instructional strategies in the Kentucky and North Carolina study samples

from about half of to most of the time and taking about one-third of the average period. In addition, teachers spent considerable time reviewing material that had already been presented. However, despite the prominence of these more traditional activities, teachers reported that activities requiring active student participation were also occurring regularly. Notable was the amount of time students spent working in small groups. The overall picture is of a slight preference for more traditional strategies, but an equal reliance on traditional and reform-oriented instructional approaches. The emphasis given to different classroom approaches differed somewhat between the two state samples, but there were no statistically significant differences between the Kentucky and North Carolina teachers in this study in the frequency or duration of their instructional strategies.

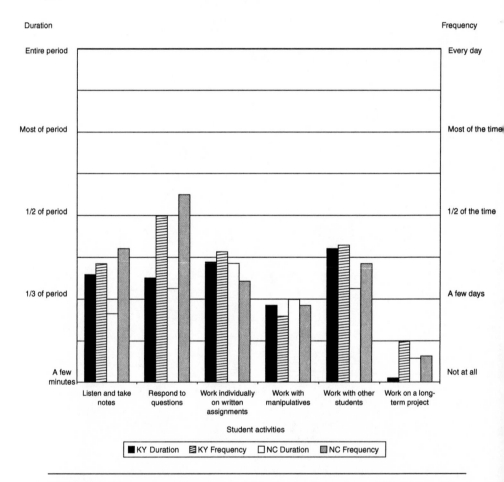

Figure 5.4. Comparison of student activities in the Kentucky and North Carolina samples

Although it appears that teachers across both state samples were balancing reform approaches with more traditional ones, it could be argued that by taking a mean score we were masking substantial variation among teachers, and that some teachers might have used reform-type strategies exclusively and others might have used only traditional approaches. Indeed, fairly large standard deviations suggested a good deal of variation. As a second, "teacher-specific" test, we created two summary scores for each teacher in the two state samples based on the teaching strategies variables. Using the classification scheme developed by Burstein and his colleagues (1995) as a basis, each strategy was first categorized as either traditional, reform, or neutral. Two additive indices were then created using the frequency variables, one indicative of traditional strategies, the second indicative of reform. Each teacher received a summary score reflecting the extent to which he or she used the two strategies. We then subtracted one score from the other to give a summary judgment about the balance (or lack thereof) between strategies in the classroom.[9]

For example, if the average score across the reform variables for a particular teacher were 3 and his or her average score for the traditional variables were also 3, the difference would be 0, indicating that this teacher showed a balance between reform activities and traditional activities. If the reform score for a particular teacher were 5 (the highest) and the traditional score were 1 (the lowest), the difference would be +4, indicating that the teacher heavily favored reform-oriented strategies. In effect, we created a nine-point scale ranging from −4 (very traditional) to +4 (very reform-oriented). The results are displayed in Figure 5.5.

The vast majority of the teachers cluster around 0, indicating that our initial conclusion about a balance between traditional and reform instructional strategies appears to be correct. There is, however, a noticeable tendency toward the negative (traditional) end of the continuum, suggesting that traditional strategies still have an edge in teachers' instructional repertoires. On balance, however, we see a pattern identified in other studies of teachers' responses to and understanding of curricular reforms (for example, Burstein et al., 1995; Cohen and Peterson, 1990). In accepting new instructional approaches, teachers tend not to reject more traditional ones. Rather, they combine the old and the new, adding those aspects of reforms that make sense to them, while still relying on traditional strategies with which they are most comfortable and which they believe have been effective in the past. Consequently, teachers can exhibit traditional and reform instructional approaches simultaneously.

ASSIGNMENTS REFLECTING THE STATE ASSESSMENT. One of the arguments in favor of the new forms of assessment, introduced in the early

1990s, was that they could measure higher-order skills and were linked to specific curricular standards. The expectation was that teachers could teach to these tests, and avoid the curricular narrowing that had occurred when they had geared their instruction to basic skills tests. In fact, because the hope was that these new assessments would change instruction, policymakers and reform advocates expected teachers to teach to the test. Nevertheless, testing experts continued to warn that "excessive reliance reliance on direct test preparation runs the risk of inflating scores (and siphoning limited instructional time away from other activities)" (Koretz et al., 1996, p. 43).

We asked the teachers in both states to submit examples of assignments that they felt were similar to the state assessment in purpose and format, including any assignments that they took directly from the state-released items. We asked that they submit all assignments from the entire semester that they felt most reflected the state assessment. On average, only 43 percent of the assignments were, in fact, similar to the state assessment. The breakdown by state is more striking, with only 32 percent of the North Carolina "most similar" assignments judged by our coders to be similar to the state

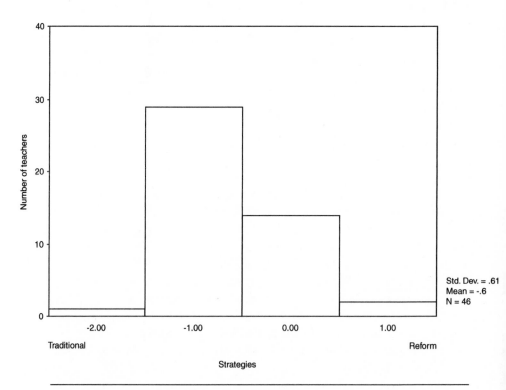

Figure 5.5. Balance between reform and traditional strategies

assessment, compared with 53 percent for Kentucky. We assumed that the assignments judged by teachers to be "most similar" would most closely mirror the purpose, content, and format of the state assessments and would be the best examples of teaching consistent with state goals. These findings, however, seem to indicate that the teachers in both states lacked complete information about the objectives of their state assessments.[10]

Indeed, there were no significant differences between the Kentucky teachers' everyday assignments and the ones that they thought were closely aligned with the state assessment. We had expected to find that the "most similar" assignments would incorporate more of the state goals than would the everyday assignments, but this proved not to be the case.

In evaluating the assignments that teachers judged as "most similar" to the state assessment, the coders considered whether they paralleled both the format and the purpose of the test. Thus they were judging whether an assignment resembled any of the items on the state assessment and whether it measured student mastery of skills and knowledge tested by on the assessment. Teachers' misjudgments about the similarity of their assignments to the assessment typically stemmed from failing to recognize the full complexity of the skills being measured on the state test. Two examples illustrate the problem. A fourth-grade social studies teacher in Kentucky submitted a "most similar" assignment that required students to locate certain geographical features of states. Although the assignment incorporated geography, it did so in a very basic way, without making the required connections associated with the state learning goal for geography: "Understanding the relationship between people and geography and applying this knowledge in real-life situations." In the same way, a North Carolina seventh-grade mathematics teacher submitted assignments that required students to make basic mathematical computations, with no effort to gauge their understanding of the underlying concepts, the solution process, or how they might apply the algorithms to unfamiliar situations.

We assumed that the variation among teachers (in the extent to which their "most similar" assignments were consistent with the goals of the state test) might be explained by the type of professional development they received in preparation for the new assessment. However, there was no significant correlation between teachers' level of preparation and their ability to identify "most similar" assignments.[11] There were, however, some differences among subject areas. For example, mathematics teachers in both the Kentucky and North Carolina samples were more likely to judge assignments correctly than were teachers in the other two subject areas. One possible reason for this difference was that mathematics teachers had more extensive experience with the kinds of goals embodied in the state assessments, because the NCTM standards had been issued in 1989. These had become the exemplar for curricular and assessment standards in a number of states, including Kentucky and North Carolina. Professional associations in the other subject areas issued their standards several years later, often without the wholesale state adoption that had characterized the mathematics standards.

CONSISTENCY WITH KENTUCKY'S AND NORTH CAROLINA'S STATE-SPECIFIC GOALS. Up to this point, teachers' instructional artifacts have been compared with the state tests using similar criteria that, while compatible with each state's assessment, are quite general. A more precise test of the extent to which teaching was consistent with state policy goals is a comparison of teachers' assignments with the specific learning goals and academic expectations that Kentucky outlined in its curriculum framework, *Transformations,* and with the competency goals included in North Carolina's *Standard Course of Study.*

However, because the study samples for the two states are small, the analysis is less precise and largely qualitative. Although the sample includes a large number of assignments, once it is disaggregated by state and subject, the numbers are too small to allow for robust, quantitative comparisons. In addition, the assignments represent the work of only a small number of teachers. For example, the Kentucky sample includes 213 regular class assignments, but when those are disaggregated by subject, there are only about 70 per subject, and they are drawn from eight language arts teachers, eight social studies teachers, and seven mathematics teachers. To further complicate the situation, North Carolina's competency goals, with their even more detailed objectives, or "subparts," make it very difficult to systematically measure the consistency of assignments with specific goals.[12]

In order to maximize the number of teachers and assignments analyzed, we first examined two Kentucky goals that applied to all subjects. Table 5.1 summarizes the extent to which these common goals were reflected in the teaching of the Kentucky sample. The mean for most of these state goals is about 2, indicating that the goal was reflected *in a few* assignments. There are several exceptions, however; Goals 6.2 and 6.3 have noticeably higher means than do the others. This is not too surprising with respect to Goal 6.2; the substantive content as well as the broad phrasing suggest that it would be included more frequently in assignments. However, Goal 6.3 had the highest mean of all, with about 63 percent of the Kentucky sample requiring students to make connections between knowledge already acquired and new knowledge in half or more of their assignments. The notable exception on the low end is Goal 5.5, with more than half of the teachers not reflecting it in any of their assignments.

Table 5.1. Consistency of classroom assignments with Kentucky's critical thinking goals (in percent)

	Goal 5.1[a]	Goal 5.3[b]	Goal 5.5[c]	Goal 6.1[d]	Goal 6.2[e]	Goal 6.3[f]
1. Not reflected in any assignment	26	32	52	50	23	11
2. Reflected in a few assignments	48	55	43	40	41	26
3. Reflected in about half of the assignments	22	14	5	5	27	47
4. Reflected in a substantial majority of the assignments	4	0	0	5	9	11
5. Reflected in all or almost all assignments	0	0	0	0	0	5
Mean (SD) on the five-point scale above	2.04 (.82)	1.82 (.60)	1.52 (.60)	1.65 (.81)	2.23 (.92)	2.74 (.99)

N=213 class assignments from 23 teachers.
a. Students use critical thinking skills to solve a variety of problems in real-life situations.
b. Students organize information to develop or change their understanding of a concept.
c. Students use problem-solving processes to develop solutions to complex problems.
d. Students connect knowledge and experiences from different subject areas.
e. Students use what they already know to acquire new knowledge and develop new skills.
f. Students make connections between existing knowledge and new knowledge.

One example from a Kentucky fourth-grade teacher illustrates how a particularly innovative teacher could incorporate critical thinking skills into her assignments. The teacher used a social studies unit on Pilgrim stories as a base for different activities. One assignment that exemplified Goal 5 was a worksheet to be completed by students after reading a story in which characters faced a moral dilemma: Should they take food that was not theirs if they planned to pay for it later? The worksheet asked the students to divide what they had read into four categories: facts, opinions, inferences, and assumptions. In addition, the students were asked what additional information they would like to have. The emphasis here was similar to Kentucky learning Goals 5.3 and 5.4. The students were required both to organize information as a way to develop their understanding, and to use decision-making processes to make informed decisions. That the students were asked to make distinctions between facts and opinions is of particular note. The students were also asked to make a list of possible options, as well as to predict the consequences of each. This type of activity clearly reflected Goal 5.1, which emphasizes analytical skills applied to real-life situations.

Learning Goals 5 and 6 required that teachers present material in new ways and help students to gain deeper conceptual understanding of that material. It is not surprising that these substantive goals tended to be reflected in teachers' assignments less often than the activity-based goals, such as having students write more or work in groups. Although having students work productively in groups takes skill and planning, it is probably easier than teaching students problem-solving skills that allow them to develop solutions to complex problems and to acquire academic content knowledge at the same time.[13]

Keeping in mind that we are talking about only a few teachers and a smaller number of assignments when we compare by subject area, we now turn to Kentucky's subject-specific goals. A significantly higher proportion of the mathematics assignments reflected the state mathematics goals than did the language arts and social studies assignments reflect state goals in those two areas. On average, the state mathematics goals were found in slightly more than half of the mathematics teachers' assignments, while social studies teachers incorporated the social studies expectations into only a few of their assignments. The language arts goals were also reflected in only a few of the daily assignments, although slightly more than in social studies. While we can only speculate on why the mathematics teachers' assignments were more consistent with state goals, we again suspect that it was due to the influence of the NCTM standards, which were clearly reflected in the state goals. More instructional materials reflecting these goals were available, thus giving mathematics teachers greater guidance than was available to those teaching the other two subjects.

Although the small numbers mean that the results are only suggestive, a pattern was evident across the Kentucky teachers' instruction. Teachers' assignments and instructional strategies were more likely to reflect the classroom activities associated with curricular reform—such as more student writing and a greater emphasis on student-directed learning—than the deeper conceptual understandings associated with helping students acquire critical thinking skills in the context of academic content knowledge. To the extent that state learning goals were reflected in the assignments of the teacher sample, traditional goals associated with learning mathematical procedures and improving reading comprehension were more prevalent than those that required the acquisition of sophisticated content knowledge (for example, statistics, using appropriate forms in writing).

The mathematics teachers in the North Carolina sample tended to stress patterns, relationships, and problem-solving in their assignments. They placed relatively little emphasis on understanding the collection, presentation, and interpretation of data, and on measurement, even though the state had stressed "real-world" applications in its curriculum and assessments. The social studies teachers stressed geographic concepts and themes in their assignments significantly more than any other competency goal. Our interviews suggested that this relatively greater attention to geography may have been due to the inclusion of map-related items on the end-of-grade tests. Several social studies teachers mentioned that not only did they now have to pay more attention to strengthening the map-reading skills of their students, but that the skill had to be taught holistically, with an emphasis on the practical applications of map-reading (knowing "how you get from here to there").

The language arts teachers in the North Carolina sample paid considerable attention to communication strategies in their assignments, but they placed little emphasis on helping students to learn how to assess the validity and quality of information. The emphasis on communication strategies was not surprising, since they related directly to two key foci of the end-of-grade test: student writing and reading comprehension. In fact, several language arts teachers in our sample were explicitly using various preparation strategies as part of their writing instruction. At the same time, teaching students to assess the quality of information and ideas would seem crucial to improving their writing. We can only speculate on possible reasons for the difference in emphasis, but it does seem easier to teach elementary and middle school students to outline and summarize new facts, information, and ideas than to distinguish between representations of fact and of opinion. The challenge for most teachers at the time of our data collection was to encourage students who typically did not like to write to write more than a few words in response to writing prompts. Consequently, what seemed to be rather straightforward writing strategies presented major challenges for many students.

The Effect of Testing on Teaching: Results from Other Recent Studies

The inferences that can be drawn from analyzing these Kentucky and North Carolina teachers and their instructional artifacts are limited because of the small sample sizes. Nevertheless, this research has distinct advantages compared with many traditional implementation studies, for several reasons. It is explicitly comparative in focus, looking systematically across two states that chose very different approaches to assessment. In addition, it attempted to validate teachers' self-reports about changes in instruction with an examination of their actual classroom assignments. Still, because data collection is so intensive and expensive, studies such as the one reported here will necessarily be based on small samples. While they provide valid pictures of the effects of policy on the classrooms studied, it is unclear whether they reflect the true effects of that policy in all the schools and classrooms subject to it.

One way to compensate for this shortcoming is to examine other recent studies that have measured the effect of testing on teaching. Some have focused on the effect of KIRIS, while others have examined testing in other states. Some are based on surveys of representative teacher samples; others have used observational techniques or the analysis of instructional artifacts; while others have relied on a combination of techniques. Although these studies vary somewhat in their results, all have identified outcomes sufficiently similar to suggest that the Kentucky and North Carolina results are generalizable, at least in their overall patterns. This section summarizes these other studies, and discusses their broad implications for the ability of testing policies to change classroom behavior.

Three other studies have examined the effect of KIRIS on classroom practice. All are based on data collected several years after the research reported in the previous section. Consequently, they provide an overview of KIRIS's effects further along in the implementation process. Kelley (1998) interviewed teachers in 1996 in 16 Kentucky schools selected to represent the range of KIRIS award patterns, including some that had received awards, others that were improving but fell short of their goals, and others that were "in decline" because they fell below their baseline scores. In contrast to those in low-success schools, teachers in schools that had received awards reported aligning their curriculum with the state curricular goals. These schools were also characterized by a focus on test-taking skills that placed a heavy emphasis on teaching writing across the curriculum, and by teacher professional development programs concentrated on student skills specified in the state accountability goals. However, teachers reported that they were motivated to change their teaching practices not because of the potential for monetary awards, but "more by a fear of sanctions, by positive public recognition, and by an interest in seeing students achieve" (p. 314).

Wolf and her colleagues (2000) collected data in four "exemplary schools" identified by Kentucky educators as places "where good things were happening" in the reform movement. The researchers visited each school three times between the spring of 1997 and the spring of 1998, interviewing teachers and principals, observing writing and mathematics teachers in their classrooms, and collecting instructional artifacts (including teacher lesson plans and student work).

The teachers in these exemplary schools reported having changed their classroom practice, and the researchers found that they were teaching to KIRIS, but also teaching "beyond it." For example, teachers indicated that before KERA, they had taught writing more as a grammatical skill than as an opportunity for self-expression. When personal narratives became one of the KIRIS writing portfolio requirements, teachers began including them in the curriculum. However, the researchers concluded that teachers "taught the genre not as one more hoop to jump through, but as a unique opportunity for written expression" (p. 379). They also found that teachers were teaching more consistently with the deeper aspects of the curricular reform, rather than just its more superficial manifestations in KIRIS—a characteristic likely related to the schools' exemplary status. Even though two of these schools were in poor rural areas, all four had strong teaching staffs and histories of innovation that were augmented by the additional professional development resources KERA provided.

The final study of the effects of KIRIS was based on two surveys of a state representative sample of fourth-and seventh-grade writing teachers and fifth-and eighth-grade mathematics teachers conducted in 1996–97 (n = 391) and 1997–98 (n = 365) (Stecher et al., 1998; Stecher and Barron, 1999). Although no attempt was made to validate teacher self-reports, the survey findings are quite consistent with the more in-depth investigations of smaller samples. For example, in the first survey, more than 75 percent of the fifth-grade mathematics teachers reported integrating math with other subjects at least once a month, and two-thirds reported integrating math with writing at least once a week. The high proportion of teachers combining some work across subjects is almost exactly the same as in our sample of mathematics teachers, while the relatively low incidence of reported integrated assignments is consistent with the low incidence of interdisciplinary assignments identified in the Kentucky and North Carolina samples. Similarly, the surveyed teachers reported using a combination of traditional and reform or standards-based activities in much the same way as was evidenced in the instructional artifact sample. In addition, a majority of mathematics teachers reported that the state standards embodied in *Transformations,* the state's mathematics curriculum documents, and KIRIS portfolio and open-response items all had a "great deal of influence" on the content of their teaching.

In analyzing the second survey, Stecher and Barron (1999) found that teachers allocated instructional time in ways that reflected which subjects KIRIS tested at a particular grade level, with some tested subjects receiving 50 percent to 60 percent more instructional time in tested grades than in non-tested ones. The authors concluded that teachers changed their classroom behaviors in ways consistent with the skills and content that KIRIS tested. At the same time, however, teachers focused more on the demands of the test than on the broader curricular goals KERA sought to promote across the entire curriculum and the educational system as a whole.

From all these studies, then, a consistent picture emerges of the effects of KIRIS on teaching. Teachers changed their classroom instruction to reflect the curricular values underlying KIRIS. They introduced the reform-oriented instructional activities that were being tested in KIRIS, most notably through the emphasis on writing in portfolios and open-ended items. Teachers combined more traditional instructional strategies and classroom activities with reform-oriented ones, but the degree to which they were able to do so at levels reflecting deep understanding of the curricular goals depended on their professional capacity and that of their schools.

Although there are no other studies of the effects of North Carolina's end-of-grade tests on classroom teaching, several studies based on other states substantiate our finding that hortatory testing policies may have as significant an effect on teacher behavior as those that result in tangible consequences. Firestone and his colleagues (1998) examined the effect of state tests on eighth-grade mathematics teaching in Maryland, where schools with consistently declining scores can be reconstituted, and in Maine, which attaches no consequences to its assessment. The researchers collected data on four Maryland schools and six in Maine during the 1994–95 school year; they interviewed a combined total of 82 teachers, principals, and district officials and twice observed the classrooms of teacher respondents, for a total of 91 observations.

The findings from this comparative study are quite similar to the one comparing Kentucky and North Carolina teachers. Although more Maryland teachers than Maine teachers changed their content coverage in response to the state's test, shifts in teaching practices across the two states were comparable. Despite the changes, however, the instructional strategies used by teachers in the two state samples were slanted toward the traditional. Nevertheless, within this traditional framework, teachers used strategies relevant to the state tests, such as hands-on activities, manipulatives, and group work.

The authors concluded that performance-based assessments of the type used in Maryland and Maine can change specific classroom behaviors and procedures to a limited extent. Although the assessments may motivate teachers to change their practices, they do not necessarily give them the opportunity and capacity to (for example) develop the deep understandings necessary "to help students learn to reason mathematically while calculating accurately" (p. 112). Consequently, most of the classroom observations in the Maine and Maryland samples revealed traditional approaches, with teachers explaining to students how to solve small problems and students then practicing those calculations. Only a small minority of the observational data (20 percent or less) involved students applying mathematical concepts and procedures to new situations or working to solve larger, more complex problems.

A final study, useful for understanding the effects of a state assessment on classroom behavior, was not specifically designed for that purpose. Rather, for more than a decade, it tracked the implementation of California's effort to improve elementary school mathematics teaching through the use of curriculum frameworks (Cohen and Peterson, 1990; Cohen and Hill, 2001).[14] Because CLAS was administered during this period, the study provides insight into its effect, albeit short-lived, on classroom teaching, and on the role that state assessments can play in larger curricular reforms. In 1994–95, survey data were collected from a state representative sample of 595 second-through fifth-grade teachers.

From these data, Cohen and Hill (2001) were able to construct a scale they called "Attended to CLAS" that measured teachers' self-reported attitudes toward CLAS and the extent to which it had changed their teaching. Respondents' scores on the scale were largely a function of whether or not they had administered the test to students or had participated in activities that provided them information about CLAS (for example, staff development, pilot testing, and assessment scoring). "Attended to CLAS," in turn, was significant in predicting whether teachers reported having conventional ideas about mathematics teaching and engaged in practices compatible with those ideas, or whether they subscribed to the reform ideas underlying the state mathematics framework and used practices consistent with the framework. The relationship was in the expected direction: teachers' familiarity with CLAS made them more likely to accept and to use reform approaches to mathematics teaching.

Cohen and Hill were also able to examine the relationship between teachers' involvement in CLAS activities, their reported teaching practices, and student scores on the 1994 fourth-grade CLAS. The authors caution that their analysis is only exploratory because the relationships are difficult to model, and only one year's scores could be used. Nevertheless, they found that schools in which teachers reported classroom practice geared more to the state framework had higher average scores on the mathematics portion of the 1994 fourth-grade CLAS, even after controlling for the schools' demographic characteristics. Similarly, teachers' attendance at curricular workshops and opportunities to learn about CLAS positively affected students' test scores. Cohen and Hill note that only about 10 percent of California's elementary teachers had substantial opportunities to learn about the new mathematics instruction embodied in the state framework and CLAS. Consequently, while this small group of teachers reported more innovative classroom practice, for most teachers, "a few new practices were added around a quite conventional pedagogical core" (p. 154).

Despite their different research methods and different state samples, the five studies summarized in this section and the earlier one comparing Kentucky and North Carolina teachers show very similar results. Classroom practice did change in response to state assessments that espoused particular curricular philosophies, and these changes seem to have occurred whether or not the state used the test to impose meaningful consequences on schools. At the same time, the extent of change was limited. It depended heavily on the nature of the professional development opportunities offered to teachers and it typically involved shifts in classroom activities rather than in how students were taught conceptual understandings of subject matter.

Conclusions

The data presented in this chapter suggest that testing policies can prompt teachers to change their modes of instruction in ways consistent with the theoretical assumptions that define hortatory policy. In the Kentucky and North Carolina cases, teachers neither fully understood nor completely accepted the aims of the state assessments. Nevertheless, the perception that KIRIS and the end-of-grade tests would produce positive benefits for students—combined with the glare of public scrutiny in North Carolina and the threat of sanctions in Kentucky—led them to change their classroom practices. While some teachers were skeptical or even critical of their state's assessment policy, they never mobilized in opposition to it as some parents and members of the public had. The teachers' responses provide an indication of the extent to which targets need to accept a policy's underlying values if it is to work as a hortatory instrument. In cases such as the assessment policies, whole-hearted acceptance of critical values may not be necessary as long as strong opposition does not form in the target group, and as long as the group perceives that there are other incentives or reasons for it to act. Those incentives can include a major reference group endorsing the values, a situation that might help explain why mathematics teachers who were familiar with the NCTM standards seemed to be teaching more consistently with the state tests' curricular values. But another incentive emerges from the informational aspect of hortatory policies: they are often designed to produce information that will be publicly available and that is intended to motivate a range of targets to act on it.

In the North Carolina, Maine, Maryland, and California cases, it appeared that the ability of the state assessment to generate information for public review was as powerful an incentive as the threat of sanctions was in Kentucky. Teachers acknowledged that they cared about public judgments of them and their schools, whether they came from test-score reporting in the newspaper or informal discussions among colleagues and parents. The fact that teachers responded in similar ways to these very different policy instruments raises the question of whether the additional threat of serious sanctions or the promise of substantial rewards significantly increases teachers' incentives. The growing emphasis on high stakes testing implies that policymakers believe that tangible consequences will strengthen teachers' motivations to teach consistently with state curricular standards. In essence, the message of recent assessment policies is that hortatory instruments alone are not sufficient incentives to change classroom behavior.[15]

The conclusion that hortatory assessment policies are inadequate on their own is probably correct, but the reason may have less to do with teachers' incentives to act than with their capacity to do so. Transforming the essence of instruction through assessment is not a self-implementing reform. The assessment itself does not carry within it sufficient guidance for teachers to change; all they really get from the assessment are whatever clues they can glean from released test items. Using state assessments to alter instruction can be effective only if it is supported by a strong infrastructure of teacher training and instructional materials. As Cohen and Hill (2001) argue, the success of policies that seek to change what and how teachers teach depends on the extent to which teachers are given extended opportunities to learn new curricular approaches. Yet one finding consistent across a variety of studies of curricular reforms and testing is that teachers rarely are given such opportunities. Most professional development opportunities are brief and focus on the specifics of a state test, rather than on its broader curricular implications. Even in a state such as Kentucky, where teacher professional development was a high priority, the investment in capacity-building fell short of the need. Consequently, it is not surprising that the changes that did occur in most classrooms were quite shallow.

One of the defining characteristics of hortatory policy that makes this strategy so appealing to elected officials is its seemingly low costs borne primarily by policy targets. The studies reviewed in this chapter vividly demonstrate this dimension of hortatory policy, but they also illustrate that policy costs are often not fully visible until well after a policy is operative. Policymakers in these cases understood that state assessments, intended to shape classroom practice, involved more than just test design, administration, and scoring. However, they failed to understand and acknowledge the full range of costs associated with preparing teachers to act consistently with the curricular values that the assessments embodied.

6

Aligning Politics, Policy, and Practice

Anyone who has followed student testing policy during the past decade would probably agree that it has become highly politicized. At the same time, many observers, particularly professional educators, argue that politics has compromised, if not corrupted, the educational functions of testing and that assessment should be removed from the political arena. This book has taken a different perspective. Rather than view the politics of testing as an aberration that diverts attention from assessment's educational functions, it has examined student testing through an explicitly political lens, and has shown that assessment policy cannot be understood independently of its persuasive and political functions.[1]

In this chapter, the implications of the California, Kentucky, and North Carolina cases are discussed in light of the current politics of high stakes testing. The chapter revisits the three arguments introduced in Chapter 1, and recommends strategies for reconciling the political and educational demands on student testing. A final section outlines the significance of this study for the design of hortatory policies in other issue areas.

Today's opponents of standardized testing may have different reasons for their opposition than the opponents of 10 years ago had, yet calls for either the abolition of state assessments or greater restrictions on their use continue. Nevertheless, the use of assessments is widespread and unlikely to diminish as a tool of education reform any time soon. Two powerful reasons explain why. First, along with vouchers and other forms of parental choice, standards and assessment are currently the only big ideas animating discussions about education reform. Consequently, policymakers wishing to address their constituents' concerns about school quality would have few alternatives from which to choose if they were to diminish testing's preeminence as a reform strategy. A second, related reason stems from the need for a broadly acceptable mechanism to ensure the political accountability of schools and to allocate scarce resources in a seemingly fair and impartial way. Although policymakers and the public appear to understand

176

that tests are limited in the quality and comprehensiveness of the information they produce, large majorities continue to support their use, partly because no alternatives have been identified to serve these critical political functions. Therefore, it makes sense in the current context to focus on improving existing assessment systems since the basic concept is likely to persist in one form or another. Recognizing the values that underlie assessment policies and understanding how such policies operate to change behavior are crucial in any effort to improve them.

Viewing Student Assessment through a Political Lens

This book argued first that standardized tests, despite their traditional function as tools for measuring student and school performance, are also strategies for pursuing a variety of political goals. The history of state testing policies during the past decade has demonstrated the validity of this assumption: the psychometric and political objectives of student testing are now linked in a tight, but uneasy, relationship. Consequently, state assessments cannot be considered independently of their political functions. Those functions stem from the schools' status as public institutions legitimated and funded by the citizens of a state and therefore accountable to them and to their elected representatives. The specifics of how this relationship should operate have long been in dispute. As this book has illustrated, one of the most enduring issues continues to be how citizens' diverse and often conflicting preferences for what schools should teach ought to be weighed, particularly in relation to the judgments of professional educators. State policymakers have decided in the case of testing that schools should be held accountable to externally imposed standards, and that information should be produced to make schooling more transparent to parents and the public. It is due to public education's standing as a democratic institution, then, that student testing has come to serve a significant political function.

Part of that function is a symbolic one. Assessment policies send a message to educators that the schools' performance is a high priority and that their work will be publicly scrutinized. At the same time, these policies also serve instrumental purposes: they are premised on assumptions about how to induce change in classrooms and are designed to improve student achievement. Today's policies are rooted in the same assumptions and goals as those formulated a decade ago. They share a common definition of the problem to which standards and assessment are the solution—namely, inadequate and unequal educational achievement. This framing has broad-based appeal, most recently evident in the passage of NCLB. However, as the history of state assessments suggests, implementation may be difficult and problematic.

Although different groups with an interest in education may agree about the nature of the problem, they often disagree about its causes and the specific solutions. One major source of disagreement involves the extent to which solutions should be designed and imposed by politicians, rather than educators. State and federal policymakers recognize that they have limited strategies for effecting change at the classroom level, but they continue to view such interventions as part of their responsibilities to their constituents. Consequently, they have chosen three related strategies to influence classroom instruction: (1) statewide academic standards and standardized assessments to measure student performance on those standards; (2) greater transparency within public education through requirements to make information about schools more widely and systematically available; and (3) the imposition of rewards and sanctions based on test scores and other data.

Even when policymakers emphasize the third strategy and the results of state assessments have tangible consequences, much of their force depends on whether the social and curricular values they embody are broadly accepted by parents, educators, students, and the public. With the growth of high stakes state testing and the passage of NCLB, the emphasis has moved from assessment policy as a tool to influence instruction toward its uses as an accountability device. Although curriculum debates about the most effective ways to teach mathematics and reading continue (Loveless, 2001), they are now less intense. The politics of testing is now less about curricular values and more about whether some students are unfairly disadvantaged by high stakes tests and their consequences. Values now focus on whether performance standards are reasonable and whether high stakes tests are effective tools for improving learning that are used in ways that are fair to all students and schools. The underlying pedagogical theories have become less important, both as a policy motivator and as a focus of political debate. Nevertheless, newer testing policies continue to be based on state curriculum standards, and recent federal and state policies articulate clear preferences for particular approaches to teaching subjects such as reading. The experience of the 1990s suggests that ignoring these political dimensions of testing policy jeopardizes a policy's survival and its potential effectiveness.

The political and technical dimensions of testing come together in the question of whether the emphasis on academic standards and assessment during the past decade has resulted in higher test scores that represent real gains in student learning. Unfortunately, the answer at this time is that we really do not know. Consequently, decisions about continuing to rely on assessments as a reform strategy will primarily be political ones, since the available evidence about testing's effectiveness is limited. The issue is not just the interpretation of test scores, but also the extent to which policy can shape educational change.

While acknowledging that test scores still are not as high as they should be and that the gap between Caucasian students and students of color persists, most states have proclaimed that test scores have risen during the past decade and have suggested that the rise is due at least partly to the standards-based reforms they have implemented. Scholarly reviews of the data have been considerably more cautious, yet have generally agreed with the states' basic conclusions. For example, in their review of recent research on the effects of state accountability systems, Hanushek and Raymond (2002) conclude:

> The clearest story is simply that schools do in fact respond to accountability systems. When introduced, schools appear from the outcomes that are observed to react to the varying incentives . . . In most cases studied, the introduction of a performance system will in fact lead to achievement improvements. Moreover, the response not surprisingly is more concentrated on the aspects of learning that are measured and assessed as opposed to those that are not. (p. 31)

At the same time, the authors note that the newness of the current versions of most state accountability systems limits the scope of analysis, and they point to evidence that schools attempt to "game" the system through actions (such as excluding some students from testing) that may raise test scores but not really improve students' overall achievement.

Currently, the research evidence for state assessment systems making a positive difference in student learning is ambiguous at best. Part of that ambiguity stems from questions about what test scores really mean. Researchers have offered a variety of caveats on the interpretation of test score gains, with one of the most serious being the possibility of score inflation. As we saw in Chapter 3, questions were raised about the validity of test score gains in Kentucky because they were significantly greater than those demonstrated by Kentucky students on both the ACT and NAEP during the same time period (Koretz and Barron, 1998). A study of score trends on the Texas Academic Assessment System (TAAS) raised similar questions about the widely touted gains on that test (Klein et al., 2000).[2]

Although assertions about the existence and extent of widespread score inflation remain in dispute and await more systematic research, it is reasonable to assume that there are significant limits on the validity of the inferences that can be drawn from scores on state assessments, particularly as their consequences for schools and students have increased. As noted in previous chapters, considerable evidence indicates that in response to state assessments, schools stress tested subjects and skills more than non-tested ones, and teachers frame more of their teaching to reflect the tests' foci and formats. Such teaching behaviors make the state assessment less accurate as a basis for inferring what students actually know. In this context, reported achievement gains can be misleading because they may reflect not general mastery of a subject, but mastery of only those aspects of it emphasized on the assessment. In sum, strong circumstantial evidence suggests that increases in state test scores are inflated, but the data are imprecise. Even those researchers most associated with identifying the problem have argued that "methods for evaluating the validity of gains obtained under high stakes conditions are poorly developed," and have not kept pace with the expansion of large-scale, high stakes testing (Koretz, McCaffrey, and Hamilton 2001, p. 1). This lack of systematic, precise data contributes to technical considerations being sidelined in political decisions about testing.

Ideally, decisions about testing's effectiveness as a reform strategy should rest on more than the validity of scores. Even if scores can be shown to be meaningful indicators of students' learning, an additional question remains about the extent to which standards and assessment policies are responsible for improvements in student test scores. It is always difficult to assess the independent effect of any policy intervention, and it is especially problematic with standards and assessments because in many states other significant policies are implemented at the same time. In California, for example, a variety of policies—including class-size reductions, a major change in bilingual education, and significant shifts in the reading and mathematics curricula—all were implemented during the 1990s. Consequently, it is next to impossible to ascertain exactly what effect either CLAS or the shift to high stakes testing had on student scores. Likewise in Kentucky, KIRIS may have been the centerpiece of KERA, but it was implemented simultaneously with other reforms that increased the resources available to schools, restructured the primary grades, and brought a variety of social services into schools. Conversely, as some commentators have argued, if test scores do not improve or improve too slowly, a number of factors, including ones beyond the control of schools, may be more responsible than standards and assessment policies (Rothstein, 2002).

It is in this context—high political visibility for assessment policy coupled with technical ambiguity about its effects—that we need to consider the implications of states' experience with standardized testing in the 1990s.

Moving from Politics to Policy and Practice

This book's second argument focused on the informational and curricular values dimensions of student testing. In an analysis premised on the assumption that information and values are critical in advancing state education policy goals, the previous chapters illustrated the theory of hortatory policy and the limits of this strategy. To a large extent, state assessments represent a successful application of the theory and its causal assumptions. Information about student performance was disseminated in more systematic and public ways, and curricular values were promulgated and appealed to through state standards frameworks, instructional materials, and state assessments. Despite focused resistance from some groups, and teachers' limited ability to respond, classroom behaviors changed. Furthermore, even if the results are still in question, student test scores are generally moving in a direction consistent with the policy's intended goals. Yet in the cases analyzed, the path to even a partial validation of this policy theory was strewn with significant obstacles, and together these cases illustrate several of the most significant conditions that limit the use of hortatory policy in education.

Those limiting conditions can best be understood as a series of tradeoffs in which officials must balance key elements of the policy strategy so as to advance their goals while minimizing unintended consequences. For example, value appeals have to be strong enough to motivate action, but not so strong that they divide potential targets. The values invoked must also be sufficiently general to have broad appeal, but if they are too general in the messages they send, targets may lack adequate guidance about exactly what is expected of them. Similarly, hortatory policies are often chosen as alternatives to other types of instruments because they may be more politically palatable, less costly, and more respectful of the professionals charged with implementing them than policy strategies based on the imposition of tangible consequences. Yet relying solely on hortatory strategies may fail to motivate targets adequately, or may leave willing targets with insufficient capacity to meet a policy's intended objectives. The implications and lessons discussed in this section and the next point to the importance of understanding such tradeoffs and how their effects can be reduced.

The recent history of state assessments suggests three perspectives from which to consider the design of education policy. The first stems from the fact that many of the older policies were hortatory in design, grounded in a set of values about the goals and methods of schooling and aimed at persuading participants to buy into those values. Second, standards and assessment policy, like most education policies, is formulated by politicians at one governmental level and then implemented in schools and classrooms several levels below that. Third, assessments generate information that is used differently by actors at different levels of the system. Consequently, efforts to improve such policies must consider political imperatives, norms of educational practice, and the uses of test data. Each perspective and the lessons it generates is discussed below.

Political Imperatives and Policy Design

Several points become relevant when we think about standards and assessment as hortatory policy. Above all, it is important to keep in mind that even though newer policies such as NCLB are high stakes, they still embody a set of ideas and values about educational goals and the strategies for achieving those goals. Those ideas include the beliefs that schools should be held publicly accountable for their students' academic performance and that the achievement gap between affluent and poor students and among students from different ethnic groups can be closed by mandating that states establish academic standards, test all students on those standards, publish school-level scores, and impose consequences on those that do not improve. As commentators have noted, the ideas behind NCLB integrate the traditionally liberal goal of greater educational equity and a policy focus on poor children with conservative strategies of choice and competition, accountability, and a focus on educational fundamentals (Wilgoren, 2001; Lemann, 2001).

One of the most critical lessons drawn from the recent history of testing is that ideas and values matter. They mattered to those who opposed CLAS and KIRIS, and they mattered to teachers who responded to them by changing their classroom teaching even without the promise of rewards or the threat of sanctions. Admittedly, the power of the tests was buttressed by other education policies premised on similar ideas, and teachers often lacked the capacity to respond to the pedagogical expectations embodied in the standards and assessments. Nevertheless, those values and expectations did work as policy instruments, providing an alternative vision of schooling and persuading people to accept (and sometimes reject) that perspective.

The implications for NCLB and other state assessments is that a more equal balance could be struck between ideas and mandates. The move to high stakes testing reflects a belief that assessments require tangible consequences because neither the values embodied in them nor the information they generate are sufficient in themselves to change classroom behavior and raise student achievement. Yet considerable evidence suggests that public disclosure of test scores and appeals to professional values can change educators' behavior. So it is reasonable to assume that although hortatory instruments are often combined with mandates and inducements, the rush to high stakes testing could be slowed and balanced by a greater emphasis on underlying policy goals. Even if it were proven conclusively that teachers and students require the rewards and sanctions associated with high stakes testing to be sufficiently motivated, there is enough evidence to indicate that an appeal to values can enhance that motivation, at least for teachers. However, because research on the effects of high stakes testing is limited, finds mixed results, and suggests unintended consequences, the informational and persuasive dimensions of testing will continue to be critical to the success of this policy.[3]

NCLB stresses the moral and economic necessity of closing the achievement gap, standards-based strategies for achieving that goal, and the reasons schools should be held accountable to externally imposed standards. Although it is premised on somewhat different values than those animating earlier state testing policies, NCLB can also appeal to teachers' sense of professional responsibility and their interest in appearing competent in their communities. Consequently, even if they decide to maintain a focus on high stakes, policymakers should not forget that appealing to values can be as powerful as imposing consequences.

Regardless of the balance between tangible consequences and hortatory appeals, policymakers' responsibilities do not end with the passage of legislation. Because testing policies serve political as well as educational purposes, elected officials need to exert regular oversight over the experts developing the assessment. This recommendation is not a suggestion that politicians micromanage the test development process. However, legislators who are in regular contact with constituents and who must run for office every few years bring a real-world perspective—sometimes lacking in people who are primarily concerned about effective teaching or the technical quality of the test.

The need to balance a real-world perspective with curricular and psychometric expertise leads to another lesson: The development of new curriculum standards and assessments cannot be solely a technical process with participation limited to experts. This recommendation is not a suggestion that parents become test item writers. But decisions as significant as what knowledge is most important for students to learn, and how they should be tested on their mastery of it, require open, public deliberation.[4] That participation can be organized in any number of ways, including state-level review committees; community forums sponsored by PTAs or the League of Women Voters; informal "coffees" in people's homes; and exchanges on the Internet, radio, and television, and in local newspapers. Clearly, in large, culturally diverse states, reaching acceptable levels of consensus is difficult. But not to try is to make a mockery of the notion of common standards for public schools. Parents and other members of the public who voice concerns about new assessments need to be treated with respect, and not dismissed as either uninformed or politically extreme.

Above all, those responsible for designing new assessments need to recognize that the process is inherently political in the best sense of that word, because it involves public deliberation about what skills and knowledge are most important for a productive life and active citizenship.

Policy Implementation and Norms of Educational Practice

Not surprisingly, the experience of California, Kentucky, and North Carolina has several implications for how testing policies are implemented. Those lessons are similar to ones learned from other studies that have examined the implementation of top-down policy: seemingly inexpensive reforms, from the perspective of policymakers, simply shift the cost and time burden to lower levels of the system; and reforms cannot succeed unless those charged with implementing them have both the will and the capacity to change.

The first lesson is often forgotten or at least ignored by federal and state policymakers, but they need to acknowledge that the lowest levels of the system typically bear the heaviest policy costs. Some of those costs are financial, and the history of testing policy during the past decade illustrates how a seemingly inexpensive policy can impose high costs on local districts and schools that must not only administer tests, but also prepare teachers to teach differently. Enhancing the capacity of local implementors is critical to successful implementation. Yet few states have made the kind of investment necessary for teachers to be truly prepared to reorient their instruction. As was evident in the studies summarized in Chapter 5, even in states such as Kentucky, where substantial funds have been committed to professional development, training was limited. Although most teachers were introduced to the format and scoring of their state tests, many had only cursory exposure to its curricular implications. Consequently, it is not surprising that although a variety of studies have found that teachers do respond to state tests, the changes they make typically involve shifts in classroom activities rather than in how they convey conceptual understandings of subject matter. Unless teachers are provided with substantial opportunities to learn about deeper curricular implications and then to reshape their instruction in light of that knowledge, superficial "test prep" will continue to be the norm.

Although it has only indirect financial implications, time is another cost whose burden is most acutely felt at the local level. Besides illustrating the usual dimensions of capacity-building necessary for any classroom-based reform, this study has also shown the importance of sufficient time for implementation. It seems fair to conclude that with few exceptions, most states have linked the implementation of their assessment systems to political and electoral cycles rather than to educational ones. Even in Kentucky, where policymakers have exhibited considerable patience in "staying the course" for more than a decade and not demanding final results for 20 years, the assessment system was expected to be operational within a very short period. So, as in most states, implementation was compromised by significant time constraints. The same problem is likely to arise with NCLB. Although schools have until 2014 to reach required proficiency levels, states need to make major changes in their assessment systems within four years, and sanctions become operative even sooner.

The issue of time requires skillful balancing by policymakers. It is difficult for them to sell patience to parents worried about the quality of their children's education or to voters without personal knowledge of the schools but skeptical of additional investments in them. Delaying implementation also runs the risk that those invested in the status quo or opposed to new testing regimes will mount opposition or simply dig in their heels and resist change. Yet rushed implementation has led to serious technical problems, undue stress on teachers and students, and an emphasis on testing formats at the expense of clear connections to the broader curriculum.

Most policymakers—especially those who have staked their reelections partly on improved student achievement—may prefer not to heed this advice. However, the only alternative to such problems is to slow the implementation process. New assessments and the systems that undergird them require three to four years for development. In addition, no significant consequences should be imposed on schools or students until an assessment has been thoroughly piloted, its validity and reliability assessed, and necessary modifications made. But a slower, more thoughtful implementation process can work politically only if policymakers can communicate a complex reality to their constituents in understandable and credible terms. The message they must convey is that testing alone will not improve student achievement. Any assessment must be integrated into a comprehensive strategy that provides students with opportunities to be taught by qualified teachers and to learn a rich array of skills and knowledge. Furthermore, even the best tests are only one measure of educational progress. This reality may be apparent to educators and educational researchers, but it is not obvious to the general public or even to many parents. Those politicians who support strong and effective testing regimes need to persuade their constituents of this complexity, while also demonstrating that attention is being paid to educational quality, that schools are moving toward that goal, and that political leaders will stay the course in the face of opposition or resistance to change. This kind of message has been more successfully communicated in other policy areas—ranging from the environment to medical research—suggesting that a much better job can be done in education, and also that the American public is sophisticated enough to hear such a message.

Other costs, in addition to financial burdens and time, are often imposed most heavily on the lowest levels of the educational system. Especially evident from this study is that local districts and schools often bear the brunt of opposition to state assessments. Although protests against mandated assessments may eventually target state or national policymakers, they typically start as grassroots efforts, attempting to change practices in local districts and schools. As such, they can disrupt established relationships between parents and teachers and between schools and communities. The key participants in anti-testing protests are often parents active in their children's schools. When they begin to raise questions that cannot be adequately answered by teachers and school officials, they may trigger concerns and skepticism even among those parents highly supportive of the schools. In the most extreme situation, such as what occurred in some California schools, bonds of trust among parents, teachers, and even students are broken — a high price to pay for schools heavily dependent on parental and community goodwill.

Opposition is likely to be endemic to any policy as value-laden as student testing, and those designing such systems may be unable to discourage it. But they can reduce its costs to local districts. The first way, discussed earlier in this chapter, is to ensure that tests and the policies governing them are formulated through an open, inclusive process. Just as they should meet psychometric and curricular standards, tests should also be defensible to the parents and members of the public to whom schools are accountable. This requirement does not mean that parents or the public should be allowed to act as a veto group, but it does mean that a range of lay citizen views should be represented in the development process. Policymakers and assessment designers also need to be explicit about an assessment's underlying values, format, and potential uses, and to be prepared to defend them. They also need to develop common understandings of the assessment policy's purpose and the information it generates. Local educators and school officials can neither defend a policy's merits nor engage in a thoughtful debate about it if they do not fully understand its intent or share policymakers' vision of what it can accomplish. Building that common understanding should ideally be done before a new test is first administered, and certainly before consequences are imposed. Policymakers should also be prepared to defend policies and possibly modify them in the face of legitimate concerns.

California's and Kentucky's contrasting responses to opposition to their assessments provide another lesson about how states should structure implementation. State assessments are designed primarily to generate publicly available information about educational performance. As such, their operations should be transparent to all interested citizens. Any adult who wishes to see a copy of a test should be allowed to do so as long as he or she signs a statement promising not to disclose its contents. In addition, although resource constraints and the need to reuse items to maintain trend data may prevent states from releasing all test items immediately after each administration, a comprehensive sample should be made publicly available.[5] Enough states have followed these or similar procedures to demonstrate that they are both feasible and politically advisable.

The experience of the past decade has shown that policymakers cannot control how various policy targets will respond to values-based policies, and such policies typically lack frameworks of rules and procedures to structure those responses. Still, policymakers can create processes that make their intent clear, and that allow dissent to be expressed in ways that encourage informed discussion and constructive policy changes. Such processes require time, patience, and leadership, but the payoff is likely to be more durable policy and smoother local implementation.

Just as the various costs imposed by state assessments have multiple implications for future policy implementation, the question of local will and capacity generates a second set of implications and lessons. Past research has consistently shown that policymakers need to consider whether those charged with implementing assessment policies have the will and capacity to do so. The lack of adequate local capacity and the serious need to enhance it have already been discussed. Equally important is the question of local will, especially that of classroom teachers. Research on teachers' willingness to implement testing reforms presents a mixed picture. As we saw in Chapter 5, they have been skeptical about the benefits of such initiatives, but willing to do what is required of them.

This situation raises questions about the long-term effect of assessment policies on teachers' sense of professionalism. Externally imposed assessments vividly illustrate the tension between two competing models of accountability in public education. The first, based on notions of democratic or political control, can be traced back to the Founders and is reflected in the current standards and accountability movement. It assumes that as governmental institutions, schools derive their legitimacy from the consent of the electorate and should be held publicly accountable. This model further assumes that as public employees, educators' behavior should be restricted by externally imposed constraints. A contrasting model stresses professionalism as a basis for accountability. It assumes that educators possess a specialized body of knowledge and that, because their work poses complex and nonroutine problems, their application of that knowledge should be regulated by a code of ethics internal to their profession. In other words, educators should be held accountable using standards and procedures articulated and enforced by their peers, not by externally defined and enforced criteria (McDonnell, 2000).

To the extent that curriculum standards reflect public preferences for what children should learn, and to the extent that assessments shape classroom teaching, they constrain professional judgment and autonomy. Thus, appealing to teachers' sense of professionalism as a motivation for complying with policies such as NCLB can be problematic. Many teachers may comply to avoid public embarrassment and some may do so out of genuine support for the policy's goals, but it may be difficult to develop a deep sense of ownership if teachers feel that NCLB and state assessments compromise their ability to act in the best interests of their students.

Yet, the choice for policymakers is not "either-or" between the political and professional models. Because both embody legitimate values, the challenge is to find an appropriate balance between the two. Even as external accountability measures have been implemented during the past decade, the emphasis on strengthening teaching as a profession has continued, with initiatives such as peer review, academic standards defined by subject-matter groups like NCTM, and increased teacher involvement in curriculum development. The link between these initiatives and the current state of public education is by no means clear. Nevertheless, part of the motivation for current accountability policies is policymakers' perception that although the professional model is necessary if teaching is to attract qualified people, it has not been an adequate mechanism for raising student achievement. Furthermore, they recognize that the downside of strong professional norms can be educators' insulation from the preferences and expectations of the broader political community. Consequently, newer reform policies have stressed the political model, with the balance now shifted in that direction, and popular, lay notions of how schools should be organized coming to the forefront.

Where the balance should be struck between political and professional accountability is partly an empirical question about the conditions that lead to effective classroom behavior, and partly a normative question about who should define and enforce accountability standards. Although the experience of states during the past decade provides only a limited basis for resolving these questions, it does point to several important considerations in deciding how to balance these two visions of education governance.

First, as the analysis in Chapter 5 indicated, teachers typically have only a limited and somewhat diffuse understanding of what policymakers expect assessment initiatives to accomplish. Although they recognize that policymakers see standards and assessment as a strategy for improving educational quality, many teachers are unclear about the dual goals of accountability and curricular change that policymakers often hope to accomplish, and therefore have only a superficial understanding of what is expected of them beyond simply raising test scores. Second, national opinion polls have found that teachers support the high stakes use of tests for student promotion and graduation at about the same rate as the public (Public Agenda, 2001), and that a majority of teachers in states with graduation tests view them as written at appropriate levels with students well-prepared to meet the tests' standards (Belden, Russonello, and Stewart, 2001).[6] At the same time, the overwhelming majority support a system that allows educators to make promotion and retention decisions based on their consideration of test scores, grades, and their personal evaluations of students. Teachers also see significant drawbacks to assessment systems. For example, in an *Education Week*–sponsored poll conducted in 2000, two-thirds of a national sample rejected a statement that state testing was helping focus their teaching on what children really needed to know in favor of one arguing that it was "forcing [them] to concentrate too much on information that will be on the test to the detriment of other important areas." Survey respondents also reported that they had too little time to cover what is in the state standards (Belden, Russonello, and Stewart, 2001). Finally, although systematic data on the scope of the problem are scarce, this study and others have found that state assessments can be a considerable source of stress for teachers and their students, with stories now circulating about teachers leaving the profession or transferring to non-tested grades to avoid the pressure. In sum, policymakers looking ahead to the implementation of NCLB and a new generation of state assessments face a teacher corps generally supportive of this policy strategy, but not completely understanding its full intent; alert to its adverse effect on their teaching, particularly as it relates to their ability to exercise their professional judgment; and already somewhat demoralized by testing's classroom effects. At the same time, most teachers believe that students are now being taught a more demanding curriculum and that educational quality will improve.

The challenge for policymakers is to communicate their goals and intentions more clearly to teachers, while also listening to teachers' "bottom-up" classroom perspectives. This process can happen formally, when policies are being formulated, through structured teacher participation in legislative hearings and agency committees, but it should also happen informally, through school visits and forums when legislators are in their home districts. Each group needs to understand the other's preferences and concerns better than it has in the past decade. Policymakers especially need to consider more carefully what types of incentives are likely to motivate teachers in the longer term—beyond fear of public embarrassment. Teachers need to be persuaded that as public employees, they should be held accountable by means of external standards and mechanisms. But they also need to be convinced that such accountability measures serve the interests of their students and can be accomplished in ways that allow them to exercise reasonable independent judgment about how best to teach individual students. Ideally, if teachers and their representatives are routinely consulted in the design of assessment systems, achieving a balance between political and professional accountability will become a more explicit dimension of education policymaking than it has been in the past. Once implementation of assessment policies begins, policymakers also need to monitor their effect on individual teachers and on the ability of the profession to attract and retain competent people.

The Uses of Test Data

Test use goes to the heart of hortatory policy and the role of information in motivating policy targets to act. A causal assumption underlying hortatory policy is that people cannot act on information unless it is reliable, understandable, and useful to them. In the case of assessment policy, the assumption is that the information produced by standardized tests will motivate students to be more attentive to their learning, teachers to teach more effectively, and ideally, motivate policymakers, parents, and the public to act to improve the schools, or at least to become informed about the status of educational achievement. However, this assumption has different implications if one approaches it from an expert, psychometric perspective rather than from a political one.

Perhaps the area in which the divergence between the two perspectives is greatest is in matching a test and its uses. Even a decade ago, when a higher proportion of state assessments were largely hortatory and imposed no consequences on individual students or schools, policymakers assumed that the same test could be used for multiple purposes. These uses ranged from providing aggregate information about the overall condition of education, to bringing greater curricular coherence to the system, aiding in instructional decisions about individual students, and holding schools and educators accountable. These varied purposes reflect the distinct information needs of different audiences: Policymakers and the public want general information about the status of education in particular communities, including if schools are improving and how they compare on widely accepted standards; parents need information about the academic strengths and weaknesses of their children; and educators require information both about their own students and about the curricular implications of an assessment. The differing detail and levels of aggregation required to accommodate these diverse audiences affects which students are tested, how many items are used to measure their performance, and what levels of reliability and validity are acceptable. Consequently, even under low stakes conditions, it is unlikely that one test can adequately meet all these different information needs.

The problem has become more serious as federal and state policies have moved toward greater high stakes use of assessment data, particularly since most of these policies also assume that one test can be used for multiple purposes. In assuming this, policymakers are at odds with the professional standards of the testing and measurement community. Those standards stress the need to base high stakes decisions on more than a single test, validate tests for each separate use, and provide adequate resources for students to learn the content being tested, among other principles (American Educational Research Association, 2000). In disregarding these standards, policymakers are using assessments in ways that exceed the limits of current testing technology. As the National Research Council's report *High Stakes* noted:

> Policy and public expectations of testing generally exceed the technological capacity of the tests themselves. One of the most common reasons for this gap is that policymakers, under constituent pressure to improve schools, often decide to use existing tests for purposes for which they were neither intended nor sufficiently validated. So, for example, tests designed to produce valid measures of performance only at the aggregate level—for schools and classrooms—are used to report on and make decisions about individual students. In such instances, serious consequences (such as retention in grade) may be unfairly imposed on individual students. That injustice is further compounded if the skills being tested do not reflect or validly measure what students have been taught. (Heubert and Hauser, 1999, p. 30)

The saga of assessment policy and politics during the past decade suggests a major reason for this disjuncture between standards of good testing practice and policymakers' actions. Policymakers often decide to rely on existing tests because they perceive a fleeting political opportunity to act, necessitating that they move quickly while they have an open policy window. Alternatively, they believe that, even with imperfect tests, more good than harm will result. Policymakers often acknowledge that critics of testing systems are making valid points. However, from their perspective, the technical constraints identified by testing experts are problems that should be remedied to the extent possible, but in an iterative fashion simultaneously with the implementation of test-based policy (McDonnell, 1994). Although the political imperative is a dominant motivation, several others were discussed previously in this chapter. Cost is one. Although tests are relatively inexpensive compared with overall expenditures for education, policymakers have been reluctant to invest in multiple tests, especially the more costly ones designed for ongoing classroom-based assessments. In a world of tight fiscal constraints, using the same test for multiple purposes has seemed a defensible economy to many policymakers. Another explanation was alluded to in the discussion of teacher professionalism: policymakers, testing experts, and educators operate in very different worlds, with each group having only a limited understanding of the others' incentives, constraints, and day-to-day work. For many politicians, this lack of understanding means that they are crafting policies with limited knowledge about the nature of teaching, learning, and testing.

There is no easy solution to the tension between political imperatives and professional standards that is so evident in questions of test use. Mitigating this tension requires that policymakers become more accepting of the limitations of tests and their potential uses. To some extent, they have done so by incorporating provisions in their policy designs that reflect professional testing standards. For example, although test scores remain the dominant data source for the state and local report cards mandated by NCLB, the legislation also requires that states report on other measures of educational quality, including graduation rates and the professional qualifications of teachers. This provision partly addresses the experts' call for multiple measures and for not reducing judgments about educational quality or high stakes decisions to a single test score.

Nevertheless, NCLB's use of "adequate yearly progress" (AYP) — requiring that school-level scores be disaggregated by demographic and educational subgroups and that sanctions be imposed on schools not meeting their targets within two years — remains a source of great concern to testing experts and educators.[7] NCLB's emphasis on assistance to schools needing improvement and supplemental student services is consistent with professional norms of providing adequate resources so students have an opportunity to learn the content on which they are tested. However, because the rate of improvement assumed by the AYP mandate will likely require far more time and resources than are available, NCLB appears to be at odds with professional assessment norms.

The NCLB provisions and their counterparts in state legislation acknowledge some of the technical requirements for appropriate test use. Yet without a fundamental rethinking of the uses of high stakes tests and a time frame that allows testing technology to catch up with policy expectations, political imperatives and professional standards will continue to be at odds. However, the blame does not lie completely with policymakers. The tendency has been for testing experts to identify the shortcomings of current systems by noting what is not working as it should and indicating when harmful or unintended consequences are likely to occur. However, the events of the past decade suggest that if testing experts want their admonitions to be heeded, they may need to move beyond criticism and provide policymakers with feasible alternatives that address the public's desire to have more accountable, responsive, and effective schools.

Like policymakers' accepting the limits of testing, moving from critics to system-builders will be a difficult change for many members of the testing and measurement community. Without compromising their research-based principles, they will need to accept that in a democracy, authority for deciding on the form of testing systems rests with elected officials, and that accountability to the electorate is at least as equally legitimate a claim as scientific knowledge. In the short term, the most effective strategy would be for testing experts to identify changes that could be made within existing assessment systems to make them reasonably consistent with standards of good testing practice. In doing so, testing experts would need to take into account the political incentives that press for information about students and schools that: (1) is valid, comparable, and understandable to the public; (2) can be used to leverage and motivate educators' and students' behavior; and (3) can produce tangible and credible results within a reasonable time frame.

One concrete strategy for achieving a better balance between these two sets of norms is to combine the political and professional oversight of testing and assessment systems. Often in state systems, these functions are separate: expert panels evaluate and advise on the technical aspects of a test, while decisions about its uses are made independently, often by state legislators. More closely integrating the two functions would allow each group to understand better the other's values and concerns, and to consider ways to accommodate the other's perspective. It would also make differences between them and the tradeoffs involved in favoring one perspective over the other more obvious to an assessment system's various publics.

As a technical term, *reliable* or *reliability* refers to the stability or reproducibility of a test's results—that assessments measure student performance consistently across tasks and parallel forms of a test, and on different occasions (Heubert and Hauser, 1999). However, in its more general use among laypeople, *reliable* also calls to mind notions of credibility—that information comes from trustworthy sources, that it is believable and makes sense. One may think of *credibility* from a lay perspective as encompassing expert notions of both reliability and validity (whether a test measures what it purports to measure and what kind of inferences can be drawn from it). But credibility includes more than even these key technical standards. Maintaining credibility with the public also requires that it views state education agencies and local school districts as trustworthy sources of information. Public perceptions will partly depend on how those agencies' overall performance is viewed beyond their function as a source of test scores and other data. However, perceptions are also shaped by how they handle test administration and score reporting. As we saw in the contrasting California and Kentucky cases, how a state agency handles the inevitable problems and conflicts that accompany testing will affect not only its public image, but also that of local districts. Trust and credibility are central to the legitimacy of any assessment system, and they must be considered in designs for test use.

One way is to include capacity-building for greater public understanding as a central component of assessment and accountability systems. Credibility requires that information is understandable to its various targets. If people cannot interpret the data, draw inferences, and apply them in informing their decisions, they are not useful. As noted in Chapter 2, reporting complex data to the public presents significant challenges. Goals of accessibility and ease of use push for reliance on simple statistics and statements—such as single test scores and brief hazard warnings on product labels. Such an approach may not only lead to misinterpretation, but also fail to provide an adequate context for understanding information, and may give users a false sense that there are simple answers to complex questions. For example, the use of a single test score may lead to incorrect assumptions that the score represents the full measure of a student's or school's performance, and it certainly does little to inform targets about the factors that might explain low scores.

Experience has shown that expert caution about test use has not been particularly effective as a remedy for oversimplification, nor has the simple provision of additional data been an especially successful strategy for enhancing public understanding. Informed public understanding of test data and their appropriate uses is unlikely to increase without sustained investment in efforts to increase the capacity of various stakeholders to interpret and apply that data. The necessary investment includes providing indicator data that can give context to test scores and help explain why they are rising or falling—for example, data concerning student demographics, the distribution of qualified teachers and curricular opportunities across schools, and the relationship between these factors and test scores. But more data will be of little use if people lack the tools to understand them. Consequently, key target groups, such as educators, the media, and parent groups, need assistance in understanding accountability system data. This might come in the form of software that allows schools and teachers to disaggregate data, import data from a variety of sources, and then manipulate them in ways that can identify the specific academic strengths and weaknesses of different groups of students and analyze trends.[8] Such software, along with technical assistance to facilitate its use, would both encourage informed school-level decision-making and allow schools to customize the reports they disseminate.

One could also imagine similar databases and software being made available to the media and parent groups, although they would have to be constructed so as to protect the identity of individual students and classrooms. The largest national and regional newspapers already have such analytic capabilities and often publish quite sophisticated analyses of test scores and school quality data, but they are the exception. Smaller media outlets, particularly local television and radio stations, need considerable assistance if they are to report anything more than that test scores are up or down, and that some schools are "winners" and others "losers."

Similarly, few parent groups have the capacity to analyze data in ways that inform their efforts to assist their own children or improve the schools they attend. However, among stakeholder groups, parent groups are some of the most motivated to use test data. We also know from a variety of sources that much of what parents know about schools they learn from teachers and other parents, and that these two sources are viewed as significantly more trustworthy than either the media or elected officials (Public Education Network, 2001). Consequently, parents are a critical link in ensuring that test data are understandable and used appropriately. Yet little is known about the kinds of test-based information parents want most or how they interpret what is available to them. Although officials' ignorance of parental views and perceptions was considerable in the case of CLAS, it was not unusual. As an initial step, then, researchers, policymakers, and educators need to obtain more systematic knowledge about how parents are currently using test data and what types of information and formats they would find most useful. That knowledge could then be used by federal, state, and local governments to invest in strategies to build greater public understanding of test data and more general indicators of educational quality. Those strategies might include broad dissemination of user-friendly software, web sites, workshops, and public information campaigns that could range from television spots to fact-filled placemats in fast-food restaurants.

Most discussions of appropriate test use focus on the technical requirements of reliability and validity and increasingly, on issues of public credibility and understanding. But there is another, more normative dimension that also deserves consideration. That dimension is *fairness*, and it extends questions of appropriate test use beyond reliability and validity to incorporate notions of equity and social justice. In its narrowest sense, fairness refers to a test "that yields comparably valid scores from person to person, group to group, and setting to setting" (Heubert and Hauser, 1999, p. 78). Included in this definition are the absence of cultural bias in tests, and assurances that all examinees are treated equitably during the examination process. However, there is another dimension that has been alluded to several times in this chapter: the opportunity for all students to learn the academic content and skills on which they are tested. If one group of examinees has such an opportunity and another group does not, their scores will have very different meanings and cannot be compared fairly. Furthermore, it would be unjust to impose negative consequences on individuals or groups who have not been given the opportunity to learn the content being tested.

Opportunity to learn (OTL) poses the greatest challenge to the legitimacy of any accountability system because it highlights serious curricular inequities across schools and communities, and it belies the notion that high stakes testing is a relatively inexpensive reform. Although policymakers typically pay lip service to the concept and the standards movement is an attempt to articulate a common set of OTL goals for all students, it is unlikely that the federal government or individual states have the political will or the capacity to ensure that all students are actually afforded equal opportunities to learn (McDonnell, 1995).[9] Consequently, even as testing policies have moved away from their hortatory roots and become high stakes, OTL and fairness standards have not been enforced, nor tangible consequences imposed, on schools that fail to provide their students adequate learning opportunities. If OTL is to remain a professed goal of accountability systems, its advocates must rely on persuasion and appealing to Americans' belief in fair play and equal opportunity.

The belief that accountability is a two-way process that lies at the heart of Americans' social contract with the public schools is perhaps the least visible and broadly accepted aspect of assessment and accountability systems. Nevertheless, it may be the most important value supporting appropriate test use and opportunity to learn. If the relationship between the public and the schools is viewed as a series of mutual obligations, then opportunity to learn becomes a shared responsibility, and accountability requires that schools be held to account for students' learning and that the public and their elected representatives provide the resources to ensure the necessary level of schooling. Test scores and other indicators of educational quality then become not just tools with which to "bash" schools, but also sources of information for determining the extent to which schools and the public have met their responsibilities. Assessment policies will work as the accountability mechanism for this social contract only if educators and their fellow citizens are persuaded to accept such a vision of public schooling. Whether a consensus about curricular values can be developed, whether all students are given adequate opportunities to learn, and how tests are designed and their results used—all depend on how beliefs about civic obligation, fairness, and accountability are translated into policy and practice. In a sense, then, any consideration of the current politics of high stakes testing must return to the role of ideas and values in assessment policy. The fate of high stakes testing in the next decade will depend just as much on broad acceptance of a few core values as it will on sound test design and careful implementation.

Designing Hortatory Policies in Other Issue Areas

As its third and final argument, this book contends that assessment policy is a useful lens for understanding other policies that rely on information and values to accomplish their purposes. Clearly, there are limits to what can be learned from three comparative cases in one policy area. However, because those cases differed in systematic ways and changed over time, they provide both a reasonable test of the theory underlying hortatory policies and insight into the limiting conditions on such policies. Since the most important lessons usually come from understanding the limiting conditions on policy strategies, this final section focuses on such constraints, and outlines five general conclusions about hortatory policy gleaned from the study.

First, a hortatory instrument may work better for some types of policies than for others. This conclusion relates to the assumption that if hortatory policies are to be motivated using values, those values need to be sufficiently strong and broadly accepted to prompt widespread action. The cases examined in this book illustrate the limiting conditions on that assumption, and suggest that hortatory policies may work better for some types of policies than for others. Assessment policy sharply contrasts with a policy such as recycling, a policy with underlying values that are relatively uncontroversial and likely to be accepted by a large proportion of the relevant public. It also differs from policies such as product labeling requirements in which the government intervenes to address information asymmetries. Opposition to such a policy may arise, but it will stem from competing economic interests, rather than ideological differences. Opponents' demands and strategies will likely fall within the realm of conventional politics, and can be predicted by which interests will bear the highest costs or gain the greatest benefits. In contrast, we have seen that policies that appeal to ideological values can be more divisive and opposition to them less predictable or controllable by policy elites through bargaining or "splitting-the-difference" compromises.

This caution about relying on a hortatory instrument when the values appealed to are not widely accepted does not necessarily mean that such a strategy should not be used. It just means that the political costs may be high. As outlined in Chapter 2, there may be situations in which it is rational for policymakers to bear those costs. The most obvious is those policies for which targets must change their behavior, but policymakers and their agents lack the capacity to observe targets' actions or to enforce and sanction non-compliance. Policies that attempt to regulate private behavior are one example, as are many educational reforms. In these instances, most inducements are relatively weak and mandates cannot be effectively enforced once home or classroom doors are closed. For these policies, then, the long-term effect of appealing to values may outweigh the short-term political costs.

Second, policy designers should consider the likely responses of all potential target groups, and develop common understandings of the policy and its intent. The theory of hortatory policy requires that a series of assumptions about targets be valid if the policy is to work. These include: the information produced is useful to them and they act on it; they accept the values appealed to by the policy; they have sufficient incentive and capacity to respond; and their responses are consistent with the policy's goals. However, in many cases, targets are not a monolithic category, and include diverse groups of people whose behavior is expected to change. Not all these groups share interests or view the policy in the same way. Yet policymakers often do not make distinctions among them or anticipate their different responses. So, for example, the targets of assessment policies include local school officials, teachers, students, parents, the public, and to some extent, testing experts. However, earlier state assessment policies seemed to have assumed that teachers were the primary targets, that parents would respond much like teachers would, and that parental reactions would be reasonably uniform across the ideological spectrum and various demographic categories. NCLB is more highly differentiated in how it treats targets in that it includes specific provisions dealing with educators and parents. Still, it is not clear that its sponsors have considered the range of likely responses—for example, those of states with more rigorous content and performance standards as compared with those with lower ones, or those of state and local officials.

So one implication of this research is that policymakers need to identify the full range of targets who are likely to be affected (intentionally or unintentionally) by a particular policy and take their interests and concerns into consideration. It is highly unlikely that a particular set of policy values or incentives will resonate positively with all potential targets, but prior consideration of their various viewpoints can at least minimize the kinds of unanticipated reactions that CLAS prompted in California. Even when potential targets disagree with a policy's goals and underlying values, if they at least share an understanding of it, debate and opposition can proceed in a more thoughtful manner. Understanding targets' diverse responses and developing common understandings of policy intent will increase the likelihood that problems can be resolved and a policy modified instead of abandoned.

Third, a low-key enactment process may not always be a good predictor of what happens during implementation. Assessment policy, like a variety of information-based policies, was traditionally framed as a technical issue of concern to only a limited subsystem of professionals, interest groups, education agencies, and a small group of legislators. This policy subsystem was accustomed to operating outside the public limelight and reaching a consensus through years of working together. Such an arrangement allowed for a relatively noncontroversial, low-visibility enactment process, and under ordinary circumstances, straightforward implementation. To a large extent, that is what happened with the end-of-grade tests in North Carolina. But the situation has changed considerably as assessment policy has come to reflect more explicit values and to play a more dominant role in education reform. Consequently, low-key policy enactment in California and Kentucky did not lead to a smooth implementation process.

This disjuncture between the tenor of enactment and that of implementation usually occurs when a policy is in transition from a closed subsystem to a broader public arena. Despite its infrequency, that transition usually signals a major widening of a policy's constituency and its movement closer to the core policy agenda of an issue. As with the previous discussion of policy targets, the remedy is to design a more inclusive process. The more open the policymaking process, with input from a broad range of stakeholders beyond just technical experts and those most directly affected by a policy, the greater the likelihood that the enactment and implementation processes will be congruent. If participation is relatively open, the issues raised during the policy formulation stage will better reflect the full range of factors that will shape (or inhibit) implementation. If these issues can be successfully addressed during enactment, implementation will not become another arena for playing out unresolved conflicts. If policy advocates and opponents are allowed or even encouraged to air their views during enactment, any countermobilization around competing values will emerge then, rather than during implementation. The advantage is that policymaking institutions, such as legislatures, have better-defined procedures for resolving conflicts than do implementing institutions, in which processes are often less structured and certainly less able to cope with controversy.

Fourth, although hortatory policies can be quite efficient in that they can lead to significant change for a relatively small investment, they often have hidden costs. As we have seen with assessment policy, many costs are not completely visible until a policy becomes fully operative. Hortatory policies can also be particularly problematic because not only do total costs in financial resources, time, and expertise not become manifest until well into the implementation process, but also the governmental level least able to handle these costs often bears the greatest burden. In pushing the costs down to the local level, hortatory policies are similar to a variety of other policies that higher levels of government use to impose their will on lower levels. So the cost calculus for hortatory policies is not unlike that for other types of domestic policies: how to change targets' behavior at the lowest cost to the level enacting the policy, while also ensuring that the cost to targets is not more than they are willing to bear. However, estimating true cost and willingness to pay are considerably more difficult for hortatory policies because the costs are not as obvious as they are for mandates and inducements. In addition, providing information and making persuasive appeals can be deceptively cheap strategies. Clearly, hortatory policies can be quite cost-effective in the degree of change they can elicit for relatively small investments. Nevertheless, effective implementation requires accurate estimates of the true costs and agreement on who will bear them.

Finally, hortatory policies often need to be combined with other policy instruments as much to augment targets' capacity to act as to enhance their incentive to do so, particularly in cases in which the expected actions are complicated. Although they may not always be explicit about it, the typical reason policymakers switch from purely hortatory policies (such as low stakes testing) to ones that combine other policy instruments is a belief that information and values alone will not induce expected levels of change. They assume that targets need more powerful incentives in the form of coercive mandates or tangible inducements such as money, particularly if change is to be sustained for the long term. Although this study has shown that a hortatory policy and one that incorporates strong inducements may produce similar levels of change, it has not directly tested these policy assumptions. Consequently, it cannot determine if policymakers' beliefs are generally valid, nor can it specify the conditions under which hortatory instruments should be joined with mandates and inducements.

However, this research can speak to the relationship between hortatory instruments and those designed to build targets' capacity. For those hortatory policies where the expected action is relatively straightforward, such as consumer recycling, the need for capacity-building is minimal. Consumers must be motivated through appeals to their concern for the environment and sense of civic responsibility, but instruction in the necessary actions can be limited to a few straightforward messages delivered in a variety of formats. Assessment policy, in contrast, requires a considerable investment in capacity-building strategies. Even as state content and performance standards have become more specific, they still do not communicate the full range of what is expected of students and educators. Not only does the hortatory message lack precision, but it is not easily acted upon even after targets understand its full implications. It often requires additional resources and usually new learning. Consequently, if either the information requirements or the values-based messages of a hortatory policy are complicated and demand a variety of complex or unfamiliar actions, capacity-building strategies are necessary.

Conclusion

This book began by admitting that state assessments, now such an integral part of elementary and secondary education, might seem to be an unlikely lens through which to view broader political and policy issues. Because these policies have changed so much during the past decade, it might also seem as if little can be learned from their earlier incarnations. Yet by looking beyond the technical challenges these policies pose and examining them as vehicles to promote both educational goals and broader political purposes, the recent history of educational testing tells us much about the range of policy strategies for addressing a variety of social problems, about the distance between political expectations and expert capabilities, and about the link between abstract values and the actions that promote them. Just as educational tests inform us about the status of student learning (albeit incompletely), an assessment of the politics of testing helps us better understand the gap between political aspirations and policy actions and how it might be narrowed.

Appendix: Sample Characteristics and Data Collection Instruments

This appendix describes the Kentucky and North Carolina local samples on which the analysis in Chapter 5 is based, and includes several of the interview guides and one of the daily teacher logs used to collect local-level data. Two of the interview guides used to collect data from the California respondents, analyzed in Chapter 4, are also included.

In selecting districts within Kentucky and North Carolina, the first priority was to represent the geographic diversity of the two states. Kentucky is divided into three distinct regions: Appalachian eastern Kentucky; the central Pennyrile; and the triangle of Lexington, Louisville, and the Cincinnati suburbs that includes most of the state's urban population, industrial production, and wealth. North Carolina has a similar geographic division: the western mountainous region, the eastern coastal counties, and the central Piedmont that includes most of the state's urban population. In both states, one district was selected from each region, and within each of these districts, two schools.

In selecting districts and schools within a region, I sought to reflect the racial diversity of the states and to ensure that the sample was balanced in its inclusion of tested grades. At the time of data collection, Kentucky was testing students in the fourth, eighth, and twelfth grades, so the sample is evenly divided among elementary, middle, and high schools. In North Carolina, I was primarily interested in the instructional effects of the end-of-grade test which is administered to students in grades three through eight, so the sample includes four elementary, two middle, and no high schools. I consulted with university faculty, staffs of independent groups working in education reform, the state teachers' organization, and state department of education staff within each state to ensure that the schools selected were not atypical—either positively or negatively—in their quality or in how they adapted to externally mandated change. The telephone sample of schools was selected in the same way. Table A.1 summarizes the characteristics of the six schools in each state where the field interviews and collection of instructional artifact data occurred.[1]

Principals selected the participating teachers. However, I specified the grades and subjects from which they should be chosen. Consequently, in most schools, principals were typically choosing from only two or three teachers at a specific grade or teaching a particular subject. Table A.2 provides an overview of the teacher sample.[2]

Table A.1. Kentucky and North Carolina school sample

School	Level	Location	Enrollment	Percent Minority	Percent Free/ Reduced-Price Lunch
Kentucky					
1	Elementary	Rural	520	10	40
2	Elementary	Rural	350	2	65
3	Middle	Urban	950	26	67
4	Middle & High	Rural	650	0	53
5	High	Urban/Suburban	950	32	31
6	High	Urban	850	10	40
North Carolina					
1	Elementary	Urban	450	40	42
2	Elementary	Rural	450	7	18
3	Elementary	Rural	460	66	59
4	Elementary	Suburban	840	32	34
5	Middle	Suburban	925	11	17
6	Middle	Urban	700	32	18

Table A.2. Teacher sample

	Kentucky	North Carolina
Grade		
Elementary	6	11
Middle	5	12
High	12	—
Subject		
Language Arts	8	8
Mathematics	8	8
Social Studies	8	8
Sex		
Female	18	22
Male	6	2
Median years of teaching experience (S.D. = 9)	16	17

1993

Interview Topics: Elementary Teachers

In our interview today, I would like to explore with you several topics related to (new state assessment) and its effect on instruction here at (school). First, however, I would like to ask you several questions about your own professional experience.

1. a. How long have you been teaching?
    b. How long have you been teaching at (school)?
    c. What grade are you currently teaching?

As I mentioned, we are particularly interested in finding out how (new state assessment) may have affected instructional practices at your school. I would like to begin by asking you about the logistics involved in administering (state test), and then move on to questions about its impact on the curriculum and on teachers' work.

[*Include this statement only if respondent does not teach at one of the grade levels being tested:* I realize that some of these questions may not apply to you since you don't teach at one of the grade levels at which students are tested. However, we are also interested in understanding how teachers in other grades may be affected by (state assessment). So I would like to ask you about your own experience and reactions. But if a question does not apply to you, just let me know.]

2. a. What kind of information did you and your colleagues receive prior to the first administration of the test?
        e.g., — written materials, workshops, meetings with school testing coordinators
        Who provided the information?
    b. Did that information discuss the curricular implications of (state assessment), or did it just focus on topics directly related to the test such as its administration and scoring?
    c. In your view, how adequate was the information you received?
    d. Were you given the name of a contact person that you or other school staff could call if you had questions or encountered problems?
    e. Did you and your colleagues encounter any significant problems in administering (state assessment)?
3. a. How much time does the (state assessment) require of students each year?

PROBES:

- preparing for the test
- taking the test

  b. How much time does it require of you?

PROBES:

- preparing students for the test
- administering the test
- (if applicable): scoring the test
- meeting to discuss test results

  c. Has the time that you have devoted to (state assessment) meant that there have been other activities related to your teaching that you have either been unable to do, or on which you have had to spend less time?
  If yes: — What are those activities?

4. a. What aspects of (state assessment) have evoked the most positive and the most negative reactions on the part of students?
   b. What aspects of the assessment have evoked the most positive and the most negative reactions on the part of teachers?
   Have you noticed any significant differences in the attitudes of teachers working at the grade level or with the subject matter being tested, as compared with those teaching at grade levels or subjects not being tested?
   c. Have the school, the district, and the state department of education been able to provide teachers here at (school) with all the support that you have needed or requested while working on (state assessment)?
   If no: — What kind of support has been unavailable to teachers?

5. *Ask Q5 only if school has already received test results from state*
   a. Does the state return test results promptly so that you can use them in planning for the next year?
   b. Did teachers here at (school) meet to discuss test results?
   If yes: — Please explain the purpose of these meetings.
   c. Is the information provided by the state about (school's) scores and how they should be interpreted understandable to you and your fellow teachers?

6. *Ask Q6 only of Kentucky schools*
   a. What do you expect will be the trend in your school's test scores and "accountability index" over the next two years?

b. How have teachers in this school responded to the test results that were released several weeks ago?

c. Does __(school)__ have a strategy for raising the test scores?

d. How do you motivate students to try and do their best on __(state test)__ when there are so few personal consequences for them, but major consequences for the school?

7. a. Do you foresee any major changes in curriculum content or instructional strategies here at __(school)__ as a result of __(state assessment)__?

b. At this point, does __(state assessment)__ affect your own teaching in any way?

PROBES:

- curricular goals
- choice of curriculum content
- sequencing of topics or skills
- instructional strategies
- grouping practices

c. *Ask Q7c only of those teaching at the grade levels being tested*
  Are there any students in your class who are having serious problems doing well on __(state test)__?
  If yes: — What is being done to assist these students?

8. a. What do you think state policymakers expected to accomplish with __(state assessment)__?

b. Is __(state assessment)__ likely to produce the kind of effects here at __(school)__ that state policymakers intended?

9. a. In your view, how well does __(state assessment)__ relate to other state policies that deal with curriculum, school organization, and related student services?

b. How well does __(state assessment)__ fit with district-level priorities?

c. What state and local policies exert the greatest influence on the curriculum here at __(school)__?

1994

Interview Topics: Elementary Teachers

Thank you for agreeing to help us again with our study of the implementation of new student assessments. What I would like to do today is to ask you a few questions that follow up on the discussion we had about __(state)__ at this time last year. Then I will explain the kinds of materials that we would like to collect from you over the next several months.

1. First, as you look back over the past year, has much changed in terms of how you, your students, and your colleagues are responding to __(state assessment)?__

    PROBES:

- the amount of time students spend preparing for the test (including portfolio pieces in Kentucky)
- the amount of time you spend related to all aspects of the state assessment, including preparing students, scoring the test, meeting with other teachers or specialists, and implementing new curriculum related to the test
- student and teacher attitudes toward the assessment
- the effect of an additional year's scores on the school's response to the assessment
- what the school or individual groups of teachers are doing to improve the school's scores

2. a. Last year when we talked you mentioned that the assessment was influencing your teaching in the following ways: *(summarize respondent's answer to #7 on last year's interview guide).* Have there been any changes or would your answer be the same now?

    PROBE:

- whether there have been any changes related to implementation of the state standards and curriculum

    b. As you think about your teaching since __(state assessment),__ are there any strategies or activities that you use that are explicitly intended to prepare your students for the test and that differ from your regular instruction?

3. *Ask Q3 only of mathematics and writing teachers in Kentucky*
    a. What characteristics do you look for in a portfolio task?

    PROBES:

- importance of subject matter content
- importance of particular skills such as problem solving
- whether tasks should focus on content covered in class or contain new topics
- student interest

    b. What sources do you use in designing or selecting portfolio tasks?

PROBE:

• proportion of tasks made up by you versus obtained from other sources

   c. Do the state's scoring criteria ever influence your choice of portfolio tasks?

   d. What are your guidelines for how many times you allow or encourage students to revise their portfolio pieces?

Now I would like to describe the kinds of materials that we would like you to provide us between now and the end of the semester.

• *First, make certain that the respondent is teaching the appropriate subject. Then have high school teachers (and middle school teachers where appropriate) select a particular course period and ask them to supply information for only that class. Make it clear to elementary teachers that we are asking for information in only one subject.*

• *Obtain textbook information (including the ISBN number) for all teachers who use texts.*

• *Review the summary guide to instructional materials collection with the respondent:*

   —the ten consecutive days of data collection—logs, assignments, and pre-printed labels; when to start the process, and how to provide information about assignments from the primary textbook; why the log forms may seem generic, stressing that teachers should feel free to write any comments that will help us in understanding their classes.

   —the collection of all assignments most like the state assessment and all portfolio prompts, to be labeled and sent to us at the end of the semester.

• *Explain about the honoraria; stress our attempts to minimize burden; and urge daily completion of the logs.*

NC

NAME

SCHOOL

DATE

COURSE/SUBJECT

1. List the content covered in today's class by briefly describing it or by providing examples.

TOPICS

2. List the most important skills or knowledge that you wanted students to learn from today's class.

INTENDED OUTCOMES OF TODAY'S CLASS

3. What modes of instruction did you use? (For ALL THAT APPLY, circle the approximate amount of time spent on the activity during today's class.)

	Just a few minutes	About half the period or lesson	Entire period or lesson
Lecture or talk to entire class	1	2	3	4	5
Use manipulatives or audio-visual materials	1	2	3	4	5
Lead question-and-answer session	1	2	3	4	5
Work with small groups	1	2	3	4	5
Work with individual students	1	2	3	4	5
Review material already presented	1	2	3	4	5
Administer a test	1	2	3	4	5
Correct or review student work	1	2	3	4	5
Other (please specify)			

4. What activities did students engage in during this period?
(For <u>ALL THAT APPLY</u>, circle the approximate amount of time spent on the activity during today's class.)

	Just a few minutes		About half the period or lesson		Entire period or lesson
Listen and take notes	1	2	3	4	5
Work exercises at board	1	2	3	4	5
Work with manipulatives	1	2	3	4	5
Collect or analyze data	1	2	3	4	5
Use calculators	1	2	3	4	5
Respond to questions	1	2	3	4	5
Discuss topics from lesson	1	2	3	4	5
Work on computer	1	2	3	4	5
Work individually on worksheets	1	2	3	4	5
Work with other students	1	2	3	4	5
Work on an assignment from another subject (e.g., science, social studies) that also involves math	1	2	3	4	5
Prepare written assignment (e.g., entry in math journal)	1	2	3	4	5
Make an oral presentation	1	2	3	4	5
Work on a long-term project	1	2	3	4	5
Work on next day's homework	1	2	3	4	5
Other (please specify) _____					

If there is anything else that you think is important for us to know about today's class, please note it below.

Comments: _____

_____

_____

_____

Figure A.1. Daily teacher log

Interview Topics: Parents (California)

Thank you for taking the time to meet with me. One of the reasons that we are interested in talking with parents about CLAS is to help inform those in other states who are planning to implement new types of student assessments and who want to take parents' views into consideration in designing new tests.

Consequently, I would like to ask you about your involvement in the local schools and your opinions about CLAS.

1. a. How many children do you have attending __(school)__?

PROBES:

• length of time attending __(school)__
• grade level(s)

    b. Did you choose __(school)__ for your child [children] or was he [she/they] assigned there?

    c. Has your child [children] been happy attending __(school)__?

2. a. How often do you typically come to __(school)__ and for what purpose?

        e.g., —when called by the principal, counselor, or child's teacher

        —to attend regularly scheduled parent-teacher conferences

        —to attend athletic events or student performances

        —to attend or participate in PTA meetings

        —to initiate discussions with school personnel about child

        —to volunteer

        —to serve on the school-site council

    b. How often do you typically help your child [children] with his [her/their] homework or other school assignments?

       Do you regularly check assignments for completion?

3. a. How did you first become aware of the CLAS test?

        e.g., —from the media

        —saw a copy of the test

        —from other parents

        —at church or other group meetings

    b. When you were first making up your mind about CLAS, did you talk to anyone else about it?

        e.g., —school principal or teachers

        —other parents

        —leaders of local parent groups

        —fellow church members

4. *Ask only of CLAS opponents*

What were your major reasons for opposing the CLAS test?

5. *Ask only of CLAS opponents*
   a. What did you want your local school district or the state to do about the CLAS test?
   b. How did you go about expressing your opposition to CLAS?

   PROBES:

- whether joined a formal group
- whether concentrated efforts at the school or district level
- whether involved in any lawsuit over CLAS
- whether decided to keep her [his] children from taking the CLAS test

   c. Did you contact any of the following to express your opposition to CLAS:
      —local newspaper, radio, or television station
      —a state or local elected official
      —a group opposed to CLAS located outside   (local community)
   d. One of the issues that arose during the controversy over CLAS was the accusation that a lot of items attributed to CLAS were not really on the test itself. How did you verify which specific items were on the actual CLAS test?

      Similarly, there were a lot of rumors floating around about how the test was being scored and how student information from the test was being used. How were you able to check on the kinds of things that you were hearing about CLAS?

6. *Ask only of parents who were not vocal opponents of CLAS*
   a. Did you have an opinion, either positive or negative, about the appropriateness of CLAS as a way to assess students?
      If yes: —What were your reasons for feeling that way?
   b. Did you make your opinion known to either school staff or district authorities? Why or why not?
   c. Did any of your children take the CLAS test?
      If yes: —What did they think of it?

7. a. Are you satisfied with the way the CLAS controversy was handled:
      —at your child's [children's] school?
      —in this district?
      —at the state level?
   b. In your view, is there any way that CLAS could have been modified to make it acceptable both to parents who supported and who opposed it?

8. *Ask only of CLAS opponents*
   a. Prior to CLAS, were you active in any political or civic activities?
   b. Has your involvement in CLAS changed your level of involvement in school politics or other political activities?

9. a. How satisfied are you with the quality of schooling your child is receiving at __(school)?__
   b. How would you rate the quality of public education generally in California?
   c. What do you think are the most important things that schools ought to be doing for your child [children]?
   d. What steps do you think should be taken to improve public education?
10. a. Do you feel that the schools respect your rights as a parent?
    b. Do you think that there are some values that schools should teach, or should that responsibility be left to parents?
11. a. Would you characterize yourself politically as conservative, middle-of-the-road, or liberal?
    b. How would you describe your overall philosophy about what the proper role of government should be in educating children?
12. What would you like to see happen with student testing in California in the future, either at the state or local level?
13. Finally, if you were to give advice to parents in other states where new kinds of student assessments are being considered, what would you tell them?

Interview Topics: Local CLAS Opposition Groups

Thank you for taking the time to talk with me. As I mentioned in my letter to you, one of the reasons why we are analyzing the experience of states that have implemented new forms of student assessment is to help inform other states that are now considering similar policies and that want their efforts to benefit from what others have learned in the process.

In our interview today, I would like to ask you about your group's concerns regarding CLAS and what you did to make those concerns known.

1. How did your group first become aware of the CLAS test?
   e.g.,—newspaper articles
   —local parents or teachers expressing concern
2. What were the major reasons for your group's opposition to CLAS?
3. a. What kinds of strategies did your group use to mobilize public opposition to CLAS?

PROBES:

• whether any organizing at individual schools
  If yes:—How did you decide which schools to target?
  —How did you make contact with individual parents or teachers?

- any attempts to contact the media (e.g., press conferences, calls to reporters, writing of op-ed pieces)
- whether __(group)__ filed any lawsuits or requests for injunctions

  b. One of the issues that arose during the controversy over CLAS was the accusation that a lot of items attributed to CLAS were not really on the test itself. How did you verify which specific items were on the actual CLAS test?

  Similarly, there were a lot of rumors floating around about how the test was being scored and how student information from the test was being used. How were you able to check on the kinds of things you were hearing about CLAS?

  c. Did the fact that the CLAS controversy occurred during an election year help or hinder your efforts?

  d. In opposing CLAS, did you work with any other groups that shared your concerns about the test?

4. a. Could you tell me something about the group you represent?

PROBES:

- size
- membership characteristics
- financial support

  b. How do you attract or recruit new members?

  c. How would you describe the overall philosophy of your group?

  d. Is your group affiliated with other groups either in the state or nationally that have similar concerns about current education policies?

  e. Is your group currently working on any education issues, or is it involved in school politics in __(local area)__?

  If yes: — What are you doing and what do you hope to accomplish?

5. a. Do you think that CLAS raised broader issues about the respective rights and responsibilities of the state, as compared with those of parents, in educating children?

  b. Did __(group)__ also support Proposition 174, the California school voucher initiative?

  c. Do you see the issues that your group and others are raising as confined to CLAS and public education, or are they related to broader political and social concerns?

6. What would your group like to see happen with student assessment in California in the future?

7. If you were to give advice to policymakers in other states about new student assessments, based on California's experience, what would you tell them?

Notes

1. Testing from a Political Perspective

1. A standardized test or assessment is administered and scored under uniform conditions in order to ensure that the results will be comparable across everyone taking the test. Any type of test—multiple-choice, essay, oral—can be standardized if the testing conditions and the scoring procedures are uniform for all testing situations and test-takers.
2. Examples of studies that focus on the consequences of testing include Heubert and Hauser, 1999 and Office of Technology Assessment, 1992.
3. Despite the move toward greater uniformity within states in the content that students are expected to master, state standards vary in their specificity and use. In some states, content standards are no more than broad, rhetorical goals that local districts are urged to follow. In others, they are considerably more precise, with textbooks and assessments linked directly to the standards, and efforts made to train teachers in a pedagogy consistent with the curricular philosophy underlying the standards.
4. Because standardized tests in the past were typically not tied to specific curricula, most disputes focused on textbook adoptions by local school boards, and were usually pursued by religious fundamentalists. A court case that exemplifies the tension between religious and secular values in textbook decisions is *Mozert v. Hawkins Public Schools*, in which the court required the schools to provide a plaintiff's children with alternative reading material. The court determined that the plaintiffs were arguing from a sincere religious position and that the government's interest in maintaining consistency in textbooks did not warrant interference with the plaintiff's free exercise of religion. Several political theorists have argued that "a civic education that satisfies the Mozert's parents' objections . . . would interfere with teaching the virtues and skills of liberal democratic citizenship" (Gutmann, 1995, p. 572; see also Macedo, 1995).
5. The effects of state assessments on classroom teaching are explored in Chapter 5.
6. Deukmejian vetoed the CAP appropriation in a funding dispute with the Democratically controlled legislature. He argued that the $11 million to support CAP should come from funds that had been specifically reserved for education through a ballot initiative, rather than from the state's general fund.
7. As in California, the format and content of the KIRIS assessment represented a marked departure from more traditional forms of testing. Students were required

to write more; the initial stages of some tasks were performed in groups although students gave individual answers; and students were given real-world problems to solve, such as siting a new Wal-Mart in their community or designing an experiment to determine which of two spot removers worked better (both examples are from the fourth-grade test). Student portfolios in mathematics and writing contained five to seven examples of students' work and were selected to show the breadth of their understanding of core concepts and principles.

8. In addition to the end-of-grade tests for elementary and middle school students, North Carolina also administers end-of-course tests to high school students in about 14 different subjects. However, these tests consisted largely of multiple-choice items, and were only gradually revised to include some open-ended items. This study focuses only on the K–8 end-of-grade tests.

9. Forty-eight teachers and 12 principals who were interviewed in person in 1993 were interviewed a second time in 1994.

10. The exception to this was our systematic coding of all the articles on CLAS appearing in the *San Diego Tribune* and the *San Francisco Chronicle* between 1994 and 1996. We had the sense that the CLAS controversy was more visible in some parts of the state than in others, and the newspaper analysis provided one way to test that hypothesis.

11. In addition to the newspaper data, a variety of other documentary data was also collected and reviewed. These included copies of all the relevant legislation; materials produced by groups supporting and opposing the state assessments; state curriculum documents, including curriculum standards and frameworks; technical reports on the state assessment produced by the state department of education and by outside monitoring bodies; test items that have been publicly released; and in the case of Kentucky, several public-opinion polls on its larger education reform and state assessment.

12. Because of family illness, one teacher in the original Kentucky sample and one in the North Carolina sample were unable to provide instructional artifact data.

13. The log form asked teachers to list which topics they covered during a class period and what the intended outcomes of the class were. They were then asked to indicate on a checklist all the modes of instruction they used and the activities in which students engaged. For each activity, teachers were asked what proportion of the class period it consumed. There was also a *comments* section, in which teachers were asked to provide any information about the lesson that they felt was important (for example, that class time was reduced by other school activities, that something particularly different or innovative occurred that day). A copy of the log form is included in the appendix.

14. Each teacher was paid an honorarium of $200 for participating in two interviews and for providing instructional artifacts during the course of a semester.

15. We asked teachers to provide us with all the assignments they made during two consecutive weeks. However, we also requested that if they were within several days of completing a unit or a topic at the end of the 10 days, that they continue to complete the logs and provide assignments until they had finished the unit. Hence, the number of assignments and logs exceeds what would have been collected during only 10 days.

Elementary teachers who were teaching in self-contained classrooms were asked to provide assignments in only one subject area. We designated the subject, in order to maintain an equal representation among mathematics, language arts, and social studies assignments.

16. Our rationale for collecting both a sample of assignments made during a time period of our choosing and all those assignments that teachers judged to be most similar to the state assessment was to learn how teachers translated their understanding of the purpose and format of the state assessment into their own assignments, and to see if assignments they judged to be like the state test were similar to assignments associated with their ongoing teaching. In essence, we have collected "typical" assignments as well as those that teachers judged "best" in reflecting the state assessment.

17. The artifacts from 20 percent of the teachers (n = 9) were coded independently by two coders to check for intercoder reliability. The rate of exact agreement between coders was 80 percent (out of 1,551 separate judgments, the coders made the same judgment in 1,239 instances). If we relax the criteria and consider those judgments where the coders differed by only one (for example, in calculating the number of assignments reflecting a particular goal), the rate of agreement increases to 87 percent. Hence, we feel quite confident that the discussion of assignments' consistency with state goals is based on reliable data.

2. Persuasion as a Policy Instrument

1. U.S. education policy has always included a strong hortatory component, not just in its focus on the goal of preparing students for democratic citizenship, but also in how the public school system was originally created. In describing the growth of local schools in the early nineteenth century, James (1991) notes that states lacked the administrative capacity and financial resources to mandate that communities establish such schools. Rather, "without regulating schools directly or belaboring the details of what should happen in classrooms, states constituted schooling as a public good in American society. They did this not by bringing the institution into being—the people and their communities did that—but by framing the activity as a desirable element of the political culture and permanent institutional base of the state" (p. 179).

2. An exception is Weiss's (1990) study of ideas as one policy instrument that federal officials used to shift mental health care away from centralized, state mental institutions toward outpatient care.

3. Relative to a discussion of values-based policy, speed limits are essentially mandates, defined by a clear set of rules. But they also embody values that form the basis of appeals to the driving public. Motorists are encouraged to obey speed limits because this saves lives, conserves fuel, and is simply the right thing to do. For this policy, the hortatory aspect is designed as a secondary instrument to enhance the mandate, since policymakers recognize that enforcement mechanisms are often inadequate.

4. Graham (2000) enumerates some of the mandatory disclosure laws that have been enacted at the federal and state levels to increase the information available to the public on varied activities and products such as on-time airline departures;

the gasoline efficiency of automobiles; the proportion of lead in faucets; the release of toxic chemicals; the geographic distribution of mortgage and home improvement loans by race, sex, and income of applicants; and the level of contaminants in drinking water.

5. The lack of enforcement is one of the TRI's most obvious design flaws. One-third of the facilities covered by the TRI law fail to report their emissions each year, and the EPA inspects only about 3 percent of firms annually to check the accuracy of emissions reports (Fung and O'Rourke, 2000).

6. An example of a more structured approach to citizen participation is community right-to-know rules under EPCRA, mandating that state and local emergency planning committees allow citizens to be members and to participate in managing the reporting and planning processes. In addition, citizens can request that businesses supplement their existing right-to-know reports with additional information (Black, 1989). For this policy, the mandate requiring that information be reported also provides a framework for encouraging and organizing some aspects of the expected public participation.

7. It is important to note that, in the case of hazard warnings, a more accurate estimate of costs would also take into consideration the probability and value of potential benefits, such as fewer accidents and adverse health effects. In fact, much of the research on risk has examined how policy targets value costs and benefits in deciding whether to heed hazard warnings.

   Magat and Viscusi (1992) make a sharp distinction between programs designed only to impart information and ones that exhort people to engage in particular behaviors. They argue that exhortatory programs are "more dictatorial than informational in nature" and are less effective than purely informational ones. They also note that for these programs, "it is especially important to ascertain whether the benefits of the prescribed behavior exceed the costs that we impose both in terms of the costs of the precautions as well as the costs of information transfer" (p. 182).

8. Chapter 5 presents limited evidence that a low stakes state assessment with only a hortatory element can be as effective, at least in the short-term, in influencing teachers to teach consistent with the state test as a high stakes approach that attaches consequences to test performance.

9. Schneider and Ingram (1997) make a different argument for why AIDS policy has relied on a hortatory strategy. They argue that hortatory tools "will commonly be used for dependent groups even when the pervasiveness of the problem would suggest that more direct intervention is needed" (p. 131). In their view, informational tools are likely to be used (as in the case of AIDS prevention programs) even when direct resources are needed, because policymakers are reluctant to spend money on dependent groups, and they will typically not empower such groups to find their own solutions, but will require them to rely on established agencies for assistance.

   This argument may be valid for groups such as those at risk for AIDS or the victims of domestic violence. But even in these instances, the need for a motivating mechanism in addition to rules, money, and power remains strong. For other policies, such as food labeling and hazard warnings, the effect of the hortatory policy is to make the targets *less* dependent and to achieve a more equal relationship with food producers and users of hazardous chemicals. The argument that hortatory tools are commonly used for dependent groups also does not apply to assessment policy. Students are a dependent group and a major target of this policy, but other targets include relatively powerful groups such as business leaders, teacher unions, and school board members.

10. Mandated reporting requirements are currently popular as an alternative or supplement to direct regulation because they are viewed as less intrusive and therefore politically more defensible. But growing dissatisfaction with direct regulation (Gormley and Weimer, 1999), coupled with a normative belief that informational strategies are more consistent with democratic values (Sunstein, 1993), also explain the increasing use of this policy tool.

3. The State Politics of Testing

1. The curriculum standards developed by NCTM combine critical thinking skills — such as problem-solving and making connections between topics and their applications—with specific content knowledge. The standards are characterized by learning goals that emphasize understanding the conceptual basis of mathematics, reasoning mathematically and applying that reasoning in everyday situations, offering alternative solutions to problems, and communicating about mathematical concepts in meaningful and useful ways. Consistent with those goals, NCTM advocated changes in both mathematics content and instructional strategies. Particularly prominent in this reform vision of the mathematics curriculum is a changed view of the teacher's role. Because students are expected to play active parts in constructing and applying mathematical ideas, teachers are to be facilitators of learning rather than imparters of information. This shift means that rather than lecturing and relying on textbooks, teachers are to select and structure mathematical tasks that allow students to learn through discussion, group activities, and other modes of discovery.

2. Payzant then served for nearly three years as the assistant secretary for elementary and secondary education in the Clinton administration; he then became superintendent of the Boston City Schools.

3. About half the states resemble Kentucky in enhancing the hortatory component of their assessment policies with some kind of inducement and in defining educational accountability as the rewarding and sanctioning of schools, based largely on assessment results. The other states, however, resemble North Carolina before 1997 and California before 1999 in considering the accountability functions of their assessment systems to be informational. Their assumption is that, when student scores are sent to parents and when school, district, and state scores are publicly reported, parents and concerned members of the public will act on that information by pressuring for improvement where it is needed.

4. Opposition to specific provisions of KERA was greater in the house than in the senate, as indicated by the margins on the final KERA vote in each chamber: 58 to 42 in the house and 30 to 8 in the senate.

5. Part of the reason that opposition was limited may be the process by which KERA was enacted. It was essentially the product of negotiations among legislative leaders and the governor. According to a study of KERA's passage, most major decisions were not debated or discussed openly. Public discussion was minimized so that individual legislators would not water down or significantly change the bill by adding amendments. The legislation was then enacted along with a large number of public works projects (such as road construction) that were funded out of the major tax increase attached to KERA (Bishop, 1994).

6. Although North Carolina's per-student costs were lower than Kentucky's, the fact that there are more students in North Carolina and that the state tested all students in grades 3–8 (and all high school students at the end of required courses) meant that its total testing costs were significantly higher than Kentucky's. Picus (1996) estimated North Carolina's annual costs to have averaged about $9.2 million, while Kentucky's annual costs averaged about $6.7 million.

7. In each of the three states, the initial assessment policy assumed that the state-administered test would be supplemented by classroom-based assessments linked to the state curriculum frameworks, but administered by classroom teachers when they felt they were appropriate. However, those plans were abandoned because of fiscal constraints.

8. The relationship between resources for professional development and local responses to the state assessment is discussed in greater detail in Chapter 5.

9. One high-level official in the SDE offered the following as an example of how KIRIS was meant to influence curricular content: "Physical science content is not covered in the eighth-grade course of study; most schools emphasize life science at that level. That's why so few students scored *distinguished* in science. But about one-third of the eighth-grade assessment in science deals with physical science. That message will get out and schools will emphasize physical science more."

10. It is not entirely clear why the testing program in North Carolina did not face the kind of opposition encountered in the other two states. It may be because the test there represented a less radical departure from more traditional approaches, that it was tied to a curriculum which had been in place for some years, or that the state was careful to limit to a few pilot projects its foray into outcomes-based education, an approach that became a major target of opposition groups in California, Kentucky, and many other states.

11. National public opinion data are summarized here, because no polls were conducted specifically on a California sample. Surveys were conducted, however, in Kentucky. Probably the most important finding to emerge from those polls was the public's limited knowledge about KERA. Despite the facts that KERA had dominated the media for close to five years and that state and private groups had sponsored many public information campaigns, a statewide survey conducted in 1994 found that more than half of the general public—and more than 40 percent of parents with children in public schools—reported that they still knew either little or nothing about KERA. The same survey found that less than half of the general public judged KIRIS to be working well (Wilkerson, 1994).

12. Focus on the Family has been described as a "$100-million-a-year Christian broadcasting and publishing empire" (Stammer, 1995, p. E1). Its leader, child psychologist James Dobson, reaches 3 to 5 million people weekly through his radio broadcasts, and is an influential figure in conservative politics nationally. Dobson's radio program is broadcast on 1,800 local stations, and has the third-largest daily audience of any radio program, ranking behind only Paul Harvey and Rush Limbaugh, two other politically conservative commentators (Guth et al., 1995). Dobson sees his mission as altering modern cultural values as they affect families, and stopping "the nation's moral free fall" (Stammer, 1995, p. E1).

13. In a *Sacramento Bee* article published several months after the height of the CLAS controversy, Delsohn (1994) reported that more than 200 California lawyers had volunteered to assist the Rutherford Institute in its work for Christian and other related causes. He also reported that the national office raises more than $6.5 million a year in direct-mail solicitations and that it produces radio messages that are broadcast on more than 1,000 local stations. Although most of its cases involve Christians, the institute has also defended Hare Krishnas, Orthodox Jews, and other non-Christians. To date, the Rutherford Institute's most celebrated case was its representation of Paula Jones in her sexual harassment lawsuit against former president Bill Clinton.

14. The Family Foundation is the only one of the Kentucky opposition groups that has paid staff members (two full-time and three part-time) in addition to volunteer assistance. The other groups are run entirely by volunteers. Because the California groups have more resources, most of them are able to employ some staff.

15. In some cases, concerns about the test became rather exaggerated. Perhaps one of the strangest instances was when two members of the state board of education proposed deleting an excerpt from Annie Dillard's *An American Childhood* because it was about children throwing snowballs and therefore might be viewed as violent. The same two board members argued against including Alice Walker's "Am I Blue?" because it could be interpreted as advocating a vegetarian lifestyle. They maintained that the "anti-meat-eating" excerpt should be excised from the test to protect the sensitivities of rural students whose parents might raise poultry or livestock (Ingram, 1994). The state board subsequently reinstated the passages after being accused of censorship by civil libertarian groups.

16. The criticisms of CLAS and KIRIS were similar to ones made by religious and cultural conservatives about other education issues, such as textbook selection. For example, in the late 1980s and early 1990s, conservative groups in California, including the Traditional Values Coalition, attacked a reading textbook series (*Impressions*) that was marketed as a whole language program. In those attacks, they expressed criticisms similar to ones made against CLAS—that the reading series undermined authority or showed disrespect for parents, teachers, and others in authority; that it was morbid and violent; and that it undermined traditional family roles or values (Adler and Tellez, 1992).

17. This charge was made by Rev. Joe Adams, a KERA opponent and chairman of the Christian Home Educators of Kentucky. He argued that KERA mandated ethical values and beliefs that were not those of most Kentucky parents. He also

said that ignoring Christian views of Christmas in the schools, while celebrating Halloween, amounted to an endorsement of witchcraft (Ward, 1993).

18. The question of which items publicized by the opposition groups were really from the CLAS test was complicated by the fact that the SDE released very few test items because it hoped to save money by using them in successive administrations of CLAS. In addition, those who saw the test, such as teachers administering it, were not supposed to discuss its contents or distribute copies to others. However, several opposition group leaders admitted that they received copies of the test from teachers upset about CLAS, or that copies were left anonymously in their offices or sent to them through the mail. One group was given a complete set of the tests by a policymaker sympathetic to their cause who had obtained them from the SDE. In addition, once the opposition groups filed lawsuits, they collected sworn statements from students about the test content as they remembered it from the previous year's administration.

19. One example of an item on a locally developed tenth-grade sample test, but not on the official CLAS assessment, was a story by Hernando Tellez titled "Just Lather, That's All." It includes an incident of a barber contemplating killing a murderer who has come in for a shave. The barber does not kill the murderer, and the story ends with the murderer saying, "They told me you would kill me. I came to find out. But killing isn't easy. You can take my word for it." Critics portrayed this story to the media as an example of a CLAS item that abandoned academics to focus on subjective, personal, and invasive material (Hageman, 1993). The *Riverside Press-Enterprise,* which initially published a story about the item, subsequently printed a correction stating that the SDE had never considered including this story on CLAS. The paper also noted that parents throughout Riverside County were outraged that the story might be used on the test.

20. One example that seemed to conflict with the public's notion of what constitutes acceptable academic performance became a topic at a legislative hearing. In solving a problem on the KIRIS test, a student multiplied four times four and got 17 as the solution. The student was able to explain the rationale behind his solution, and the response was scored as "proficient." However, one Democratic legislator questioned whether KIRIS was measuring a student's ability "to shoot the bull" more than the academic content the student had mastered. Thomas Boysen, the state commissioner of education, promised to change the scoring rubrics to reflect this concern, saying that precision was important (May, 1994b).

21. Public concern about the reading curriculum grew more intense after fourth-grade NAEP scores in reading showed that in 1993, California ranked higher than only Mississippi, the District of Columbia, and the island of Guam among the fifty states and the U.S. territories. NAEP reported that more than half of the students tested could not understand simple texts, identify themes, or summarize what they had read. CLAS scores identified similar problems in students' reading achievement (Colvin, 1995a).

22. Cothran was credited by other opposition leaders with effectively focusing their arguments on issues of broad interest to the general public, such as the use of a traditional academic curriculum. Cothran's communication skills were evident in the CARE platform that helped transform the image of the opposition groups

from that of extremists accusing the state of encouraging witchcraft to one of responsible citizens who were espousing greater academic rigor in the schools.

23. During 1994, at the height of the controversy in the two states, the *Lexington Herald-Leader* published 320 articles about KERA and KIRIS, compared with only 171 about CLAS in the *Los Angeles Times*.

24. One of the opposition leaders in Kentucky explained that the groups there would have liked to have a legal fund, but did not have the resources. They had been talking with a lawyer representing the Rutherford Institute in Kentucky, and were hoping to be able to file a suit if any districts began to use the twelfth-grade KIRIS test as a condition for high school graduation.

Only one lawsuit was filed in Kentucky, by a family that wanted its children exempted from taking KIRIS because it argued that the test "promoted environmentalism, animal rights, feminism, multiculturalism, socialism, humanism, evolution, liberalism, and gun control," as well as overstressing "imagination," "negativism," and "depressive content." The case was dismissed in circuit court, with the judge considering each of the objections separately and finding no basis for them. In response to the charge that the test lacked traditional content, he wrote: "from Appalachian craft to the inner cities, from stories of Lincoln to the strengths of American industry, there evolves a glowing account [in the test] of a country teeming with opportunity and liberty for all persons regardless of their race, color, creed, or religion" (Associated Press, 1996).

25. In addition to the legal action initiated by the opposition groups, the school boards in five of the state's districts (out of more than a thousand) decided not to administer CLAS, arguing that while they were required by law to administer state tests, the test did not have to be CLAS. The SDE subsequently had to take legal action against the recalcitrant districts.

26. In 1995, the state legislature enacted a new assessment program, and despite the opposition of conservative groups, the governor signed the legislation. The legislation was nearly defeated in the legislature and Wilson, then running for president, waited until the last possible day to sign it. However, the new testing program was supported by the state's Business Roundtable, representing the largest businesses in the state; and by the school boards association; the Parent Teachers Association; and the teachers' unions. The new assessment system was to have two tiers, with the first one allowing local school districts to use a commercial, "off-the-shelf" basic skills test for students in grades 2 through 10. This testing was to be voluntary: local districts would receive $5 per student if they chose to participate, and they could select from among several tests approved by the SDE and designed to produce comparable scores across districts. The second tier was to consist of a mandatory statewide test of applied academic skills produced by an outside contractor and administered to students in grades 4, 5, 8, and 10. However, the two-tiered system was soon abandoned because fewer than half of the local districts in the state chose to participate, and contrary to the test publishers' promises, student scores on different types of tests could not be validly compared.

27. Not only were the participants in this second round more difficult to characterize politically, but the debate also divided academic experts. For example, the chair

of the mathematics department at the University of California, Berkeley strongly supported the commission's standards, while the former chair of the Stanford University mathematics department opposed them and helped the state board rewrite the standards.

28. Looking back on the controversy and the SDE's response, another SDE official admitted that tactical mistakes were made, but blamed them on the constraints placed on the testing staff by the department's lawyers once the lawsuits were filed:

> Secrecy for security's sake was a good idea until CLAS blew up. It much too quickly became a legal issue. I put the blame on the legal people who said that we didn't have enough passages to release them and still use them on the test. By that time, we were in court. The lawyers refused to let us tell a press person whether or not a particular passage was even on the test. As a result, we had to sit back while the press reported that all kinds of bizarre passages were on the test, like the one about the cat being dragged across nails. It was so ludicrous not to let us respond to the press because we were being crucified.

29. In an analysis of the role of Christian conservative influence in the 1994 California election, Soper (1995) notes that Wilson's pro-choice stance had been a source of friction with Christian conservatives in the past. However, during the campaign, Wilson signed or vetoed several bills that had high public support for the Christian Right position; among those was the CLAS veto. After Wilson vetoed CLAS, Sheldon "began referring to the governor as his good friend" (p. 217).

30. Subsequently, the state decided to reduce the testing burden on students and teachers by spreading the testing over six grades instead of three, thus reducing by half the classroom time devoted to testing in any one grade. As of 1998, fourth-grade students were tested in reading and writing and submitted science and writing portfolios; fifth graders were tested in mathematics, social studies, arts and humanities, and practical living, with an optional mathematics portfolio; seventh graders in reading, science, and writing; eighth graders in mathematics, social studies, arts and humanities, and practical living, with an optional mathematics portfolio; eleventh graders in reading, mathematics, science, social studies, writing, arts and humanities, and practical living; and twelfth graders submitted a writing portfolio and an optional mathematics portfolio.

31. The Partnership for Kentucky School Reform was founded by the chairmen and chief executive officers of United Parcel Service, Ashland Oil, and Humana, all Fortune 500 companies headquartered in Kentucky. The group was established in March 1991 with the intention of supporting KERA for 10 years.

32. Although rank-and-file legislators understood KIRIS less well than did the leadership, and were less vocal in their support, most endorsed the concept. A telephone survey of 102 of the 135 members of the general assembly conducted during the summer of 1994 found that only 11 percent considered the assessment successful, with another 59 percent judging it somewhat successful. Ninety percent of the legislators surveyed had fielded some negative complaints about

226 | Notes to Pages 91–96

the assessment program, with the accuracy of the assessment program and its overall appropriateness among the major concerns voiced. Slightly more than half had received some positive reports from constituents. Nevertheless, 69 percent agreed that the state assessment should be primarily performance-based (Office of Education Accountability, 1994).

33. Although the state did report significant gains in student scores during a two-year period (for example, the percentage of fourth graders scoring at the proficient level increased from 7 percent to 12 percent), 85 percent of the students who were tested were still performing at either the novice or apprentice level. In other words, the overwhelming majority of students could not be considered proficient on the state's performance standards.

34. Another study, completed at about the same time, examined the validity of KIRIS score gains in reading and mathematics, and also concluded that they were inflated (Koretz and Barron, 1998). Its conclusions were partly based on a comparison of KIRIS fourth- and eighth-grade mathematics scores with those on NAEP. The KIRIS mathematics framework was explicitly linked to NAEP's, yet score increases on KIRIS were about four times larger than for NAEP. These researchers also found that scores improved for those KIRIS mathematics items that were reused from one year to the next, with performance dropping when new items were introduced. This finding suggested that teachers might have been engaging in item-specific coaching tailored to reused items, although no systematic evidence was available to confirm this hypothesis.

35. The multiyear design of this study allowed a predictive test of the theory of hortatory policy, as outlined in Chapter 2. During most of the period that data were collected, California's and North Carolina's policies seemed to belie the theory in that they continued to rely solely on value appeals. The analysis presented in Chapter 5, showing how North Carolina's low stakes testing had as much effect on classroom teaching as Kentucky's, seemed to suggest that, at least in the short term, policies based solely on value appeals could change behavior as much as those using both value appeals and tangible consequences. However, by the end of the decade, policymakers in both states had acted consistently with the theory by enacting policies that assumed rewards and sanctions were necessary to promote significant, sustained change in both educators and students.

36. The legislation also called for the number of affected teachers to expand to cover all those working in schools deemed low-performing, regardless of whether or not a state assistance team had intervened.

37. At the time the legislation was changed, there were more than 47,000 teachers working in North Carolina's elementary and middle schools (National Center for Education Statistics, 1997); 247 of whom were working in the 15 schools with state intervention teams. Of these, approximately 50 had received poor teaching evaluations, but only 20 of those were due to a lack of general content knowledge.

38. The district also noted that if students fail the test after several tries, but have passing grades, their cases can be reviewed by their principals who make recommendations about whether or not to promote them based on review of the students' work and consultation with their teachers (Quillin and Kurtz, 1997).

39. The 285,000-member California Teachers' Association had contributed more than $1 million to Davis's campaign, with the smaller California Federation of Teachers contributing $71,000 (Colvin, 1999; Pyle, 1999a).

40. However, this change was less than what the unions had pressed for in their lobbying efforts. They had hoped to make the program entirely voluntary, with no penalties for a district's non-participation. But the governor held firm in the face of these demands and insisted on financial penalties for non-participating districts (Pyle, 1999b).

41. The certificated staff rewards program has experienced several problems. For example, in 2001, a scoring error by the state's testing contractor, Harcourt Educational Measurement, led to the state allocating $750,000 to professional staff in six schools that were ineligible for the rewards (Groves and Smith, 2001).

42. However, it should be noted that the exam covers the state mathematics standards through first-year algebra, and reading and writing standards through the tenth grade. Consequently, some educators have argued that it is not surprising or particularly alarming that only a minority of ninth graders passed a tenth-grade test that "is widely considered the most difficult of its kind in the nation" (Bergan, 2001).

4. Local Testing Controversies

1. Recent studies that have examined parents who oppose district and school policies include those by Apple, 1996; Adler, 1996; and Farkas, 1993.

2. These interviews occurred about nine to 10 months after the height of the CLAS controversy. The time lag meant that we could not observe these schools as the controversy unfolded, and that participants had had sufficient time to put a particular "spin" on their interpretations of events. At the same time, these events were still fresh in participants' memories, and enough time had elapsed for them to be able to talk about the effects of the CLAS controversy on the schools and districts.

3. In addition to analyzing the 116 interviews conducted at the local level, we drew from 16 interviews that we had conducted in 1992 and 1994 with the state-level respondents. These interviews allowed us to consider the local data in a broader context.

   Data from two schools in this sample were analyzed as part of a political science honors thesis that used the CLAS controversy to examine the fundamental tensions between the rights of the state and the rights of families in educating children (Falk, 1996).

4. In several districts, the opposition group leaders were active members of Christian churches. However, the leader of the grassroots organization formed in one district during the CLAS controversy did not belong to a church, and she felt that this status may have helped in her dealings with district officials when they realized that she "wasn't a Religious Right nutcase."

5. A 1996 study, commissioned by the California Public Education Partnership and based on a review of past public-opinion surveys, a new survey of a representative sample of 2,207 Californians, and eight focus groups of parents from across the

state, found similar views about what students should be taught. This study divided the preferred skills into four tiers and called them "basics, but more." Basic computational skills and "reading, writing, and speaking English well" topped the list, but solving "real life problems" and "working in teams" were included in the third tier (California Public Education Partnership, n.d.).

6. Respondents reported widespread coverage of the CLAS controversy in community newspapers, but we did not have access to all those newspapers. In the central coast district, the local newspaper published 21 news articles, editorials, and op-ed pieces during April and May 1994. The three metropolitan newspapers covering the other three districts published one, nine, and 13 articles respectively, during the same two-month period. Considering that these newspapers primarily cover Fresno, San Diego, and Los Angeles, this level of coverage of three relatively small school districts was unusual. Respondents on both sides of the issue agreed that while the extraordinary level of media coverage heightened the controversy, coverage was generally balanced and fair.

7. The superintendent in this district was quoted in the local newspaper saying that he had looked at the eighth-grade test before the board had done so, and could see that there would be some concern. "When I look at the literature in light of the controversy surrounding the test, they could have selected less controversial passages and ones less likely to offend some people," he said. The district testing director, who is a strong advocate for performance assessment and who also described himself as a fundamentalist Christian, made a similar argument about the language arts portion of the test in our interview with him: "I thought the stories had a kind of neurosis tone to them when you put them all together . . . and maybe one story was beautiful. But when you put all eight or twelve of them together they had this kind of general undertone of sadness and despair, and I don't think that was appropriate . . . There's enough great children's literature out there that you don't have to do that. I [also] thought some of the questions and prompts were offensive."

8. The SDE's reversal was also a source of considerable irritation to local districts. The SDE had first said that districts could not exempt students from taking the test. However, after a superior court judge in San Bernardino county ruled that individual parents could have their children excused from taking the test, the SDE reversed itself and agreed to allow districts to grant individual exemptions. However, in several of the districts in our sample, local officials did not find out about the change in policy until after the opposition did, and officials found themselves defending an SDE policy that had already been altered. They reported feeling foolish and losing credibility.

9. In the other districts, information about the opt-out option was not sent home to parents; they had to take the initiative by bringing or mailing written requests to their children's schools or to district offices.

10. In this school, opposition parents and their children were particularly concerned about the data sheets accompanying the CLAS test that asked students for personal information about themselves and their parents. The state intended to use these data in the aggregate only as a basis for interpreting the test scores of different subpopulations, but parents believed that individual students' files could be accessed and that this was an invasion of students' and their families' privacy.

5. Testing and Teaching

1. A telling example of the lessons that schools learned from the released items was the response of one of the rural schools in the sample to the inclusion of art and music items on the fourth-grade test. Teachers complained that the test was biased against students who had never had the opportunity to visit art museums or attend concerts. However, a year later, reproductions of major artwork hung in the hallways and children listened to classical music as they worked.

2. One telephone poll, conducted during June and July 1994, surveyed a representative sample of the state's general public, public school parents, parents who were members of school-site councils, teachers, instructional supervisors and testing coordinators, and principals (Wilkerson, 1994). This survey focused on KERA generally, but included questions about support for KIRIS, how well it was working, and the level of information and support that teachers felt they had been provided.

   A second study, focused specifically on KIRIS, was conducted in the spring of 1995. A state-representative sample of elementary and middle school principals and a sample of fourth- and eighth-grade teachers were surveyed by telephone. In addition, the teachers completed a lengthy written survey. The survey focused on attitudes about the accuracy and usefulness of the information generated by KIRIS, how it was changing instructional practices, the extent of test preparation, and how portfolios were being handled (Koretz et al., 1996).

3. The extent to which a variety of test preparation strategies were used and even considered desirable by local educators was evidenced in the extensive, statewide press coverage of the specific approaches different schools were using. Cited below is just one example from scores of items published in the state's newspapers after the release of the 1993 test results. This excerpt refers to a high school in northeastern Kentucky at risk of becoming a "school in crisis":

   > [The principal] said Blazer teachers inject[ed] more open-ended questions throughout their classes and took writing workshops. Students were given an intensive workshop on responding to every question.
   >
   > Blazer seniors were asked to respond to school pride and offered incentives for their participation. "If they came to school every day, we gave them a free tardy pass and five days of early lunch," [the principal] said. "If they answered every question on the test—and I checked all the papers—they were allowed a 2 percent bonus on the grade in the class of their choice." (Collard and Wolfford, 1994, p. 6)

4. Teachers identified specific changes in content coverage, such as placing greater emphasis on probability and statistics in middle school mathematics and spending more time on poetry in an eighth-grade literature class.

5. The 1993 interviews with principals presented a picture of fewer changes in instruction than had the interviews with the teachers. For example, of the 40 principals interviewed in the two states, only five reported that more writing was occurring in their schools as a result of the new state assessments. A similar number reported an increase in discovery learning and hands-on instructional activities. Only three reported that students were doing more work in groups.

However, one-third of the North Carolina principals reported that the curriculum in their schools was being aligned with the state's *Standard Course of Study*.

6. p <.05.

7. p <.05.

8. KIRIS contained items that measured how well students integrated content from several different academic and applied subjects (for example, arts and humanities with reading, vocational studies with mathematics, science, and social studies).

9. The traditional and the reform scores were means because we did not have the same number of traditional and reform strategies.

10. Only 11 percent of the "most similar" assignments from the Kentucky teachers, and 9 percent from the North Carolina teachers, were released items from previous state assessments. The small proportion is especially striking in the case of Kentucky, since the state had released all performance event prompts and a significant number of open-response items. North Carolina, in contrast, had not released as many items, but it did maintain an unofficial "item bank," from which teachers could select items for classroom assessments. Teachers reported in the 1994 interviews that their districts were having them use the item bank several times a year in preparation for the end-of-grade test. However, the 9 percent includes only items that were actually on the end-of-grade test.

11. Three variables, coded from the teacher interviews, were used to measure type of preparation: (1) received an introduction to the new assessment, (2) participated in an in-service on curriculum related to the assessment, and (3) participated in an ongoing professional development network such as a mathematics or writing project.

12. Because North Carolina's goals were so specific, many were likely to be reflected in assignments at one specific point in the curriculum, and therefore could not be measured with data collected during only about two weeks. For example, a specific objective such as *use a variety of models to illustrate acute, right, and obtuse angles* (North Carolina fourth-grade mathematics Goal 2.5) is likely to appear at one distinct point in the curriculum and not to be interwoven at multiple times in the way that *understand space and dimensionality concepts and use them appropriately and accurately* (Kentucky mathematics Goal 2.9) is likely to be.

The difference in the specificity of North Carolina's competency goals and Kentucky's learning goals is illustrated by mathematics, in which Kentucky had eight goals for student performance that applied to all grades, whereas North Carolina had many separate goals for each grade level—for example, the goals for fourth-grade mathematics numbered 58.

13. Another study that examined changes in instruction at one high school in Kentucky reached a similar conclusion. It noted that teachers "do not seem to recognize that changing the format of instruction—for example, using small groups instead of individual seatwork—does not ensure more authentic instruction. Without addressing the substance of instruction as well as its format, KERA's aims cannot be realized" (Gamoran, 1996).

14. During the first phase, a team of researchers collected data in 1988 and 1989 from a purposive sample of 23 elementary teachers working in six schools. The teachers were interviewed before and after researchers observed their classrooms

for two days on the first site visit and for one day during the second visit (Cohen and Peterson, 1990). State and district officials were also interviewed about the implementation of the mathematics frameworks. The researchers then continued to track the implementation process in California, and five years later, collected survey data as a way of situating the earlier case studies in a broader context.

15. Two recent studies found that teachers in states with high stakes assessments that have consequences associated with them in the form of rewards and sanctions imposed on schools, educators, or students perceive the assessment's effects on classroom teaching to be greater than what teachers in states with low stakes assessments perceive them to be. One study was based on a nationally representative mail survey of 4,195 teachers (Pedulla et al., 2003), and the other on interviews with 120 educators in each of three states—Kansas, Massachusetts, and Michigan—that vary on the level of consequences associated with their assessments (Clarke et al., 2003). While the latter study considered the policy characteristics of each state's assessment, the former did not report state-specific results and used only generic categories of assessment consequences in its analysis. Neither study considered state-specific implementation processes or attempted to validate educators' perceptions.

Nevertheless, the scope of the findings suggests that policymakers may be correct in assuming that policies with meaningful consequences do give them greater leverage over classroom practices than ones that rely only on values and information. However, some evidence from these studies suggests that the added power of high stakes tests may be less than policymakers assume. For example, even in states with moderate or low stakes tests, a significant proportion of teachers reported that the test influenced the amount of time they spent on activities such as critical thinking (63 percent), concept development (48 percent), and cooperative learning (41 percent) (Pedulla et al., 2003, p. 54). In addition, two-thirds of the teachers in high stakes states and low stakes states alike reported that the state-mandated test was compatible with their daily instruction (p. 37), suggesting that a low stakes, hortatory assessment can exert considerable influence on instruction.

6. Aligning Politics, Policy, and Practice

1. In starting with the assumption that politics is an integral part of public education and needs to be considered in scholarly analyses of it, this book joins a growing body of research. For example, in their analysis of education reform in 11 cities, Stone and his colleagues (2001) argue that "education reforms of the last century and this one, by building institutional walls to buffer education decision making from political 'interference,' ironically have deprived themselves of this critical tool . . . we see the solutions as well as the problems as lying within the political realm" (pp. 3–4).

2. The Texas case illustrates both the complexity of interpreting test scores and the extent to which they can become politicized. Klein and his RAND colleagues (2000) concluded in their report that the gains recorded on the TAAS were several times greater than the performance of Texas students on NAEP between

1994 and 1998, and that except for fourth-grade mathematics, gains in Texas on NAEP were not significantly different from those in other states. However, an earlier RAND report (Grissmer and Flanagan, 1998) compared score gains on NAEP between 1990 and 1997 across the 44 states that participate in the National Assessment, and found that after controlling for student demographic and other factors, North Carolina and Texas had higher average gains than other states. The researchers then concluded that the way in which standards and assessment policies had been implemented in the two states was significant in explaining the increases.

Because the two studies examined different time periods and had different bases of comparison, it is not surprising that they generated seemingly inconsistent results. Still, the difficulty in reconciling the two sets of findings to policymakers and the public meant that the two studies became fodder for the 2000 presidential campaigns, with each candidate basing campaign advertising on the study more favorable to his message.

3. For example, using data from the 1992 National Educational Longitudinal Survey (NELS), Jacob (2001) found that high school graduation exams had no significant effect on twelfth-grade mathematics or reading achievement, but did increase the probability of dropping out among the lowest-ability students. In contrast, Carnoy and Loeb (2002), using data from the NAEP mathematics assessment between 1996 and 2000, found a positive and significant relationship between the strength of states' accountability systems and gains in mathematics achievement at the eighth-grade level across all racial and ethnic groups. However, achievement gains were less pronounced at the fourth-grade level, and their results show no evidence of strong accountability systems having a positive effect on student progression through high school. Roderick, Jacob, and Bryk (2002) found strong evidence that achievement among students in the third, sixth, and eighth grades—points at which students must meet minimum test score requirements to be promoted—increased after the implementation of Chicago's accountability policy. However, the researchers also identified differential effects of the testing policy by grade and prior achievement levels, with students at greatest risk of not being promoted showing larger effects than their lower-risk classmates. In some instances, the high stakes testing had either a negative or no effect on the highest-achieving students.

4. In most states, such a process would be somewhat complicated because they hire private testing contractors such as CTB McGraw Hill, Harcourt, and Riverside Publishing to undertake some or all of their assessment tasks. In some cases, states simply purchase generic off-the-shelf tests produced and scored by these contractors. However, a growing number of states require that the contractor's standardized test be supplemented with additional items that are aligned with the state's standards. It may be particularly important in states where commercial tests are used to have public involvement in the initial standard-setting process and in review of the customized assessment, although this adds an additional layer to the process. Such inclusion would help ensure that parents and the public would view the assessment as legitimate and appropriate for the state's students.

5. Testing experts have noted that the reuse of test items contributes to score in-

flation, and have recommended that this practice be strictly controlled (Koretz, 2002). Consequently, adherence to sound testing practice would also favor allowing items to be released.

6. In a poll conducted in late 2000, the same proportion of parents and teachers (57 percent and 56 percent, respectively) supported requiring that students pass a basic skills test before being awarded high school diplomas, and an additional one-fourth of each sample supported the use of a more challenging test (Public Agenda, 2001). However, in a poll conducted a year earlier, 79 percent of the parent sample supported a standardized test for grade-to-grade promotion while only 60 percent of the teachers supported it (Public Agenda, 2000a).

7. States are required to develop measurable AYP objectives for improved achievement by all students so that all students will reach a proficient level by the end of the 2013–14 school year. AYP results must be reported by school and by student subgroups within schools. Schools that do not meet their AYP objectives for two consecutive years will be identified for improvement and must develop two-year plans to address the problem and set aside 10 percent of their federal funds for teacher professional development. Schools that have been identified for improvement will also be required to allow students to transfer to other schools within their districts. After a school has been in improvement status for a year, its local district has to make supplemental educational services such as after-school tutoring available to students. Parents can select from a list of approved providers, which can include private-sector and religious organizations. If a school is still in improvement status after two years, its district has to begin restructuring the school and formulating alternative governance arrangements that can include converting it to a charter school, replacing staff, contracting with a private management company, or turning school operations over to the state.

8. One example of such software is the Quality School Portfolio (QSP) system developed by researchers at UCLA's CRESST. QSP is both a data manager that allows schools to analyze data from multiple sources and a resource kit that includes surveys and observation protocols that schools can use to collect their own noncognitive data on school climate and instructional practices (*http://qsp. cse.ucla.edu/mainSub/what/whatRight.html*).

9. In an earlier analysis of OTL, I examined the incentives of federal and state policymakers to enact and enforce OTL standards, and concluded that they have few because of the tremendous cost and redistributive implications if resources had to be reallocated from more affluent to poorer communities or taxes had to be raised. The exception would be if civil rights groups or others were to file a lawsuit arguing that students' due process rights had been violated because their instruction had not included the skills and content measured on a particular test. A decision regarding current high stakes tests, similar to the earlier *Debra P. v. Turlington* case, could force policymakers to pay greater attention to OTL issues. In that case, the Fifth Circuit of the U.S. Court of Appeals ruled that if the test Florida required for high school graduation "covers material not taught the students, it is unfair and violates the Equal Protection and Due Process clauses of the United States Constitution" (644 F.2d 397 [1981]).

Appendix

1. The schools in the Kentucky sample differ in one important way from many schools in the state: four of the six are significantly larger than the average school in the state. Kentucky schools tend to be small, with the average enrollment for elementary schools 329, middle schools 544, and high schools 666. However, the sample schools were similar to the state average in how well they performed on the KIRIS test between 1992 and 1994. The scores of students in the sample schools were virtually identical to the state-wide averages in fourth-grade reading and social studies, and in twelfth-grade mathematics, reading, and social studies. In mathematics, the proportion of students in sample schools scoring at the proficient level or higher was four percentage points higher than the state average in the fourth grade (15 percent versus 11 percent) and three points higher in the eighth grade (22 percent versus 19 percent). The sample also deviated from the statewide average in eighth-grade reading, falling five percentage points below (13 percent versus 18 percent proficient or better), and four points below in eighth-grade social studies (12 percent versus 16 percent).

   The schools in the North Carolina sample performed at about the state average on the end-of-grade reading test, but significantly better than the state average on the mathematics and social studies tests. The percentage of students scoring at the proficient level or better statewide in 1993 in mathematics was 63 percent, in reading 64 percent, and in social studies 59 percent. The average scores for the study sample were 72 percent in mathematics, 68 percent in reading, and 67 percent in social studies.

2. In median years of teaching experience, the sample is quite typical of the teaching force as a whole. However, the proportion of men in the North Carolina sample is less than half of what it is in the state teacher population; the proportion in the Kentucky sample mirrors the state's teaching force exactly.

References

Adler, L. 1996. "Institutional Responses: Public School Curriculum and Religious Conservatives in California." *Education and Urban Society,* 28(3): 327–346.

Adler, L. and Tellez, K. 1992. "Curriculum Challenge from the Religious Right: The *Impressions* Reading Series." *Urban Education,* 27(2): 152–173.

American Educational Research Association. 2000. "Position Statement of the American Educational Research Association Concerning High-Stakes Testing in PreK–12 Education." *Educational Researcher,* 29(8): 24–25.

Appalachia Educational Laboratory. Planning, Research and Evaluation Unit. 1995. *The Needs of Kentucky Teachers for Designing Curricula Based on Academic Expectations.* Frankfort: Kentucky Institute for Education Research.

Apple, M. W. 1996. *Cultural Politics and Education.* New York: Teachers College Press.

Associated Press. 1994, May 2. "Opposition to KERA Has Led to Forming of Splintered Front." *Lexington Herald-Leader,* p. B3.

———. 1995, October 28. "Business Leaders' Group Supporting KERA through $100,000 in TV Ads." *Lexington Herald-Leader,* p. C3.

———. 1996, February 25. "Family Loses Bid to Refuse KERA Testing." *Lexington Herald-Leader,* p. B3.

Bardach, E. 1977. *The Implementation Game: What Happens after a Bill Becomes a Law.* Cambridge, MA: MIT Press.

Belden N., Russonello, J., and Stewart, K. 2001. "Making the Grade: Teachers' Attitudes toward Academic Standards and State Testing: Findings of National Survey of Public School Teachers for Education Week." *Education Week.* Retrieved August 6, 2001, from *www.edweek.org.*

Bergan, M. 2001, June 25. "Exit-Exam Story Fails the Test of Fairness." *Los Angeles Times,* p. B11.

Bishop, B. 1994, March 23. " 'Independent' Legislature Still Wheels and Deals in Secret." *Lexington Herald-Leader,* p. A9.

Black, E. G. 1989. "California's Community Right-to-Know." *Ecology Law Quarterly,* 16: 1021–1064.

Blackford, L. B. 1998, February 25. "Businesses 'Blindsided' by Bill to Revamp Test." *Lexington Herald-Leader,* p. A1.

Boyd, W. L., Lugg, C. A., and Zahorchak, G. L. 1996. "Social Traditionalists, Re-

235

ligious Conservatives, and the Politics of Outcomes-Based Education." *Education and Urban Society,* 28(5): 347–365.

Burstein, L., McDonnell, L. M., Van Winkle, J., Ormseth, T., Mirocha, J., and Guiton, G. 1995. *Validating National Curriculum Indicators.* Santa Monica, CA: RAND.

California Department of Education. 1995. *Every Child a Reader: The Report of the California Reading Task Force.* Sacramento, CA: Author.

California Public Education Partnership. n.d. *What Californians Want from the Public Schools.* Santa Cruz, CA: Author.

Capitol Resource Institute. 1994. *CLAS Information Packet.* Sacramento, CA: Author.

Carnoy, M. and Loeb, S. 2002. "Does External Accountability Affect Student Outcomes?" *Educational Evaluation and Policy Analysis,* 24(4): 305–331.

Caswell, J. A. 1992. "Current Information Levels on Food Labels." *American Journal of Agricultural Economics,* 74(5): 1196–1201.

Caswell, J. A. and Mojduszka, E. M. 1995. "Using Informational Labeling to Influence the Market for Quality in Food Products." *American Journal of Agricultural Economics,* 78: 1248–1253.

Catterall, J. S., Mehrens, W. A., Ryan, J. M., Flores, E. J., and Rubin, P. M. 1998. *Kentucky Instructional Results Information System: A Technical Review.* Frankfort: Commonwealth of Kentucky Legislative Research Commission.

Chronicle of Higher Education. 1998, September 25. "California Won't Revise Controversial Standards," p. A10.

Clarke, M., Shore, A., Rhoades, K., Abrams, L., Miao, J., and Li, J. 2003. *Perceived Effects of State-Mandated Testing Programs on Teaching and Learning: Findings from Interviews with Educators in Low-, Medium-, and High-Stakes States.* Boston: National Board on Educational Testing and Public Policy, Boston College.

Cohen, D. K. and Hill, H. C. 2001. *Learning Policy.* New Haven, CT: Yale University Press.

Cohen, D. K. and Peterson, P. L. 1990. Special Issue of *Educational Evaluation and Policy Analysis,* 12(3): 233–353.

Collard, G. and Wolfford, G. 1994, September 9. "Area Schools' Scores Please." *Ashland Daily Independent,* pp. 1, 6.

Colvin, R. L. 1995a, March 23. "State's Reading, Math Reforms under Review as Scores Fall." *Los Angeles Times,* pp. A1, A21.

———. 1995b, April 6. "Eastin Names Panels to Probe Education Failure." *Los Angeles Times,* pp. A3, A17.

———. 1995c, July 5. "School Goals Spelled Out in 'ABC Bill.'" *Los Angeles Times,* pp. A3, A12.

———. 1995d, October 2. "Pressure Mounts on Wilson to OK New Test for Academic Assessment." *Los Angeles Times,* pp. A3, A15.

———. 1995e, November 19. "Her Best Subject." *Los Angeles Times,* pp. E1, E2.

———. 1999, January 25. "Davis Ally Will Wait and See on Education Plan." *Los Angeles Times,* p. A3.

Corbett, H. D. and Wilson, B. L. 1991. *Testing, Reform, and Rebellion.* Norwood, NJ: Ablex Publishing.

Council of Chief State School Officers. 2001. *State Student Assessment Programs Annual Survey: Summary Report.* Washington, DC: Author.

Cronbach, L. J., Bradburn, N. M., and Horvitz, D. G. 1994. *Sampling and Statistical Procedures Used in the California Learning Assessment System* (Report of the Select Committee). Stanford, CA: Stanford University.

Cross, A. 1995a, October 19. "KERA Opposition Rife, Forgy Says." *The Courier-Journal* (Louisville, KY), p. B5.

———. 1995b, October 20. "New Patton TV Ad Says He'd 'Fix KERA.'" *The Courier-Journal* (Louisville, KY), p. B6.

Daniel, S. M. 1995, November 19. "KERA Teaches a Radical Agenda." *Lexington Herald-Leader,* p. E2.

Debra P. v. Turlington, 644 F.2d 397 (U.S. Ct. App. 5th Cir. 1981).

deLeon, P. 1995. "Democratic Values and the Policy Sciences." *American Journal of Political Science,* 39(4): 886–905.

Delsohn, G. 1994, September 28. "Christian Law Firm Has Clout in State." *Sacramento Bee,* pp. A1, A7.

DeNeufville, J. I. and Barton, S. E. 1987. "Myths and the Definition of Policy Problems." *Policy Sciences,* 20: 181–206.

Diegmueller, K. 1995, September 27. "More Basic-Skills Instruction in California Urged." *Education Week,* pp. 14, 17.

Elam, S. M. and Rose, L. C. 1995. "The 27th Phi Delta Kappa/Gallup Poll of the Public's Attitudes toward the Public Schools." *Phi Delta Kappan,* 77(1): 41–56.

Elam, S. M., Rose, L. C., and Gallup, A. M. 1991. "The 23rd Annual Gallup Poll of the Public's Attitudes toward the Public Schools." *Phi Delta Kappan,* 73(1): 41–56.

———. 1992. "The 24th Annual Gallup/Phi Delta Kappa Poll of the Public's Attitudes toward the Public Schools." *Phi Delta Kappan,* 74(1): 41–53.

———. 1996. "The 28th Annual Phi Delta Kappa/Gallup Poll of the Public's Attitudes toward the Public Schools." *Phi Delta Kappan,* 78(1): 41–59.

Falk, K. 1996. "The Dilemma of Public Education: The Family versus the State." Senior honors thesis, Department of Political Science, University of California, Santa Barbara.

Farkas, S. 1993. *Divided Within, Besieged Without: The Politics of Education in Four American School Districts.* New York: Public Agenda Foundation.

Firestone, W. A., Mayrowetz, D., and Fairman, J. 1998. "Performance-Based Assessment and Instructional Change: The Effects of Testing in Maine and Maryland." *Educational Evaluation and Policy Analysis,* 20(2): 95–113.

Fullan, M. G. 1991. *The New Meaning of Educational Change.* New York: Teachers College Press.

Fuller, B., Hayward, G., and Kirst, M. 1998. *Californians Speak on Education and Reform Options.* Berkeley, CA: Policy Analysis for California Education.

Fung, A. and O'Rourke, D. 2000. "Reinventing Environmental Regulation from the Grassroots Up: Explaining and Expanding the Success of the Toxics Release Inventory." *Environmental Management,* 25(2): 115–127.

Gamoran, A. 1996. "Goals 2000 in Organizational Context: Will It Make a Difference for States, Districts, and Schools?" In Borman, K., Cookson, P., Sadovnik,

A., and Spade, J. Z. (Eds.), *Implementing Educational Reform: Sociological Perspectives on Educational Policy* (pp. 429–443). Norwood, NJ: Ablex.

Gormley, W. T., Jr. and Weimer, D. L. 1999. *Organizational Report Cards.* Cambridge: Harvard University Press.

Graham, M. 2000, April. "Regulation by Shaming." *Atlantic Monthly,* 285(4): 36–40.

Grissmer, D. and Flanagan, A. 1998. "Exploring Rapid Achievement Gains in North Carolina and Texas." Paper commissioned by the National Educational Goals Panel. Washington, DC: National Educational Goals Panel.

Groves, M. and Ritsch, M. 2001, October 10. "School Improvement Brings Bonuses; Education: State to Spread $100 Million among More Than 12,000 Teachers and Others as Rewards for Student Gains on Stanford 9 Test." *Los Angeles Times,* p. B1.

Groves, M. and Smith, D. 2001, September 28. "Ineligible Schools Got Rewards; Test Scoring Foul-up Sent $750,000 to the Wrong Campuses." *Los Angeles Times,* p. B1.

Guth, J. L., Green, J. C., Kellstedt, L. A., and Smidt, C. E. 1995. "Onward Christian Soldiers: Religious Activist Groups in American Politics." In Cigler, A. J. and Loomis, B. A. (Eds.), *Interest Group Politics* (pp. 55–76). Washington, DC: Congressional Quarterly Press.

Gutmann, A. 1995. "Civic Education and Social Diversity." *Ethics,* 105: 557–579.

Hageman, B. 1993, October 11. "New State Test Spurs Criticism." *The Press-Enterprise* (Riverside, CA), p. B1.

Hambleton, R. K., Jaeger, R. M., Koretz, D., Linn, R. L., Millman, J., and Phillips, S. E. 1995. *Review of the Measurement Quality of the Kentucky Instructional Results Information System, 1991–1994.* Frankfort: Office of Educational Accountability, Kentucky General Assembly.

Haney, W. 1984. "Testing Reasoning and Reasoning about Testing." *Review of Educational Research,* 54(4): 597–654.

Hanushek, E. A. and Raymond, M. E. 2002. "Lessons on Limits of State Accountability Systems." Paper prepared for the conference "Taking Account of Accountability: Assessing Policy and Politics," Harvard University, June 9–11.

Harp, L. 1994, May 18. "The Plot Thickens: The Real Drama behind the Kentucky Education Reform Act May Have Just Begun." *Education Week,* pp. 20–25.

Herman, J. L. and Golan, S. 1993. "The Effects of Standardized Testing on Teaching and Schools." *Educational Measurement, Issues and Practice,* 12(4): 20–25, 41–42.

Heubert, J. P. and Hauser, R. M. 1999. *High Stakes: Testing for Tracking, Promotion, and Graduation.* Washington, DC: National Academy Press.

Hochschild, J. and Scott, B. 1998. "Trends: Governance and Reform of Public Education in the United States." *Public Opinion Quarterly,* 62(1): 79–120.

Howlett, M. and Ramesh, M. 1995. *Studying Public Policy.* Toronto: Oxford University Press.

Immerwahr, J. 1997. *What Our Children Need: South Carolinians Look at Public Education.* New York: Public Agenda.

Ingram, C. 1994, March 12. "Stories Deleted from Tests to Be Reinstated." *Los Angeles Times,* p. A1.

Ingram, H. and Schneider, A. 1993. "Constructing Citizenship: The Subtle Messages of Policy Design." In Ingram, H. and Smith, S. R. (Eds.), *Public Policy for Democracy* (pp. 68–94). Washington, DC: The Brookings Institution.

Jacob, B. A. 2001. "Getting Tough? The Impact of High School Graduation Exams." *Educational Evaluation and Policy Analysis,* 23(2): 99–121.

James, T. 1991. "State Authority and the Politics of Educational Change." *Review of Research in Education,* 17: 169–224.

Jenkins-Smith, H. C. 1990. *Democratic Politics and Policy Analysis.* Pacific Grove, CA: Brooks-Cole.

Johnson, J. 1995. *Assignment Incomplete: The Unfinished Business of Education Reform.* New York: Public Agenda Foundation.

Johnson, J. and Immerwahr, J. 1994. *First Things First: What Americans Expect from the Public Schools.* New York: Public Agenda.

Kelley, C. 1998. "The Kentucky School-Based Performance Award Program: School-Level Effects." *Educational Policy,* 12(3): 305–324.

Kentucky Department of Education. 1993. *Transformations: Kentucky's Curriculum Framework (Volume I).* Frankfort, KY: Author.

———. 1994. "Position Paper on Recommended Changes in the KIRIS Assessment and Accountability Program." Frankfort, KY: Author.

Khator, R. 1993. "Recycling: A Policy Dilemma for American States?" *Policy Studies Journal,* 21(2): 210–226.

Kingdon, J. W. 1995. *Agendas, Alternatives, and Public Policies.* New York: Harper-Collins College Publisher.

Klein, S. P., Hamilton, L. S., McCaffrey, D. F., and Stecher, B. M. 2000. *What Do Test Scores in Texas Tell Us?* Santa Monica, CA: RAND.

Koretz, D. M. 2002. "Limitations in the Use of Achievement Tests as Measures of Educators' Productivity." *The Journal of Human Resources,* 37(4): 752–777.

Koretz, D. M. and Barron, S. I. 1998. *The Validity of Gains in Scores on the Kentucky Instructional Results Information System (KIRIS).* Santa Monica, CA: RAND.

Koretz, D. M., Barron, S., Mitchell, K. J., and Stecher, B. M. 1996. *Perceived Effects of the Kentucky Instructional Results Information System (KIRIS).* Santa Monica, CA: RAND.

Koretz, D. M., Madaus, G. F., Haertel, E., and Beaton, A. E. 1992, February 19. *National Educational Standards and Testing: A Response to the Recommendations of the National Council on Education Standards and Testing.* Testimony before the Subcommittee on Elementary, Secondary, and Vocational Education, Committee on Education and Labor, U.S. House of Representatives.

Koretz, D. M., McCaffrey, D. F., and Hamilton, L. S. 2001. *Toward a Framework for Validating Gains under High-Stakes Conditions.* CSE Technical Report 551. Los Angeles: Center for the Study of Evaluation, University of California, Los Angeles.

Lawton, M. 1998, June 17. "Wilson Pressures Panel to Cede Standards-Setting Control." *Education Week,* p. 32.

Lemann, N. 2001, July 2. "Testing Limits." *The New Yorker,* pp. 28–34.

Linder, S. H. and Peters, B. G. 1988. "The Design of Instruments for Public Policy: A Preliminary Design for Modeling How Experts and Policymakers View Government's Policy Tools." Paper presented at the annual meeting of the Midwest Political Science Association, Chicago.

Linn, R. L. 1993. "Educational Assessment: Expanded Expectations and Challenges." *Educational Evaluation and Policy Analysis,* 15(1): 1–16.

Loveless, T. 2001. "A Tale of Two Math Reforms: The Politics of the New Math and the NCTM Standards." In Loveless, T. (Ed.), *The General Curriculum Debate* (pp. 184–228). Washington, DC: Brookings Institution Press.

Macedo, S. 1995. "Liberal Civic Education and Religious Fundamentalism: The Case of God v. John Rawls?" *Ethics,* 105: 468–496.

Madaus, G. 1988. "The Influence of Testing on the Curriculum." In Tanner, L. N. (Ed.), *Critical Issues in Curriculum, Eighty-Seventh Yearbook of the National Society for the Study of Education* (pp. 83–121). Chicago: University of Chicago Press.

Magat, W. A. and Viscusi, W. K. 1992. *Informational Approaches to Regulation.* Cambridge, MA: MIT Press.

Manzo, K. K. 1997, October 22. "High Stakes: Test Truths or Consequences." *Education Week,* pp. 1, 9.

———. 2000, April 5. "North Carolina Plan Aims to Close Achievement Gap." *Education Week,* p. 19.

Marcano, T. 1990, November 11. "Year off Might Do CAP Test Some Good." *Los Angeles Times,* p. T1.

March, J. G. and Olsen, J. P. 1989. *Rediscovering Institutions.* New York: The Free Press.

May, L. 1994a, January 16. "Some See KERA Changes as Effort to Quiet Foes." *Lexington Herald-Leader,* p. A1.

———. 1994b, March 6. "Kentucky Schools' Test Scores Are Still Full of Questions: 2 Studies to Review Validity of KERA-Required Program." *Lexington Herald-Leader,* p. B1.

———. 1994c, March 23. "Education Petition Delivered Calling for KERA Repeal." *Lexington Herald-Leader,* p. A6.

———. 1995a, February 7. "KERA Critic Embraces 'World of Controversy.' " *Lexington Herald-Leader,* p. A1.

———. 1995b, September 29. "Education Groups Unite with Concerns about KERA Testing." *Lexington Herald-Leader,* p. A1.

McCarthy, M. 1996. "People of Faith as Political Activists in Public Schools." *Education and Urban Society,* 28(3): 308–326.

McDonnell, L. M. 1994. *Policymakers' Views of Student Assessment.* Santa Monica, CA: RAND.

———. 1995. "Opportunity to Learn as a Research Concept and a Policy Instrument." *Education Evaluation and Policy Analysis,* 17(3): 305–322.

———. 2000. "Defining Democratic Purposes." In McDonnell, L., Timpane, P., and Benjamin, R. (Eds.), *Rediscovering the Democratic Purposes of Education* (pp. 1–18). Lawrence: University Press of Kansas.

McDonnell, L. M. and Elmore, R. F. 1987. "Getting the Job Done: Alternative Policy Instruments." *Educational Evaluation and Policy Analysis,* 9(2): 133–152.

McDonnell, L. M., McLaughlin, M. J., and Morison, P. 1997. *Educating One and All.* Washington, DC: National Academy Press.

McDonnell, L. M. and Weatherford, M. S. 1999. *State Standards-Setting and Public*

Deliberation: The Case of California. Los Angeles: National Center for Research on Evaluation, Standards, and Student Testing, University of California, Los Angeles.

McLaughlin, M. W. 1987. "Learning from Experience: Lessons from Policy Implementation." *Educational Evaluation and Policy Analysis,* 9(2): 171–178.

———. 1990. "The RAND Change Agent Study Revisited: Macro Perspectives and Micro Realities." *Educational Researcher,* 19(9): 11–16.

Merl, J. 1994, May 11. "Judge Finds No Privacy Invasion in CLAS Tests." *Los Angeles Times,* pp. B1, B8.

Moe, T. M. 1990. "Political Institutions: The Neglected Side of the Story." *Journal of Law, Economics, and Organization,* 6: 213–253.

Nather, D. 2001a. "As Education Bills Head for Floor Votes, Big Ideological Tests Loom in House." *CQ Weekly,* pp. 1157–1158.

———. 2001b. "Student-Testing Drive Marks an Attitude Shift for Congress." *CQ Weekly,* pp. 1560–1566.

National Center for Education Statistics. 1997. *Digest of Educational Statistics.* Washington, DC: U.S. Department of Education.

National Council of Teachers of Mathematics. 1989. *Curriculum and Evaluation Standards for School Mathematics.* Reston, VA: Author.

National Council on Education Standards and Testing. 1992. *Raising Standards for American Education.* Washington, DC: Author.

New York Times. 2001, July 8. "Teachers Vote to Let Parents Decide on Tests," p. A15.

O'Day, J. A. and Smith, M. S. 1993. "Systemic Reform and Educational Opportunity." In Fuhrman, S. (Ed.), *Designing Coherent Education Policy: Improving the System* (pp. 250–312). San Francisco: Jossey-Bass.

Office of Education Accountability. 1994. *A Survey of Legislators on Kentucky Instructional Results Information System.* Frankfort, KY: Author.

Office of Technology Assessment. 1992. *Testing in American Schools: Asking the Right Questions.* Washington, DC: U.S. Government Printing Office.

Olsen, M. E. 1978. "Public Acceptance of Energy Conservation." In Warkov, S. (Ed.), *Energy Policy in the United States: Social and Behavioral Dimensions* (pp. 91–109). New York: Praeger.

———. 1981. "Consumers' Attitudes toward Energy Conservation." *Journal of Social Issues,* 37(2): 108–131.

Olson, S. 1998, September 30. "Science Friction." *Education Week,* pp. 25–29.

Palumbo, D. J. and Calista, D. J. 1990. "Opening up the Black Box: Implementation and the Policy Process." In Palumbo, D. J. and Calista, D. J. (Eds.), *Implementation and the Policy Process: Opening Up the Black Box* (pp. 3–17). Westport, CT: Greenwood Press.

Pease, W. S. 1991, December. "Chemical Hazards and the Public's Right to Know: How Effective Is California's Proposition 65?" *Environment,* 33(10): 12–20.

Pedulla, J. J., Abrams, L. M., Madaus, G. F., Russell, M. K., Ramos, M. A., and Miao, J. 2003. *Perceived Effects of State-Mandated Testing Programs on Teaching and Learning: Findings from a National Survey of Teachers.* Boston: National Board on Educational Testing and Public Policy, Boston College.

Picus, L. O. 1996. *Estimating the Costs of Student Assessment in North Carolina and*

Kentucky: A State-Level Analysis. Los Angeles: National Center for Research on Evaluation, Standards, and Student Testing, University of California, Los Angeles.

Pitsch, M. 1994, October 19. "Critics Target Goals 2000 in Schools 'War.'" *Education Week,* pp. 10, 21.

Porter, A. C. 1994. "National Standards and School Improvement in the 1990s: Issues and Promise." *American Journal of Education,* 102(4): 421–449.

Public Agenda. 2000a. "Reality Check 2000." Retrieved August 8–9, 2002, from *www.publicagenda.org.*

———. 2000b. "Survey Finds Little Sign of Backlash against Academic Standards or Standardized Tests." Retrieved June 19, 2001, from *www.publicagenda.org.*

———. 2001. "Reality Check 2001." Retrieved August 11, 2002, from *www .publicagenda.org.*

Public Education Network and *Education Week.* 2001. *Action for All: The Public's Responsibility for Public Education.* Bethesda, MD: Author.

Pyle, A. 1999a, February 15. "Clear Case of Backhanded Backing for School Bills." *Los Angeles Times,* p. A3.

———. 1999b, March 23. "Final Approval Near on Davis' Education Plan." *Los Angeles Times,* p. A1.

Quality Counts. 2003, January 9. Special Issue of *Education Week.*

Quillin, M. and Kurtz, M. 1997, August 1. "Johnston Schools Sued over Testing." *The Raleigh News and Observer,* p. B-1.

Ravitch, D. 1995. *National Standards in American Education: A Citizen's Guide.* Washington, DC: Brookings.

Resnick, L. B. 1994. "Performance Puzzles." *American Journal of Education,* 102(4): 511–526.

Roderick, M., Jacob, B. A., and Bryk, A. S. 2002. "The Impact of High-Stakes Testing in Chicago on Student Achievement in Promotional Gate Grades." *Educational Evaluations and Policy Analysis,* 24(4): 333–357.

Rose v. Council for Better Education, Inc. 1989. 790 S.W.2d 186 (Ky. 1989).

Rose, L. C. and Gallup, A. M. 2000. "The 32nd Annual Phi Delta Kappa/Gallup Poll of the Public's Attitudes toward the Public Schools." *Phi Delta Kappan,* 82(1): 41–57.

Rose, L. C., Gallup, A. M., and Elam, S. M. 1997. "The 29th Annual Phi Delta Kappa/Gallup Poll of the Public's Attitudes toward the Public Schools." *Phi Delta Kappan,* 79(1): 41–56.

Rothman, R. 1992, September 23. "Kentucky Reformers Await Reaction to Results of Tough Tests." *Education Week,* pp. 1, 20.

Rothstein, R. 2002. "Out of Balance: Our Understanding of How Schools Affect Society and How Society Affects Schools." Paper prepared for the 30th Anniversary Conference of the Spencer Foundation, January 24–25.

Schneider, A. L. and Ingram, H. 1990. "Behavioral Assumptions of Policy Tools." *Journal of Politics,* 52(2): 510–529.

———. 1997. *Policy Design for Democracy.* Lawrence: University Press of Kansas.

Schreiner, B. 1996, January 29. "Making Waves Family Foundation Trying to Keep Issues at Forefront." *Lexington Herald-Leader,* p. B3.

Simmons, T. 1997, November 3. "Ready or Not, ABCs Reforms Are about to Hit the State's High Schools." *The Raleigh News and Observer*, p. A1.

———. 1998, August 7. "N.C. Exults in ABCs Triumph." *The Raleigh News and Observer*, p. A1.

Smith, M. and O'Day, J. 1991. "Systemic School Reform." In Fuhrman, S. and Malen, B. (Eds.), *The Politics of Curriculum and Testing* (pp. 233–268). San Francisco: Jossey-Bass.

Smith, M. L. and Rottenberg, C. 1991. "Unintended Consequences of External Testing in Elementary Schools." *Educational Measurement, Issues and Practice*, 10(4): 7–11.

Sommerfeld, M. 1996, April 24. "California Parents Target Math Frameworks: Critics Worry Schools Have Abandoned Basics." *Education Week*, pp. 1, 11.

Soper, J. C. 1995. "California: Christian Conservative Influence in a Liberal State." In Rozell, M. J. and Wilcox, C. (Eds.), *God at the Grass Roots* (pp. 211–226). Lanham, MD: Rowman and Littlefield.

Stammer, L. B. 1995, November 2. "A Man of Millions: Broadcaster James Dobson Has Become a Leading Name in Evangelical Circles." *Los Angeles Times*, pp. E1, E5.

Stecher, B. M. and Barron, S. 1999. "Test-Based Accountability: The Perverse Consequences of Milepost Testing." Paper prepared for the annual meeting of the American Educational Research Association, Montreal, Canada, April 21.

Stecher, B. M., Barron, S., Kaganoff, T., and Goodwin, J. 1998. *The Effects of Standards-Based Assessment on Classroom Practices: Results of the 1996–97 RAND Survey of Kentucky Teachers of Mathematics and Writing*. Los Angeles: National Center for Research on Evaluation, Standards, and Student Testing, University of California, Los Angeles.

Stecher, B. M. and Klein, S. P. 1997. "The Cost of Science Performance Assessments in Large-Scale Testing Programs." *Educational Evaluation and Policy Analysis*, 19(1): 1–14.

Stecklow, S. 1997, September 2. "Kentucky's Teachers Get Bonuses, But Some Are Caught Cheating." *Wall Street Journal*, pp. A1, A6.

Stenzel, P. L. 1991. "Right-to-Know Provisions of California's Proposition 65: The Naiveté of the Delaney Clause Revisited." *Harvard Environmental Law Review*, 15: 493–527.

Stone, C. N., Henig, J. R., Jones, B. D., and Pierannunzi, C. 2001. *The Politics of Reforming Urban Schools*. Lawrence: University Press of Kansas.

Stone, D. 1997. *Policy Paradox*. New York: Norton.

Sunstein, C. 1993, Winter. "Informing America: Risk, Disclosure, and the First Amendment." *Florida State University Law Review*, 653–677.

Viadero, D. 2000, May 10. "N.C. Launches Broad Assault on the Achievement Gap." *Education Week*, p. 23.

Walsh, M. 1994, September 28. "Christian Coalition Puts Education at Heart of Election Agenda." *Education Week*, p. 10.

Ward, B. 1993, November 20. "Minister Says Evidence Shows Witchcraft Taught in Schools." *Lexington Herald-Leader*, p. B3.

Washington Post. 2000. "*Washington Post*/Kaiser Family Foundation/Harvard University. Issues I: Education." Retrieved July 9, 2000, from *www.washingtonpost.com*.

Weiss, J. A. 1990. "Ideas and Inducements in Mental Health Policy." *Journal of Policy Analysis and Management,* 9(2): 178–200.

White, S. 1994, March 3. "Boysen Offers Concessions to Ministers on KERA." *Lexington Herald-Leader,* p. A1.

Wilgoren, J. 1994, June 16. "A Look at What's Really There in the CLAS Tests." *Los Angeles Times,* pp. A1, A24, A25.

———. 2001, January 23. "Education Plan by Bush Shows New Consensus." *New York Times,* p. A1.

Wilkerson, T. and Associates, Ltd. 1994. *Statewide Education Reform Survey.* Frankfort: Kentucky Institute for Education Research.

Wilson, J. Q. 2000. *Bureaucracy: What Government Agencies Do and Why They Do It.* New York: Basic Books.

Wilson, S. M. 2003. *California Dreaming: Reforming Mathematics Education.* New Haven, CT: Yale University Press.

Wise, L. L., Harris, C. D., Sipes, D. E., Hoffman, R. G., and Ford, J. P. 2000, June 30. *High School Exit Examination (HSEE): Year 1 Evaluation Report.* Alexandria, VA: Human Resources Research Organization.

Wolf, S. A., Borko, H., Elliott, R. L., and McIver, M. C. 2000. " 'That Dog Won't Hunt!' Exemplary School Change Efforts within the Kentucky Reform." *American Educational Research Journal,* 37(2): 349–393.

Zoroya, G. 1995, October 1. "Flying Right." *Los Angeles Times,* pp. E1, E2.

Index